Praise for *Origins*

"Genesis 1–11 is the foundation of the book of Genesis, which is the foundation of the whole Bible. These chapters provide the critical background for the story of Abraham, whom God would use to bring blessing to the whole world. This important part of Scripture is, however, difficult to understand. Paul Copan and Douglas Jacoby use their considerable skills to bring insight into the meaning of these chapters. I recommend *Origins* to everyone who is serious about their faith."

— **Tremper Longman III**, Distinguished Scholar and Professor Emeritus, Westmont College

"In Copan's and Jacoby's characteristically engaging style, this book successfully addresses key issues in one of the most important but controversial areas that has challenged believers' faith."

— **Richard S. Hess**, Distinguished Professor of Old Testament, Denver Seminary

"This is a remarkable book. The authors admirably meet their goal of writing in such a way that, even if one does not agree with every interpretive conclusion they come to, the biblical and extra-biblical materials from the ancient world are introduced with care and clarity. This very well written volume will carry believers through a flood of deep waters in the reading of these early chapters of Genesis. All along the way, however, there is a constant concern for the spiritual welfare of the reader, that we might all grow mature in the grace of God in Christ, our creator and our redeemer."

— **Richard E. Averbeck**, Professor of Old Testament and Semitic Languages Director, PhD in Theological Studies, Trinity Evangelical Divinity School

"An excellent, eminently readable introduction to the challenges and benefits of reading Genesis 1–11 as a genuinely ancient (specifically ancient Near Eastern) text. The authors do a great job of helping the reader understand why making the effort to read in this manner is actually *beneficial*."

— **Iain Provan**, Marshall Sheppard Professor of Biblical Studies, Regent College, Vancouver (Canada), and author of *Seriously Dangerous Religion: What the Old Testament Really Says and Why It Matters*

Origins

Origins

The Ancient Impact & Modern Implications of Genesis 1–11

PAUL COPAN
DOUGLAS JACOBY

NASHVILLE

NEW YORK • LONDON • MELBOURNE • VANCOUVER

Origins

The Ancient Impact and Modern Implications of Genesis 1-11

Published in New York, New York, by Morgan James Publishing. Morgan James is a trademark of Morgan James, LLC. www.MorganJamesPublishing.com

The Morgan James Speakers Group can bring authors to your live event. For more information or to book an event visit The Morgan James Speakers Group at www.TheMorganJamesSpeakersGroup.com.

ISBN 9781683509509 paperback
ISBN 9781683509516 eBook
Library of Congress Control Number: 2018932055

Cover and Interior Design by:
Chris Treccani
www.3dogcreative.net

Dedication

In memory of my beloved mother, Valtraut Kirsch Copan (3 September 1923–2 December 2017), who was steadfast, immovable, always abounding in the work of the Lord, and whose labors were not in vain in the Lord.

–Paul Copan

In memory of Anita Anderson Jacoby (13 November 1932–6 October 2016), a mother who always had time to talk—and listen. She believed in me and (more important) trusted the Lord. 'Til we meet again...

–Douglas Jacoby

Contents

A Note from the Authors

Genesis is the introductory volume of a 66-volume library called the Bible.[1] It is not short; in fact, to some, a thousand pages seems like a great amount. Yet many of us manage to find time to read thousands of pages of novels, magazines, and literature of mixed value. We stare (often mindlessly) in front of television sets and computer screens for countless hours a week—and for what? If we really understood that the infinite God has put his vital message in a book so thin, so compact and convenient, we would gratefully dig in.

Many start reading the Bible but then stop. It's more than busy schedules that causes us to freeze in our tracks. We feel, almost instinctively, that in this book there is something chillingly different, something transcendent. It's simultaneously unsettling and comforting—something we hide from, yet something we know we desperately need. This isn't just another book. It is the Book of all books. And Genesis is its gateway.

Eleven Chapters

Genesis is fifty chapters long—so why are we studying only eleven? In the divine drama in which we all play some role, Gen 1–11 is Act I, Scene 1. Here the plot begins to unfold, and many subplots are set in motion.

Genesis was composed in two sections. Chapters 1–11 form the "prehistory" of the ancient biblical world. Then comes the mainstream of history, in chapters 12–50. The culture, literature, religions, geography (and so on) of the ancient Near East dramatically influenced what was written and why. Without an appreciation of these elements, the purposes, structure, and message of the biblical text are easily misconstrued by modern readers. Yet even a basic familiarity with them illuminates a fascinating horizon, one that will transform your reading of Scripture.

The first section of Genesis runs from Creation to Babel, the second from God's call to Abraham to Joseph's invitation to the Twelve Tribes to escape the famine by settling in Egypt (Gen 12–50).

Relatively few Bible readers are familiar with the world of the ancient Near East, centered in Mesopotamia and its most prominent city, Babylon. Egypt is crucial too, as this is where the Hebrews spent several centuries leading up to the Exodus. Lack of knowledge of the ancient world is unfortunate, because all too often it leaves the primeval narrative as a collection of Sunday school stories. What is lost is an awareness of the radical nature of the Genesis writer's retelling of the background narrative.

Instead of reading Genesis with attentiveness to its revolutionary teachings, we can easily reduce it to a repository of principles for Christian living, quotable verses, prophecies of the end times, hidden Bible codes, or the final word on dinosaurs, aliens, or astronomy. Genesis speaks to hardly any of these matters. Such "insights" must be read between the lines and forced into the text.

Commentary, Apologetics, and Interpretation

We have sought to avoid such scenarios. It is our hope that you experience this book as a helpful running commentary on Genesis 1–11. Yet there is another reason for the book. *Origins* is also a work of Christian apologetics, and we aim to convince you that Genesis is seriously interacting with the ancient world, critiquing its polytheistic worldview while providing a credible alternative. If we can learn to engage with our culture as Genesis did in the ancient world, our own proclamation of the biblical message will be greatly enhanced. (Think of the approach the Apostle Paul took to gain the interest of the Greek audience at a meeting in the Areopagus, described in Acts 17:19–34.[2]) Further, by suggesting how these eleven chapters *should* be read, we hope to undo some of the damage wrought by those who have created unnecessary obstacles to faith, for outsiders and insiders alike, as well as for children of Christian families.

The motivated reader will probably want to take advantage of the abundant chapter endnotes, not to mention all the extra material in the appendices. There you will find not only sources for further study, but also additional thoughts that might have made the body of the book cluttered or unnecessarily lengthy had they been included there. Our websites (www.paulcopan.com and www.douglasjacoby.com) contain even more material. And if you're a Bible teacher, whether of children or adults, please be sure to read the postscript—short but important.

The Fast Track

Some readers may prefer to read straight through, skipping endnotes and appendices. They will finish the book more quickly—this is the "fast track." Perhaps on another reading they will want to go back and wade through the extra material. Other readers, however, may not want to miss anything the first time through.

In any case, there are two tracks, as well as some possible combinations of the two. You decide which course you would like to plot!

The Bible We Selected and Why We Sometimes Altered It

Hebrew is the language of 99% of the Old Testament (OT);[3] so unless you read biblical Hebrew, you depend on a translation. None is perfect, but English is blessed with a broad spectrum of options. The Bible version used throughout *Origins* is the New Revised Standard Version (NRSV), one of the most accurate English versions available. We have, however, made a few changes:

1. In the genealogical chapters 5 and 11, where the translators have written out the longer numbers in letters, we have rewritten them in numerals, for reading ease. For example, nine hundred sixty-nine (Gen 5:27) has become 969.

2. A handful of terms have been altered (retranslated) for clarity or have been commented upon. Such changes are indicated by an asterisk (*).
3. In most English versions, including the NRSV, it is conventional to render the divine name YHWH (Hebrew *Yahweh*) as LORD.[4] This is different from "Lord" (Hebrew *'Adônai*). The convention persists, although it makes things unnecessarily difficult for readers, since most people (ourselves included) seldom notice the subtle difference (Lord vs. LORD). As "Yahweh" is a perfectly good word, YHWH is always rendered Yahweh.[5]

When Christians Differ

This book is not meant to be the last word on the interpretation of Genesis—although naturally we would be gratified if it stood the test of time. Undoubtedly, many more volumes will be composed on these eleven intriguing chapters, some by those intimately familiar with Scripture (and the Lord of Scripture), others by those who have failed to take into account the essential background material.

That Bible readers should occasionally arrive at different interpretations should be no surprise. The two bookends of Scripture—Genesis 1–11 and Revelation 1–22—have always engendered controversy. (What is literal? What is figurative? How is the symbolism to be understood?) We may agree with one prominent scholar in his conclusion that:

> There can scarcely be another part of Scripture over which so many battles, theological, scientific, historical and literary, have been fought, or so many strong opinions cherished. This very fact is a sign of the greatness and power of the book, and of the narrow limits of both our factual knowledge and our spiritual grasp.[6]

Controversy surrounding the first eleven chapters of Scripture has lasted for millennia and shows little sign of abating. Fortunately, although there are important truths at both ends of the Bible—and no one should skip over

Genesis or the Apocalypse—dissent is not normally the sign of a saboteur or a wicked heart.

Our security in Christ does not depend on perfect comprehension. We are, however, called to love God with all our heart, soul, and strength—and, as Jesus amplified the original command (Deut 6:5)—with all our *mind* (Mt 22:37; Mk 12:30; Lk 10:27). Yet even when we do so, we may still disagree with others of equal sincerity, spiritual devotion, and intellectual depth. Let us do so with magnanimity. To be gracious is to be Christlike. This is, we trust, the spirit in which *Origins* was written. We hope you will extend the benefit of the doubt where our views diverge.

"Open My Eyes"

The psalmist prayed, "Open my eyes, so that I may behold wondrous things out of your law" (Ps 119:18). Genesis 1–11 is truly a treasury. Seeker, new believer, or veteran of Scripture, you may find some surprises or even see a different approach to understanding these texts. Thank you for purchasing (or borrowing) *Origins*. May your study be spiritually fruitful and uplifting.

Paul Copan
Douglas Jacoby
18 June 2018

---

1. "Bible" was not originally a religious word. It comes simply from the Greek *biblion* (book), in turn derived from *biblos*/*bublos* (scroll or paper). Many, if not most, of the world's earliest books (examples of what paleographers call a codex) were Bibles. The fact that we even have books in the first place flows substantially from the conviction of the early Christians that the books of the Bible were the word of God—to be published for all to read, hear, and understand.
2. On Paul's message to the Athenians in both its ancient context and modern application, see Paul Copan and Kenneth D. Litwak, *The Gospel in the Marketplace of Ideas: Paul's Mars Hill Experience for Our Pluralistic World* (Downers Grove, IL: IVP Academic, 2014).
3. While the entire NT was written in one language, Greek, the OT was written in two: 99% in Hebrew, 1% in the sister language of Aramaic (Ezra 4:8–6:18; Jer 10:11; Dan 2:4–7:28; and two words in Gen 31:47).
4. The letters YHWH (*yodh heth waw heth*) are called the *Tetragrammaton*, Greek for four letters. These four Hebrew consonants are conventionally rendered in English by the four English letters L-O-R-D.

5. Hebrew and OT scholars believe the word was pronounced "Yahweh." Note that the synthetic "Jehovah" is a forced combination of the consonants of YHWH with the vowels of *'Adônai.* (The Masoretic scribes supplied the vowels from *'Adônai,* which are a-ô-a. Put together, the word appeared to be pronounced YeHoWaH, or Jehovah.) In other words, the well-known "Jehovah" is found nowhere in the Bible. As for uttering the divine name, unlike Orthodox Jews, who out of reverence dare not pronounce YHWH, substituting instead the word *'Adônai* (Lord) or *ha-shēm* (the Name), Christians are free to say "Yahweh."
6. Derek Kidner, *Genesis: An Introduction & Commentary* in Tyndale Old Testament Commentaries (Downers Grove, IL: InterVarsity Press, 1967), 9.

I

–

ORIENTATION

The next four chapters cover background information without which the message of Genesis 1–11 is easily missed. We will answer the simple question, What is Genesis about? But since we all come to the text with certain assumptions and backgrounds, how can we know whether we're approaching it the right way? To answer this, we will examine the three principal written sources predating Genesis with which it is indirectly interacting. We will also become familiar with some of the gods and goddesses thought to exist by the peoples of the ancient Near East.

But first, let's take a peek under the hood, so to speak, at how the opening book of the Bible is structured. We may not be used to thinking of books of the Bible in this way, but all of them are carefully constructed, from the shortest (like Obadiah or 2 John) to the longest (Jeremiah, or the second longest, Psalms). Structure frequently enhances and reinforces the biblical message.

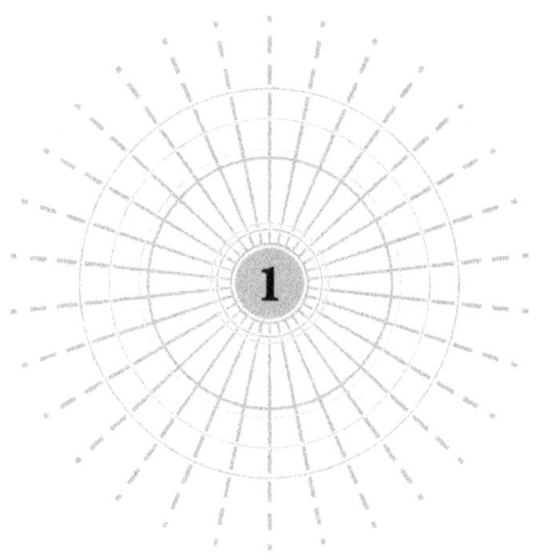

Genesis

Structure

1. The Word "Genesis"

In many Bibles and languages, Genesis is The First Book of Moses.[7] In Hebrew it is *b^{e}rē'shîth* (also the first word of the Hebrew Bible), meaning "in the beginning." Greek speakers called it *Genesis*, which means "beginning, origin, or descent." Most English speakers call Genesis by its Greek name.

Although the first book of the Bible is ancient, it resonates with all of us who live in the modern age. God, the gracious Creator, brought our world into being. Our origin lies in his personhood and will, and in aligning ourselves with his purposes is the key to the life God intended us to live (Jn 10:10). Since we have all wandered away from God, the path back to him entails appreciating where we have come from. Thus, to discover our origin is to discover our destiny. Genesis lays out basic insights vital for human life and flourishing. Whereas idolatry leads to error, heartache, and alienation, true godliness enables us to truly live.

2. Two Ages

Genesis begins with a prehistory, the Primeval Age.[8] It continues into the mainstream of history with the Patriarchal Age, which, once we reach Exodus, flows into the national history of Israel that ends in 2 Kings.[9] Creation is recounted in barely fifty verses. The focus rapidly narrows to the creation of humankind, continuing in a genealogy that leads (in the next testament) to the birth of the heavenly Savior of the earth.

Genesis spotlights four key events in the Primeval Age and four main figures in the Patriarchal Age. As a "patriarch" is "a father and ruler of a family or tribe," the term "patriarchal" refers to the era during which men—fathers and grandfathers especially—functioned as heads of society, leaders of God's people.

Primeval Age	*Patriarchal Age*
Adam and Eve (2:4–5:5)–Garden	Abraham (11:27–25:18)
Cain and Abel (4:1–25)–Field	Isaac (21:1–35:29)
Noah and family (6:8–9:29)–Flood	Jacob (25:19–37:1)
Nations and Babel (10:1–11:9)–Tower	Joseph (37:2–50:26)

The patriarchal period includes the stories of Abraham (c. 2000 BC), his son Isaac, his grandson Jacob, and his great-grandson Joseph, whose death is recorded at the end of Genesis (eighteenth century BC). If you are a newcomer to the Bible, you may find it helpful to commit to memory these sequences: *Garden–Field–Flood–Tower* and *Abraham–Isaac–Jacob–Joseph.*

When Abraham visited Egypt, he may well have seen the Great Pyramid—already over 500 years old at the time. When Joseph invited his father, his brothers, and their families to Egypt, their part of the world was suffering a terrible famine. God brought the Israelites into Egypt, which was literally their salvation (Gen 45:7; 50:20). In time, however, Egypt would mean enslavement—both in symbol and in actuality.

The author of Genesis is genealogically tracking the "chosen seed of Israel's race"[10]—that is, the generations of the chosen people, the Jews.[11] Since history and archaeology have preserved the memory of structures, like the famous Tower of Babel, and because the city of Ur, Abraham's first home (Gen 11–12), has been excavated, we can roughly date the beginning of the Patriarchal Age from about 2000 BC to the time of Moses (thirteenth century BC).

3. Ten Generations

Scripture consistently focuses on persons and relationships. The generational structure of Genesis centers on *people*—not protons, protoplasm, or pulsars. Science and technology play an important role in human culture, in investigating God's world, and even in appreciating how Yahweh accommodated his message to the ancients, coming down to their level. (More on this in Appendix D.) The ten *toledoth*[12] (generations) are as follows:

1. The heavens and the earth (2:4a)[13]
2. Adam and his descendants (5:1)
3. Noah (6:9)
4. Shem, Ham, and Japheth (10:1)
5. Shem (11:10)
6. Terah (11:27)
7. Ishmael (25:12)
8. Isaac (25:19)
9. Esau (36:1 and 9)
10. Jacob (37:2)[14]

OT scholars have detected an even deeper inner structure in Genesis, but it is beyond the scope of this book. In fact, many biblical books are carefully composed.[15] If we studied the original Hebrew text, we would notice abundant literary features that contribute to the remarkable theology and message of Genesis.

4. Twelve Themes

In addition to the organizational structure we have noted, there are several biblical themes in the early chapters of Genesis. That is, the major themes of Genesis are the themes of the Bible. As one scholar notes, "Genesis 1–11 may be seen to set out the fundamental theological and ethical assumptions that are presupposed in the rest of Scripture." For ancient—and also for modern—readers, "it distinguishes Israelite faith from the beliefs of their contemporaries in neighboring lands."[16] These themes include (though are not limited to) the following:

1. *God*—The Creator does not beg for our service or worship out of some need on his part. His blessings are generously and freely given. Outside the Bible no "god" is so desirous of a relationship with his creatures. Some may believe that humans are nothing special—mere animals without ultimate significance—but the biblical message strongly contradicts such a position.
2. *Worship*—We worship only one God, since other deities are false gods. Worship is for our benefit, not his.
3. *Order*—God is a God of order. He is consistently reasonable, not capricious or chaotic. Since God is good, his divine law enables the world to function smoothly—to be good.
4. *Sin and guilt*—Morality and evil are realities. Sin lies at the root of our problems, directly or indirectly. Sin grieves Yahweh God and causes him sorrow (Gen 6:6). Furthermore, when humans deviate from God's will, there are consequences.
5. *Sacrifice*—True religion is based on true sacrifice. God requires sacrifice of us; after all, he always gives his best without holding back. Moreover, God cannot be manipulated by sacrifice, unlike genies or ancient Near Eastern gods.
6. *Grace*—God is always willing to grant a fresh start to those who seek him. Grace is one of the strongest themes in Genesis.

7. *Providence*—God provides for his creation, anticipating needs years—even generations—in advance, and sovereignly working out all the necessary arrangements.
8. *Marriage and family*—God affirms marriage and family. If we do things God's way, these relationships bring great blessing. The ancient Canaanites and the surrounding nations were guilty of adultery, pederasty, prostitution, fertility cults, and other sexual perversions.[17] This departs from God's created order, according to Genesis. When it comes to building family, God asks us to trust and obey.
9. *Work*—Man is created to work, not to be lazy. Perhaps disappointing to some, the institution of work predates the fall, being present in the condition of "paradise" (Gen 2:15). Various natural processes need to be reined in or tamed—as all gardeners know (Gen 1:28).
10. *Justice*—Wrong must be requited. Sin is still sin, no matter how much we rationalize it. The theme of justice runs deep and strong in the OT. To truly be God, this supreme Source of all good must punish wrong and reward what is right.
11. *Seed*—This is closely connected with the generations theme. We can trace the theme from the seed of Eve (3:15) through Abraham, Isaac, Jacob, and Judah—and then, through David, all the way to the Messiah.[18] God does not permit any person or power to extinguish the line of his godly offspring.[19]
12. *Covenant*—God desires friendship with humans, and he enters into covenant relationship with them (Gen 9; 15; 17; 28; cf. Ex 19–20; etc.). Through Christ, God initiates a relationship (Rom 5:6–10), but we have a responsibility to respond to his initiating grace (Acts 7:51; 17:30) and to remain in the relationship by that same grace (Col 2:6; Jude 21).

In Genesis, God spells out how life works—not by the complex mechanisms of microbiology, not by specific instructions about every decision we will ever be faced with, and not by answers to every question we might think of, but by trusting and obeying God as we attend to his intentions for us and the rest of his creation.

This is not to say that when it comes to interpretation, anyone's guess is as good as anyone else's. Interpretation is both essential and unavoidable; otherwise we would never grasp the Scriptures at all, being unable to appreciate context, content, or application. So it's not a case of interpretation versus truth, but sound interpretation versus dubious interpretation—which is why Chapter 2, "Ancient Sources," is so important.

---

7. We will leave several introductory matters unexplored.
   - One area is authorship. Moses is responsible for part, but not all, of the Torah. And yet the entire Law is attributed to him, in the same way that the book of Psalms as a whole is attributed to David, even though many psalms themselves do not support his direct authorship (naming instead Asaph, Solomon, the Sons of Korah, and others). For more on the authorship of Genesis, see https://www.douglasjacoby.com/?p=16516.
   - Literary (or oral) sources are a second area for another study, and we trust that careful OT scholars who detect sources are as cautious as they are discerning.
   - A third area on which we will only barely touch is the debate about science and Genesis. This is generally uncontroversial among Christians in the biological sciences, and yet it can be highly divisive among believers outside the sciences, or those unfamiliar with genetics, geology, cosmology, and other fields. The fast pace of modern science means that the nonspecialist or general reader can barely manage to keep up with the trends along the frontiers of knowledge.
8. Primeval (Lat. *primum*, first + *aevum*, age) means "pertaining to the first age of the world; primitive" (*Oxford Abridged Dictionary*).
9. However, in the order of the Hebrew canon, this section is "Ruth-less." Instead, Ruth appears after the book of Proverbs.
10. The hymn "All Hail the Power of Jesus Name" was written by Edward Perronet (1779), music by Oliver Holden (1793).
11. For a fascinating study of the theme of "seed," see Appendix C, "Genesis Genealogies: Genesis 5, 10–11: The Spreading of the 'Seed.'"
12. Some scholars recognize 12 *toledoth*. The account of Esau (Gen 36:1–43) uses the word twice, emphasizing two aspects of Esau's family, while the initial "genesis," 1:1–2:3, does not use the word at all. However, in the same way that 1:1–2:3 and 36:1–43 each deal with a single topic, it is better to count 10 *toledoth*, or *geneseis*.
13. This "generation" is a sort of personification (though not deification) of heaven and earth. Perhaps the author wanted to emphasize that our ultimate origin is closely connected with the creation itself, although of course not in any pantheistic sense.
14. There are ten generations from Adam to Noah, ten from Noah to Abram. Also notice that Abraham and Joseph are absent from the *toledoth* formula. As for Abraham, Terah's line included not just Abraham, but a large number of the personae of Genesis. As for Joseph, keeping in mind that Genesis is written for Jews and from a Jewish perspective, it is fitting that the ten generations terminate in Jacob, the father of the twelve tribes. In this way, the accent is placed on Jacob's generation—Israel—thus setting the stage for the Exodus. After all,

the Exodus involved far more than the two "half-tribes" of Ephraim and Manasseh (the sons of Joseph). All twelve exited Egypt.

15. Three examples will need to suffice. Matthew is built around five tracts of teaching material—paralleling, in all likelihood, the five books of the Torah; Matthew gives the "new" law. Psalms does the same, the Psalter grouped into five books. For an even more striking example, see Ps 119. Even if you can't read Hebrew, you will easily see the repetition of letters at the beginning of each line in the original text. Lamentations is an acrostic poem. That is, each successive verse begins with the next letter of the Hebrew alphabet. Most books in the Bible have been structured—for theological purposes—and commentaries and OT and NT surveys bring this out, even though it may not be apparent in the English Bible.
16. Gordon J. Wenham, *Rethinking Genesis 1–11: Gateway to the Bible* (Eugene, OR: Cascade, 2015), 13.
17. In Eden, homosexuality, incest, and adultery were all demographically impossible. In connection with family sexual culture, surrogate childbirth was also practiced in the ancient Near East and is well documented (see Gen 16)—although this seems to be a morally neutral matter, not a sin.
18. Yet not all ten *toledoth* contain the messianic bloodline. The seventh (Ishmael) and ninth (Esau) lie outside the genealogy of Christ.
19. See, for example, Gen 38.

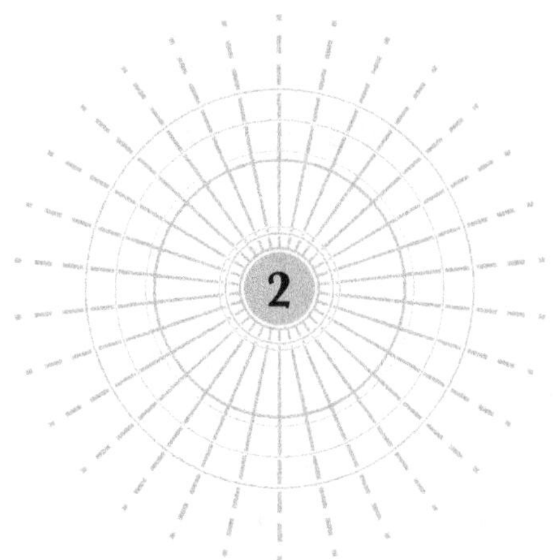

Ancient Sources

As Christian writers and university professors, we both travel a lot. It helps to know something of the culture, language, history, and geography of a country before the plane lands. What is the climate like? How do people dress? What sorts of things do they eat—and how (spoon, hands, or chopsticks)? Is the country stable? Will civil unrest, war, or high crime affect the trip? What language(s) are spoken? Do we need translators? We also try to engage with the people we meet.

Visiting the world of the Bible is like visiting a foreign country—because we *are* visiting a foreign country. The cultural gap between the biblical world and our own is enormous. Without adequate preparation, we run the risk of becoming confused or bored—or (worse) assuming we get it when we don't. Even if we were brought up around church—perhaps *especially* if we were brought up around church—chances are high that we missed out on the necessary preparation and may have some unlearning to do.

Civilizations of the Biblical World (years approximate)

Civilization (years BC)	*Ancient location*	*Modern location*
Egyptians (5000-333)	Africa	Africa
Sumerians (4500-1900)	Mesopotamia	Iraq & Kuwait*
Akkadians (2300-2100)	Mesopotamia	Iraq & Kuwait
Old Babylonians (2000–1595)	Mesopotamia	Iraq & Kuwait
Canaanites (1800–587)	Canaan/Israel	Israel**
Hittites (1600–1190)	Anatolia	Turkey
Assyrians (1300–605)	Mesopotamia	Iraq & Kuwait
Neobabylonians (626–539)	Mesopotamia	Iraq & Kuwait

* Also includes sections of Turkey and Syria
** Also includes sections of Lebanon and Syria

While the truths and commands of Scripture directed to us Christ-followers are valid and practical anywhere on the planet, the world of the Bible is remarkably small. It does not include most of Africa, Europe, or Asia. It is unaware of Australia or the Americas. Israel itself is a minuscule state. Nearly all the action takes place in the locale of the eastern Mediterranean, and even then, the setting is usually (what we call) the Middle East. The "ancient Near East" is another common term in studies on this part of the world during that age.

The biblical story does not take place in a vacuum. It takes place in our three-dimensional world—hence history's essential companion, geography. The setting for much of Gen 1–11 is ancient Mesopotamia, strategically located where trade routes from Africa, Asia, and Europe converge, and where a series of powerful city-states emerged. Mesopotamia lies between the Tigris and the Euphrates rivers.[20] These rivers, never more than 100 miles apart, flow in the same direction and frame the "Fertile Crescent," in which lay a succession of ancient kingdoms: Sumer, Akkad, Babylon, and Assyria. Ancient Mesopotamia is more or less the modern land of Iraq.

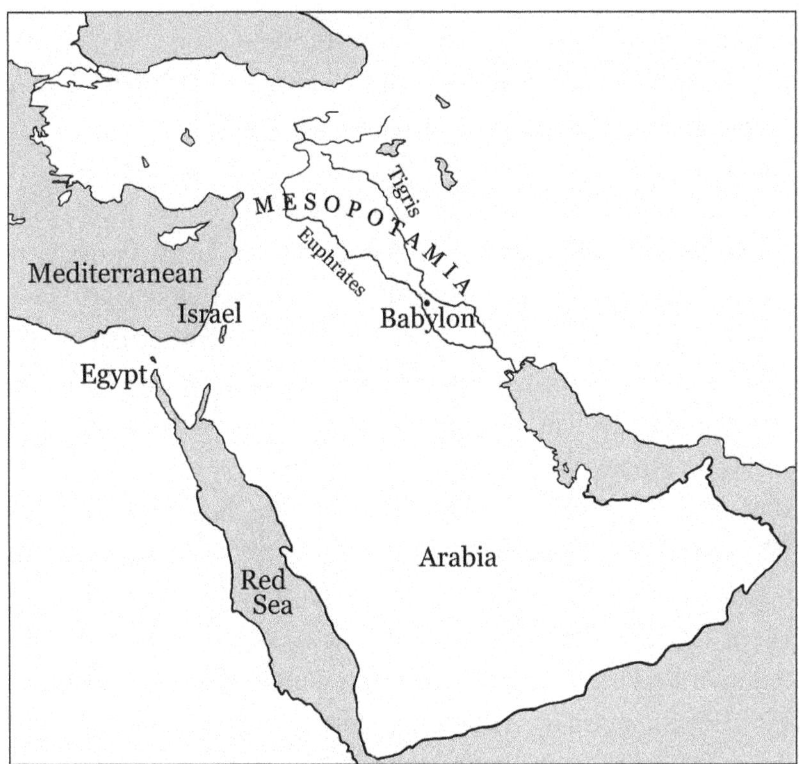

The World of Genesis 1-11 [21]

Cultural Backdrop

Egyptian and Mesopotamian civilizations had existed for over two millennia before Israel came into being. Most of the motifs in Gen 1–11 were inherited from the neighbors. Stories of origins were well known in Mesopotamia from before 1600 BC. The final version of Genesis was evidently written no earlier than 1000 BC, since the monarchy, to which the text refers, was established in the late eleventh century (cf. Gen 36:31).[22] It was only natural, then, that Genesis should speak to people in terms with which they were familiar—those of their own culture.

The biblical writers were aware of the surrounding world. They spoke often of foreign powers, trade, commerce, and war. Imports and exports led to a distribution not only of goods, but also of phrases, ideas, and even religions. When we approach Genesis without giving any thought to its cultural and historical background, we not only underestimate the author(s), but end up wresting the various accounts from their proper contexts. We are more likely to misinterpret—and to import our own ideas into the text.

It bears repeating that the environs of ancient Mesopotamia are not *our world*, which is why we need some preparation before "visiting" (through reading Scripture) the ancient world. Some believers become uneasy about using uninspired books to assist in illumination of the inspired Word. However, we are unlikely to be tuned in to the ancient world (before and during biblical times) if our knowledge of Genesis has come exclusively through a children's Sunday school curriculum, the average Bible class or sermon, or even from just reading the Bible. We need more.

Most of the material in Gen 1–11 closely parallels pagan accounts of primeval history. But although Genesis refers to the same events—creation, flood, etc.—it turns them on their heads. The folly of idolatry is exposed, often even satirized. Accordingly, several scholars have described Gen 1–11 as a "tract for the times." In the words of Gordon Wenham, "Genesis is flatly contradicting the humanistic optimism of Mesopotamia: humanity's situation in its view is hopeless without divine mercy."[23]

There is no more solid method for appreciating the world of the Bible than taking the time to study the ancient world. This is true not only for the OT, but also for the New Testament (NT). Furthermore, use of sources, even though they originate outside the people of God, should not alarm us. Many biblical writers, like Luke and Paul, freely admit to using other sources (Lk 1:1–4; Acts 17:28). In the OT, we see quotations from the "book of Jashar"—apparently a poetic work (Josh 10:13; 2 Sam 1:18). Sometimes, however, quoted material may be less obvious. The NT incorporates at least sixteen extrabiblical sources, including nine or ten pagan citations. For the OT, we count at least twenty-four sources.[24]

To connect with the people of their day, the writers of the Bible had to use words, phrases, and concepts that were familiar to their audience. They may have been writing for posterity, but surely they weren't focused on twenty-first-century issues. Their concern was *their* world, *their* era.

Few of us specialize in ancient history, but anyone can become familiar with the literary background. Might we not read the Bible in a different way—in a different light? Perhaps it's time for an illustration.

Goldilocks and the Four Bears

Like most children in the US, we were brought up on nursery rhymes and fairy tales. One of these was "Goldilocks and the Four Bears." (In some cultures, Goldilocks may not be a familiar children's story at all, and if that is the case, of course the reader is excused for not noticing our edits.) In this story, little Goldilocks has wandered deep into the forest. She comes across a cottage, and through its open windows is wafting the smell of delicious spaghetti and meatballs. The residents, four bears, have gone for a walk while the hot meal cools. Realizing no one is at home, Goldilocks sits in their chairs, samples their spaghetti, and then falls asleep in baby bear's bed. She is later startled when the bears return but is rescued when a park ranger puts the bears into a zoo.

Most kids, if they heard us tell the story above, would interrupt with squeals of "No!" and "That's not how it goes!" That's because they know there are only *three* bears; that Goldilocks ate *porridge*, not spaghetti; that Goldilocks, terrified, leaps out the window, never to return; and that the bear family returns from their walk for lunch in their cottage—not to be caged in a zoo.[25] Any changes to a familiar story tend to be highly noticeable.

What's the point?

- Creating stories, or tapping into existing ones, is a great way to engage an audience or an individual.
- When the story is familiar, the alteration of any key element will be noticed.

- There were multiple stories circulating in the ancient Near East, familiar to the local peoples—including the Israelites. Together they shaped the cultural background of the world directly addressed by Genesis.
- Since these stories promoted idolatry, immorality, and error about God/deity, they needed to be countered. One highly effective way of doing this was to retell—and reshape—them.
- The truth (biblical theology) is most visible at the points where the story has been recast.
- Yet people notice the differences only if they know the original. The original hearers of Genesis were more likely to comprehend the message than we are, especially if we have not been familiarized with the Mesopotamian background narrative.

Principal Ancient Near Eastern Texts Illuminating Genesis 1–11

Gilgamesh Epic	22nd–21st cent. BC	Garden and flood
Atrahasis Epic	18th cent. BC[26]	Babylonian creation myth and flood account, on Sumerian base
Enuma Elish	18th–11th cent. BC[27]	Babylonian creation myth

Pagan Parallels

This perspective is borne out by the OT, as observed by Conrad Hyers:

> Jewish Scripture abounds in literary allusion and poetic usage which bear some relation, direct or indirect, to images and themes found among the peoples with which Israel was in contact.
>
> An analogy may be drawn from contemporary English usage which contains innumerable traces of the languages and literatures,

> myths and legends, customs and beliefs, of a great many cultures and periods which have enriched its development. Thus one finds not only a considerable amount of terminology drawn from Greek, Latin, French, German, etc.... but [also] references derived from the myths, legends, fables and fairy tales of many peoples: the Greek Fates, the Roman Fortune, the arrows of Cupid, Woden's day and Thor's day, and even Christmas and Easter...[28]

Then Hyers puts his finger on the hub of the matter, which is not the pagan motifs themselves, but the theological points Yahweh is conveying.

> The issue, then, is not where the language (Hebrew) and certain words and phrases came from, but the uses to which they are put, and the ways in which they are put differently. The cosmogonic [birth of cosmos] form and imagery [watery chaos, separation of heavens and the earth, and other elements familiar in the Near East], in this case, is not chosen in order to espouse these other cosmogonies... or even to borrow from them, but precisely in order to deny them.[29]

Without doubt, a vital component in the historical background of Genesis is its religious milieu. Genesis was written against the backdrop of a polytheistic society and exposes the manmade religions of idolatry for what they are. The casual reader is not apt to notice that Genesis has a polemical edge, but the more one knows about the sham—and shallow—pagan background of the times, the more striking the edge appears.

If we are to be fair in our comparisons of pagan myths with the Genesis material, there is an important point we should appreciate. In modern parlance, "myth" usually implies falsehood. But if we are to be careful students of ancient religions, we probably need to revise our definition.

> Discussions about the early chapters of Genesis often focus on whether the accounts are mythology or history. It is an important

> question, but framing it this way may not be the best approach. Today, we often consider the label *mythology* to imply that what is reported is "not real." But in the ancient world, they did not consider what we call their mythology to be not real. To the contrary, they believed their mythology to represent the most important reality–deep reality, which transcends what could be reported in terms of events that have transpired in the strictly human realm. Indeed, they further considered that even the events in the human realm, which we might label *history*, found their greatest significance in aspects of the event that human eyewitnesses could not see–the involvement of the divine hand.[30]

Let us now spend a few moments becoming familiar with the principal ancient texts whose narratives were familiar to the Genesis writer(s) and with which they interacted. If through reading this book you become only generally familiar with the *top three* sources reflecting the cultural backdrop of Mesopotamia, you will never read early Genesis the same way again.

I. The *Gilgamesh Epic*

The *Gilgamesh Epic* is one of the best known of the ancient Mesopotamian sources, known by everyone from schoolboys to kings.[31]

Gilgamesh was the king of Uruk (biblical Erech)—or was he? King Arthur, c. AD 500, and Robin Hood, c. AD 1100, may well have been historical individuals—around whom was wrapped the stuff of legend. Gilgamesh was supposedly two parts god, one part man. Yet he probably *was* an actual king (2800–2500 BC), even though copious legendary material has been rolled into the epic version of his life.[32]

After the king seizes his subjects' sons for his army and lies with their virgin daughters in the practice of first night,[33] they complain to the gods. The gods create Enkidu[34] to confront Gilgamesh—in effect, Enkidu is a second Gilgamesh. He is a primitive man with shaggy hair, who drinks from the forest pools and is a friend of the animals—because he *is* an animal. Enkidu becomes "civilized" by having sex with a prostitute. He confronts Gilgamesh in Uruk; they grapple with each other, but Gilgamesh prevails—and they end up becoming close comrades. Soon the friends set out to locate and destroy the monster Humbaba—and succeed. Later, the goddess Ishtar (an insatiable sexual predator) makes an advance toward Gilgamesh, but he rebuffs her. In return, she sends the Bull of Heaven to kill Gilgamesh and Enkidu, but instead they kill the bull.

One day Enkidu dies. "Six days and seven nights I mourned, until a worm crawled out of his nose." Shamash, sun god and deity of retributive justice, says in effect, "You're mortal. Get over it!" Deeply affected, Gilgamesh sets out to find wisdom and the secret of everlasting life. After all, the pleasures of life and glories of being a hero figure all end in darkness—in meaninglessness. The Mesopotamian underworld is a dreary place.

Gilgamesh then sets out on a quest to find Utnapishtim, the only man to have received immortality from the gods. (Utnapishtim's wife had also received this gift.) Gilgamesh is taken aback that Utnapishtim isn't a hero like himself. Utnapishtim reveals a secret: a plant at the bottom of the abyss, that confers eternal life.

Utnapishtim is also the Noah of the Mesopotamian flood story, having survived the deluge. He tells Gilgamesh of his survival on a large boat, along with his family and pairs of animals. The flood is not sent to provide the human race with a new beginning (as in Genesis). It was decreed by the chief gods in council: Anu, god of the firmament; Enlil, god of earth, wind, and air; Ennugi, the god of irrigation; Ninurta, god of war and wells; and Ea, the god of wisdom and crafts. Enlil orders a flood to destroy humankind, but Ea finds a way to tip off Utnapishtim by warning his *house* about the flood—in which Utnapishtim happens to be at the time.[35]

Let us return to the quest for immortality. Gilgamesh ties heavy stones to his feet and plunges into the bottom of the abyss. He finds the plant of which Utnapishtim spoke and retrieves it. Later, however, while he is napping, a snake steals the plant. Gilgamesh, now knowing that eternal life is no longer accessible to him, returns to Uruk. The epic concludes with Gilgamesh marveling at the city of Uruk, realizing that the only "afterlife" will consist of his reputation—his royal honor and legacy. After much weeping and further reflection, Gilgamesh makes peace with his status as a mortal, continues his reign, and makes the most of life.[36] Yet the overall tone of this epic is pessimistic.[37] In contrast, Genesis neither downplays human sinfulness nor offers saccharine solutions to existential problems. Rather, it emphasizes personal accountability and consequences (as opposed to life being dictated by the whims of the gods), seasoned with divine grace.

II. The *Atrahasis Epic*

The *Atrahasis Epic* is an early Sumerian-Babylonian creation and flood story. The junior-level gods rebel after becoming frustrated with the work of digging canals, and a war between the gods ensues.[38] Now the gods are no longer willing to carry out their backbreaking work. What to do? The problem is solved by the creation of humans. Seven original males and females are made from dust combined with the blood of a sacrificed god.[39] The humans' purpose? To take over the menial labors of the gods so that they may no longer be fatigued, but content.

The story then moves on to the major characters: Anu, god of heaven; Enlil, god of earth; Enki, god of the underworld; and Atrahasis, a human king. Enlil, whose sleep has been disturbed by the noisy humans, seeks to drown them by means of a flood. Meanwhile, Enki (Ea of the *Gilgamesh Epic*) warns Atrahasis to build a boat in order to survive the calamity—not directly, but by allowing Atrahasis to overhear the news. It seems the cataclysm was a river flood (Tablet III).

Atrahasis plays the same role as Utnapishtim, except that Atrahasis and his wife are already immortal. Of the three ancient accounts (in their various iterations through the centuries), the *Atrahasis Epic* has the most points of contact with the Bible (Gen 2–8).

III. *Enuma Elish*

The Babylonian creation myth *Enuma Elish*[40] covers the sweep of history from the creation of the world—coming into existence as a result of battle between two gods, Marduk[41] and Tiamat—to the construction of the temple of Marduk. Bill Arnold notes, "Both the *Enuma Elish* and the Ugaritic *Baal Cycle* close their creation accounts in cultic dramas, in the building of great temples, and in the case of *Enuma Elish*, specifically as a place of 'rest.' Likewise, in the Memphite theology of ancient Egypt, the god Ptah rested after creating everything."[42]

In *Enuma Elish*, humankind was created to do the work the gods did not want to do themselves. Under King Hammurabi (1792–1750 BC), known for his famous law code, one of the earliest in all of history, Babylon had become the most powerful city in Mesopotamia—with Marduk being promoted to king of the gods.

IV. Other Sources

Eridu Genesis (c. 1600 BC) is a (fragmentary) Sumerian epic primarily concerned with the creation, the rise of cities, and the flood. According to *Eridu*, after the world was created out of the primeval sea and the gods were born, the deities created humans out of clay. Their purpose? To till the ground, care for flocks and herds, and perpetuate the worship of the gods. In time, cities were built and kings began to rule. At a certain point, the gods decided to destroy humans by means of a flood, although one (Enki) reveals the plan to Ziusudra (Utnapishtim). Ziusudra builds a large boat, escaping the destruction of the flood. Afterward, in recognition of his righteous life, the gods gift Ziusudra with immortality.

Egyptian creation myths are an important backdrop for appreciating the Genesis account. "Although there are nearly one dozen Egyptian creation myths, the three most dominant arose in the cultic sites of Heliopolis, Memphis, and Hermopolis.... They all feature the similar concepts of a primordial ocean, a primeval hill, and the deification of nature."[43] We'll explore this in our commentary on Gen 1–2.

Tremper Longman III and John Walton, biblical authorities who have written extensively on the background of the OT, remind us of how well poised modern scholars are to scrutinize the ancient world:

> Throughout most of history, scholars have not had access to the information from the ancient world and therefore could not use it to inform their interpretation. Even the early Christian writers

> were interested in accessing the ancient world (as indicated from their frequent reference to Berossus, a Babylonian priest in the third century BC) but had very limited resources. However, since the beginning of the massive archaeological undertakings in Iraq from the middle of the nineteenth century, more than one million cuneiform texts have been excavated that expose the ancient literature through which we can gain important new insight into the ancient world. This is what provides the basis for our interpretation of the early chapters of Genesis as an ancient document.[44]

Conclusion

Once we reach Abraham (introduced in Gen 11 and setting out by faith in Gen 12), there is no indication that we are still reading reevaluated and retooled stories from the pagan world. Genesis 1–11 gives us a compressed history that engages with themes found in ancient myths, in some cases appropriating, in other ways reworking, and at a number of points rejecting various aspects of them. To be sure, in Gen 12–50 there are still many points of cultural connection, and some passages are difficult to fathom when read simplistically and without giving proper attention to their ancient context. Yet instead of a compressed history that interacts with pagan myths, once we come to Abraham, we have the sense that we have stepped into the mainstream of history.

Some of the disagreement about Gen 1–11 may result from biases we bring to the text or perhaps from differing personal, denominational, or philosophical perspectives. That is why in the next chapter we will check our interests against ancient interests, to ascertain whether we are asking the right questions.

---

20. *Mesopotamia* is literally "[the land] between the rivers," from the Greek words *mesos* "amidst," and *potamos*, "river." Canals and irrigation ditches were dug to facilitate extensive agriculture. Unfortunately, "the Euphrates, Iraq's lifeblood, has now decreased to one-third its normal capacity." Joshua Hammer, "Troubled Water," *Smithsonian* (December 2017): 71.
21. Map created by Kedamawit Atsbeha, 19 October 2017.

22. Key moments in OT history: 1290 BC (the Exodus), 1010 (King David), 930 (Divided Kingdom), 722 (fall of Northern Kingdom of Israel to Assyrians), 587 (fall of Southern Kingdom of Judah to Babylonians), 538 (resettlement by leave of Persian King Cyrus).
23. Gordon J. Wenham, *Genesis 1–15*, Word Biblical Commentary, Volume 1 (Waco, TX: Word Books, 1987), xlviii.
24. For the NT, see the list at https://www.douglasjacoby.com/nt-extrabiblical-sources/. For the OT, the list is at https://www.douglasjacoby.com/old-testament-extrabiblical-sources/.
25. When my (Douglas's) children were young, we enjoyed such a fairy tale, "The True Story of the Three Little Pigs"—skewed in favor of the wolf: "Alexander T. Wolf was framed! All he wanted to do was borrow a cup of sugar to make a cake for his granny. Unfortunately, a bad cold and some unfriendly neighbors landed Al in a heap of trouble. Now in jail, Al recounts what really happened to the three little pigs." https://www.barnesandnoble.com/w/true-story-of-the-three-little-pigs-jon-scieszka/1102955029#/.
26. *The Atrahasis Epic* has been translated from copies (c. 650 BC) discovered from the royal library of Nineveh.
27. The oldest surviving manuscripts of *Enuma Elish* come from the 7th cent. BC.
28. Conrad Hyers, "The Narrative Form of Genesis 1: Cosmogonic, Yes; Scientific, No," *Journal of the American Scientific Affiliation* 36.4 (1984): 210a–b. Accessible at http://faculty.gordon.edu/hu/bi/ted_hildebrandt/otesources/01-genesis/text/articles-books/hyers_gen1_jasa.htm. Cited with permission.
29. Hyers, "Narrative Form."
30. Tremper Longman III and John H. Walton, *The Lost World of the Flood: Mythology, Theology, and the Deluge Debate* (Downers Grove, IL: IVP Academic, 2017), 17.
31. A fragment of the *Gilgamesh Epic* from the late second millennium BC was discovered in the excavations at Megiddo. Source: https://eprints.soas.ac.uk/3251/1/GilgameshWhat%27sNew.pdf.
32. Kenton L. Sparks, *Ancient Texts for the Study of the Hebrew Bible: A Guide to the Background Literature* (Peabody, MA: Hendrickson, 2005), 275–278.
33. *Ius primae noctis* (Lat., "the law of the first night") was a medieval custom allowing a nobleman to sleep with a virgin bride on her wedding night, before her own husband lay with her.
34. Enkidu was also the name of an actual Sumerian king, c. 2700 BC.
35. Ea even tells him what to say to the neighbors, in so many words, "I think the god Enlil has rejected me. So I must go down to the apsu [the waters of the abyss] and stay with my master Ea. Then he will shower abundance on you." This abundance includes fish. Of course, when Utnapishtim repeats these words, he is dissembling. The neighbors will have fish in abundance—because they will drown in the depths. All that will be showered down on them are the waters of the flood!
36. Glenn. S. Holland, *Religion in the Ancient World* (Chantilly, VA: The Teaching Company, 2005), 75–84. Those familiar with the classics will recognize the literary genre, from both Homer's *Iliad* and *Odyssey* (Greece) and Virgil's *Aeneid* (Rome).
37. It is possible that the *Gilgamesh Epic* influenced Ecclesiastes. There are parallels in both content and order of presentation.
38. The technical term for war between the gods is theomachy. For example, theomachy is illustrated on the friezes of the Parthenon in Athens.
39. The sacrificed God is Qingu, who is a clumsy laborer.
40. *Enuma Elish* means "When on high," as various sections of the work start with these two words. "When on high no name was given to heaven / Nor below was the netherworld called by name / Primeval Apsu was their progenitor / And matrix*-Tiamat was she who bore them all / They were mingling their waters together." See Benjamin Foster, "Epic of Creation

(1.111)" in COS 1:391, Tablet I, lines 1–5, which is the very beginning of the composition, corresponding to Gen 1:1–2. * Note: *Matrix* is Lat. for womb.

41. In the NIV; "Merodach" in the NRSV.
42. Arnold continues, "At the conclusion of each of these, the cultic drama gives reason for the preeminence of a deity, of a temple, or of a specific cultic feature of life or worship." Bill T. Arnold, *Genesis*, in The New Cambridge Bible Commentary (New York: Cambridge University Press, 2009), 29n3.

    > The major Egyptian creation myths, and the chief deities involved in creation, were celebrated in Heliopolis (Atum), Hermopolis (Thoth), Thebes (Khnum), and Memphis (Ptah). Of interest to readers of Genesis, Khnum creates humans on a potter's wheel, while Ptah speaks into creation by his powerful word. Yet the Egyptian gods took little interest in humans; apart from the pharaohs, there seems to be virtually no relationship between gods and humans—who are nothing special.

    Holland, *Religion in the Ancient World*, lesson 6.
43. The following sets the citation in its context:

    > The ancient Egyptian beliefs and concepts of creation appear in various sources: Pyramid Texts, Coffin Texts, The Book of the Dead, The Memphite Theology, as well as various hymns, Wisdom texts, and wall bas-reliefs. These sources show that Egyptian cosmology is both uniform and diverse. Although there are nearly one dozen Egyptian creation myths, the three most dominant arose in the cultic sites of Heliopolis, Memphis, and Hermopolis. These three interconnect with one another, as evidenced by the appearance of some of the gods in more than one tradition. The cosmogonies of Heliopolis and Memphis share more in common with one another than with Hermopolis. However, they all feature the similar concepts of a primordial ocean, a primeval hill, and the deification of nature. These three cosmogonies deal specifically with how the god(s) created the world. They do not directly address the creation of humans and animals.... The Egyptians developed a separate creation tradition to explain the creation of humans and animals, namely the tradition of Khnum, the potter-god.

    Tony L. Shetter, "Genesis 1–2 In Light Of Ancient Egyptian Creation Myths," paper presented at the second annual Student Academic Conference at Dallas Theological Seminary, 18 April 2005. Accessible at https://bible.org/article/genesis-1-2-light-ancient-egyptian-creation-myths.
44. Longman and Walton, *Lost World of the Flood*, 13. Not all scholars are as optimistic about our ability to generalize from the textual evidence. See Noel K. Weeks, "The Bible and the 'Universal' Ancient World: A Critique of John Walton," *Westminster Theological Journal* 78 (2016): 1–28.

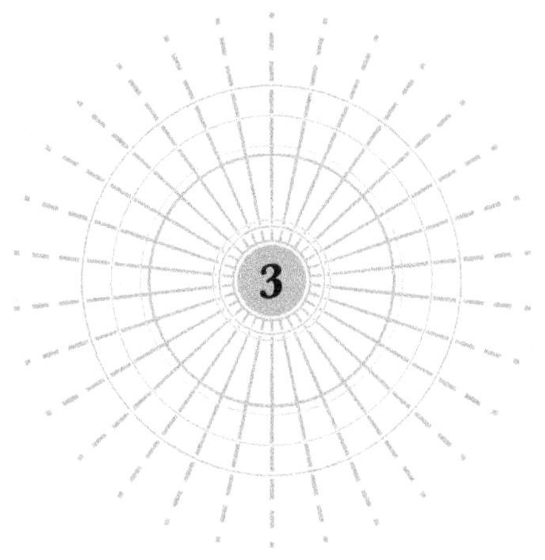

Ancient Agenda

How many modern readers care about ancient culture, history, gods, and goddesses, which are the raw materials of Gen 1–11? (Most were subject to heavy scrutiny—as well as retelling—in Genesis.) Probably not many—which is a shame, because they're missing all the good stuff! The really arresting insights come once we've "tuned in" to the correct frequencies. All of Gen 1–11 critiques ancient culture and beliefs, and if we can understand this critique, we will not only better grasp the message of Genesis, but also be better equipped to engage our own culture.

Agendas Modern and Ancient

Having taught from the Bible all over the world (frequently in academic settings), we are familiar with modern concerns about Genesis. These are reflected in questions not necessarily addressed by the text. *How long is a "day"? How could a snake talk? Did the ark have headroom for the giraffes? How did the kangaroos get there? Was the flood global or local? Was Eden wiped out in the flood? What about evolution? Where did the fossils come from if all species have been fixed since the beginning? How could Methuselah reach 969? Were there really giants, the offspring of gods and humans? Where's the original Tower of Babel? And Noah's ark? And what about the dinosaurs?*

Yet ancient concerns frequently diverge from our own. People were anxious about the threatening primordial, watery chaos ("Are we safe?"), just as they feared the powers of nature ("Are they gods? Can they hurt us? How may we appease them?"). Further concerns are reflected in the following queries: *Which gods should we follow? How many gods are there? What do the gods require? How can we ensure that crops won't fail? How should we relate to other people groups? Will I have children—sons, in particular, to extend the family line—or will the family line end with me? Is idolatry such a terrible thing? How can we preserve faith when displaced from our land? (And should we still keep the Sabbath?) Are the systems of the world (like Babylon) all-powerful? Could it be that Marduk really is the king of the gods?*

All of these are issues Genesis addresses. In other words, with a little work, we can gain insight into the concerns of our spiritual brothers and sisters of millennia past.

Questions Concerning Genesis 1–11 (typical)

Modern	***Ancient***
Was Adam a Neanderthal?	Who is Yahweh?
Did the flood cover Mt. Everest?	What about the other gods?
Have they found the ark?	Is God still with us in our exile?
How long are the days of Gen 1?	How may we please Yahweh?
Inconsequential	*Central emphasis*

In short, there are multiple differences between their concerns and our own—what roused their curiosity and what engages ours. But the divide between us is not as wide as we might think. We share many of the same concerns, especially existential ones.[45]

Gordon Wenham, a scholar of exceptional insight, comments:

> The ancient oriental background to Gen 1–11 shows it to be concerned with rather different issues from those that tend to preoccupy modern readers. It is affirming the unity of God in the face of polytheism, his justice rather than his caprice, his power as opposed to his impotence, his concern for mankind rather than his exploitation. And whereas Mesopotamia clung to the wisdom of primeval man, Genesis records his sinful disobedience. Because as Christians we tend to assume these points in our theology, we often fail to recognize the striking originality of the message of Gen 1–11 and concentrate on subsidiary points that may well be of less moment.[46]

If you are disappointed that this book sets too many modern concerns (the age of the earth, the origin of species, the location of the ark…) on the side, don't despair. The appendices and the many endnotes will prove helpful. Further, the bibliography (in the final section) could keep you busy for a long time.

Category Error

It bears repeating that reading the Bible (a) to answer modern questions it was never intended to answer or (b) to confirm previously held beliefs is a flawed approach to Scripture.

You wouldn't buy a physics textbook to find out how to improve your relationships. That's not the province of science. And next time you're at the bookstore, you won't be purchasing a new Bible to learn the latest discoveries in chemistry or physics. Nor, if we buy an international espionage novel, are we expecting to learn how to cook. If we did, our confused purchase would involve a category error. That would be fundamentally confusing the nature of the category (science book, spy novel, cookbook).

Genre

This discussion of category is integral to healthy biblical interpretation. This is true because the Bible is not a book so much as it is a library. Books in a library are organized by category: sociology, self-help, sci-fi, Asian cooking, etc.

There are dozens of literary genres (types) in the books of the OT and NT, and each genre has its own rules for interpretation. For example, a travelogue or inventory is not to be spiritualized, but taken literally (apart from figures of speech, of course). In contrast, poetry paints pictures with words, and to force a literal interpretation may dull its poetic impact. Letters are appreciated by considering such issues as author, audience, and situation.

Some Biblical Literary Genres

Allegory	Encomium	Ode
Apocalypse	Epic	Parable
Battle report	Epithalamion	Parody
Beatitude	Fantasy	Poetry
Bios	Genealogy	Prayer
Blazon	Gospel	Primeval narrative
Blessing	Hymn	Prophecy
Combat story	Idyll	Proverb
Covenant	Inventory	Psalm
Creed	Itinerary	Riddle
Curse	Lament	Romance
Dare	Law code	Satire
Diatribe	Lawsuit	Soliloquy
Discourse	Lyric	Tragedy
Doxology	Monologue	Travelogue
Drama	Myth	Treaty
Elegy	Narrative	Wisdom

The task of interpretation moves from (1) determination of genre to (2) studying the text to (3) exploring context to (4) working on content to (5) determining the main point to (6) application. Application begins with the teachers or writers themselves, before moving to application for the audience. Though it challenges our mental laziness (that idle voice that complains, "Why should Bible study be work?"), this is far and away the best method to approach God's word. [47]

In the list above, primeval narrative is its own category. In Gen 1–11 multiple genres are present: covenant, poetry, genealogy, and so on. What ties all the parts together are their cultural and theological connections with ancient Near Eastern culture, which, for the most part, stop once we reach the time of Abraham in Gen 12.

Conclusion

In light of this discussion, what should we do to become better Bible students?

- We need to get to know some of the pagan gods and goddesses, for they form an important part of the background of the world of Genesis. The more familiar they are to us, the more we will recognize the degree to which Genesis engages culture.
- We should be able to summarize the Mesopotamian religious narrative—the salient points. When we don't realize there's a backstory, we tend to ask the wrong questions (What about cavemen? How did the kangaroos reach the ark?). We end up focusing on incidental details or spinning doctrine out of the text in ways never intended by the author—much less by God!
- We should learn to recognize the tenets of pagan religion that are directly and indirectly challenged in Genesis—and in the rest of the Bible, for that matter. Some of these are highlighted in the next chapter, where we zoom in on a few of the major and minor players in the pantheons of the ancient Near East.

45. Common existential concerns:
    - Origin–Where do we come from?
    - Destiny–Where are we going?
    - Identity–Who are we?
    - Relationships–How do we relate to others?
    - Morality–What is right and wrong?
    - Ethics–How should we treat others?
    - Meaning–What is the significance of life? Of the world?
    - Purpose–For what have we been created?
46. Wenham, *Genesis 1–15*, l. Longman and Walton also express the point well:

    Even though the Bible is written *for* us, it is not written *to* us. The revelation it provides can equip us to know God, his plan, and his purposes, and therefore to participate with him in the world we face today. But it was not written with our world in mind. In its context, it is not communicated in our language; it is not addressed to our culture; it does not anticipate the questions about the world and its operations that stem from our modern situations and issues.

    Lost World of the Flood, 9.
47. For more on the importance of reading by genre, see Gordon D. Fee and Douglas Stuart, *How to Read the Bible Book by Book: A Guided Tour* (Grand Rapids, MI: Eerdmans, 2002); Leland Reyken, *A Complete Handbook of Literary Forms in the Bible* (Wheaton, IL: Crossway, 2014); Andreas J. Köstenberger and Richard Patterson, *Invitation to Biblical Interpretation: Exploring the Hermeneutical Triad of History, Literature, and Theology* (Grand Rapids, MI: Kregel, 2011); and Michael J. Gorman, *Elements of Biblical Exegesis: A Basic Guide for Students and Ministers* (Grand Rapids, MI: Baker, 2009).

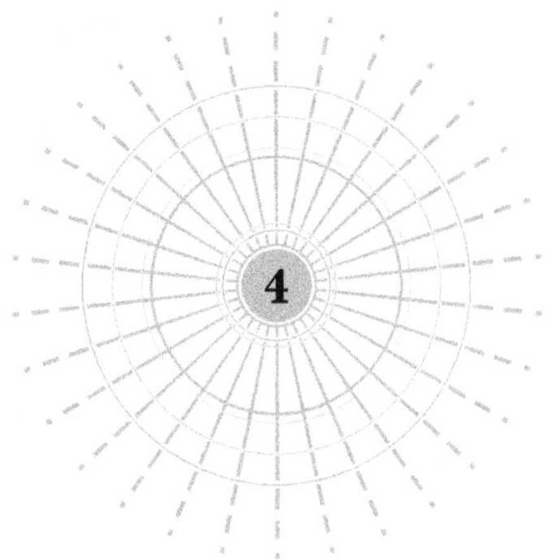

Ancient Gods & Goddesses

When I was twenty-four years old I (Douglas) met the Buddha—many times, actually. I was spending a month in Thailand, Singapore, and (mainly) Malaysia. As this was my first time in Asia, I was eager to visit temples—most of which, in these countries, were Buddhist. Although I had read about idolatry and was soon to teach a course in OT on my return to London, I had never entered (or even seen) a temple. From the Pagoda of the Ten Thousand Buddhas in Malaysia to the Temple of the Emerald Buddha in Thailand, I toured temple precincts as a respectful observer.

What was noticeable in these Buddhist temples—and this is similar to what one sees in the temples of Hinduism and other polytheistic religions—was how *dependent* the god or goddess is on humans. How so? The following are typical:

- A bell is rung in the morning to awaken the deity from sleep.
- Food and drink are brought into the temple and placed before the statue. (Temple personnel may consume the "leftovers.")

- The god is clothed, depending on the season of the year and any special occasion.
- During especially important festivals, the god is carried around town so that it may go on "tour."
- The god is cleaned and perfumed as necessary.

Mechanics

Human duty to the gods is to offer gifts and sacrifices. In exchange, the gods bring rain, cause crops to grow, and enable livestock to bear their young. Religion is a means of controlling the gods, gaining concessions from them, or keeping them at bay. Mutual manipulation is the dynamics of paganism: a dance of domination and control. It is a mechanical approach to faith, and it is still present with us today in most religions, including many strains of Christianity.

What a contrast we find in Genesis! God made us in his own image, not the other way around. We are special, not slaves of the gods; in fact, we are even coregents with God, ruling the creation with him (Gen 1:28). He owes us nothing—even as we owe him everything.

The Gods Are Not Love

This means that the biblical depiction of a God who desires to know his creatures clashes strongly with the pagan concept of divinity. Pagan gods and goddesses, such as the Greek and Roman ones we learned about in grade school, do not love us. The Norse myths present a similar scenario, as do the Celtic, Inuit, Mesoamerican, and gods of other religions—in fact, all pagan religions. One gets the impression that the gods of the ancient Near East don't particularly *like* humans—let alone desire a relationship with them. Yahweh wants to *dwell among* his people (Lev 26:11–12)—a radical concept.

Dennis Venema and Scot McKnight, scientist and theologian, respectively, team up to offer a magnificent description of Yahweh in comparison to the gods:

The gods go back and forth and get in tangles with one another while working the earth. Those deities are irritable, worn down by working, in need of help–and not entirely able to resolve their own problem without permission from the higher-up gods, who seem to be at the same time at odds with themselves. No one seems to be totally in control. The God of Genesis 1–2 is different: this God, like Michelangelo's creator God with the all-powerful, creative finger, controls the whole lot. God creates by a word deriving from God's own sovereign choice. The fundamental event of Genesis 1 is saying, "Let there be," and there is. The waters may be primal chaos, but the waters are easily and simply subdued by God's own command. The swirl of *tōhû va-bōhû*, translated "formless and empty," is untangled into orchestrated order, function, and purpose.... God, then, is not part of the created order but outside and over the created order. All of the gods of the ancient Near East are eliminated in the theology of Genesis 1, and one supreme God, YHWH, is left standing.[48]

Hadad, god of the storm, c. 2500 BC[49]

Similarly, the gods of the ancient world, whether worshiped in ancient Babylon or Sumer, or among the Canaanites and others dwelling in the promised land, needed humans to service them.[50] In distinction to the true God, they were neither omnipotent nor omniscient. Worse, they were frequently capricious, petty, and immoral. Nor did they have humans' best interests at heart. Still, in OT times the people of God constantly struggled with attraction to the religions and practices of the surrounding peoples.

Dominant Gods of the Mesopotamian Myths

Below are listed nine of the major deities of Mesopotamia.[51] Acquaintance with these gods allows us to read Gen 1 in a new light: the writer is speaking into the world of paganism, not one of monotheism. Most gods had consorts—goddesses with whom they procreated more gods. Amazingly, a document from about 2600 BC lists 560 deities by their Sumerian names![52] Sometimes the gods had union with mortals, producing demigods. Given the various pantheons and the proliferation of deities, we must be selective in our survey.

Mesopotamian Gods

- *Anu*–creator god and sky god.
- *Ishtar*–goddess of love, sex appeal, and war. The most important goddess in western Asia.
- *Inanna*–fertility goddess, transformed into Ishtar in the Babylonian period. She is noted for her beauty, ornaments, and being the very embodiment of sexual desire. She is the evening star (Venus) and patroness of prostitutes. Part of Inanna's worship entailed sacred intercourse within the temple of Inanna, between her priestess and the king of the city.[53]
- *Tammuz*–Ishtar's lover. He guaranteed seasonal fertility. Mentioned once in the Bible, in Ezek 8:14.

- *Enki/Ea*–Sumerian lord of water beneath the earth, source of magical knowledge, patron of arts and crafts. Enki was later known as Ea in Akkadian and Babylonian mythology.
- *Sin*–moon god.
- *Shamash*–sun god. See 2 Kings 23:11.[54]
- *Adad (Hadad)*–god of weather, storms, and rain. A key deity for agriculture.
- *Marduk*–god of Babylon and king over the Babylonian pantheon.[55]

While Scripture teaches that God is one, ancient religions had pantheons of gods. As with the fickle divinities of Greco-Roman paganism, there was little in these gods to admire. They were unpredictable and selfish (Judg 9:13). They were distant (Dan 2:11), not personal. Often, they were nothing more than the powers of nature personified. Several Assyrian and Babylonian—that is, Mesopotamian—deities are explicitly named in the OT: Nisroch (2 Kings 19:37; Isa 37:38), Rimmon (2 Kings 5:18), Nebo (Isa 46:1), Bel (Isa 46:1; Jer 51:44), and Marduk (Jer 50:2).

The Gods of Egypt

Since the people of God spent centuries in Egypt, a neighboring nation even after they had taken possession of the promised land (c. 1250 BC), it is not surprising that their gods and beliefs would be familiar to the Hebrews. In fact, much of the action in Genesis takes place in Egypt.[56]

Egyptian Deities

- *Osiris*, *Isis* (his sister/wife), *Horus*, *Anubis*, and *Nephthys*–funerary deities. These were gods of the underworld and judgment. The earlier belief was that only the pharaoh, or he and his family, would live again in the next world. By about 2000 BC, this had given way to the belief that all had a shot at immortality, assuming they lived righteously. Otherwise, at the judgment, if one's soul proved to be heavier than an ostrich feather, it would be devoured by the goddess *Ammit* (annihilation).

- *Atum, Khepri, Horus, Rē, Amun, Amun-Rē*–solar deities. In all ancient cultures, the sun was worshiped–not to say that this was the only celestial body considered divine. Take, for example, *Thoth* (moon, learning, and wisdom), *Khons* (moon), and *Nut* (the sky goddess).
- *Hapi*–the Nile flood. The great river itself, integral for agriculture and determining whether the people were sated or starved, was regarded as a god. *Khnum*, who lived on the Nilotic island of Elephantine, ensured the annual flood would take place. Many Egyptian gods were connected with natural phenomena.
- And there were scores more, like *Maat* (truth, justice, and order), *Ptah* (craftsmanship and creation), *Bastet* (protection from evil), *Geb* (god of the earth), *Seth* (the evil brother/husband of Nephthys), and *Hathor* (goddess of fertility, motherhood, dance, joy, mining, and music). Several will be discussed below in the section on the plagues.

Polemics

It is not only Genesis that exposes the so-called gods and goddesses for what they are—hollow, shallow, and less than nothing. Exodus, too, takes aim at the ranks of deities worshiped up and down the land. Numerous Egyptian gods were targeted by the ten plagues against Egypt (Ex 7–12), after which their king (pharaoh) finally let the people go. The Bible says that the plagues were delivered in judgment on the Egyptian gods (Num 33:4).

Since most readers are not aware of how humiliating these plagues would have been to worshipers of the Egyptian pantheon, and because of the clear polemic element in the account, it is worthwhile clarifying the connections.[57]

The Ten Plagues

1. *Plague of Blood*

   The Nile turned to blood, and so the first plague was a slap in the face to the Egyptian god Khnum, creator of water and life; to Hapi, god of the Nile; and to Osiris, whose bloodstream was a mighty river and source of life for all the land. This plague would have subjected the Egyptian economy to considerable strain.

2. *Plague of Frogs*

   The second plague was an insult to Heket (Heqt), wife of the creator of the world and goddess of childbirth; she was represented as a frog.

3. *Plague of Lice*

   Geb, god of the earth, is the likely target of the third plague, as the dust of the ground is turned into lice (or gnats), which cover man and livestock alike.

4. *Plague of Flies*[58]

   The next plague suggests the importance of Khepri, who had a fly for a head. This deity was connected with creation, rebirth, and the movement of the sun. Three of the plagues (the third, fourth, and sixth) had implications for the Egyptian priesthood, which valued smooth (shaved) skin for one to enter the presence of the "divine" pharaoh.

5. *Plague on Livestock*

   Since Hathor, mother and sky goddess, took the form of a cow, and Apis, who symbolized fertility, took the form of a bull, plague five underscored their powerlessness.

6. *Plague of Boils*

   Handfuls of soot were taken from the furnace to cause the sixth plague. This was redolent of the furnaces that were manned by Hebrew slaves. The soot caused boils, which Isis, goddess of nature, magic, and medicine was powerless to avert; similarly, Thoth, also god of medicine, was shown up as a charlatan. The stigma of the boils covered Pharaoh's sorcerers, who were unable to protect themselves–much less the Egyptian people ruled by Pharaoh.

7. *Plague of Hail*

The devastating plague of hail, which included severe lightning and thunder, made Nut, goddess of the sky, look bad. This was obviously no conjurer's trick, but the work of the true God.

8. *Plague of Locusts*

Plague number eight was aimed at Seth, who manifested himself in wind and storm; Nepri, the god of grain, and Ermutet, goddess of childbirth and crops.

9. *Plague of Darkness*

Darkness, with its association with judgment, hopelessness, and death, was the penultimate plague. This terrible plague challenged the integrity and reality of the solar deities Ra/Rē, Aten, Atum, and Horus–all associated with the sun.

10. *Plague on the Firstborn*

The final plague took the lives of the firstborn, including the son of the pharaoh, and thus can be construed as a declaration of judgment against Osiris, patron deity of the pharaoh and judge of the dead; Apis and Heket (fertility); Min, god of procreation; Isis, goddess of fertility; Selket, guardian of life; Meskhenet, goddess of childbirth; Hathor, one of the seven deities that attended births; and, perhaps most of all, Renenutet, the cobra-goddess who was the special guardian of the pharaoh. Since the pharaoh was considered to be the son of Ra, the personal nature of this tenth plague was highly discrediting. The tenth plague brought about the death of all firstborn–apart from in those houses whose doorframes were smeared with blood, in which case the destroying angel "passed over"–on the evening of the first Passover.

The failure of the magicians to replicate Yahweh's plague miracles (traditionally named Jannes and Jambres—see 2 Tim 3:8) exposed as frauds three more Egyptian divinities. First, how could the bloodthirsty Sakhmet retain credibility as god of war and protector of the pharaohs, given the subsequent loss of the Egyptian army following the death of Pharaoh's firstborn? Second, how could the Egyptian-Nubian god of wealth and incense, Dedwen, allow Yahweh to make the Egyptians give the Hebrew slaves all that they asked for in flocks, herds, clothing, silver, and gold (Ex 12:32, 35–36)? But perhaps the most amusing of all the Egyptian gods is Thoth, god of wisdom. Thoth is sometimes depicted as a baboon.[59] As the Apostle Paul would later muse, "Where is the one who is wise? Where is the scribe? Where is the debater of this age? Has not God made foolish the wisdom of the world?" (1 Cor 1:20).

Dominant Gods of Canaan

Following are some of the top gods worshiped in Canaan,[60] and to which the Israelites were perennially attracted. (Objectively speaking, Yahweh was often edged out by them. [61])

Canaanite Divinities

- *Ba'al*–Canaanite vegetation deity and father of seven storm gods. In Israelite history, more popular than Yahweh. See 1 Kings 18:16–40 for the big showdown between the prophets of Ba'al and the prophet Elijah. [62] *Ba'al-Zebub* is "Lord of the Flies" (2 Kings 1:2, 3, 6, 16). Ba'al means "lord" (or "husband").
- *Asherah*–Originally Amorite, she was the great mother goddess, mentioned in nine books of the OT. Associated with fertility. Asherah poles were set up by altars to Ba'al and Yahweh (1 Kings 14:22–24).
- *'El*–chief god of the pantheon.
- *Yam*–god of the sea, also a sea serpent.
- *Mot*–the god of death.
- *Molech*–Ammonite god of the underworld to whom babies were sacrificed. Firstborn children were burned alive. These human sacrifices often took place in the Valley of Ben Hinnom (Gehenna),

although in the earlier Canaanite period there were altars in other parts of the land.

In our time, few are allured by Ba'al and Asherah worship (we worry far less about weather and crops), yet we may worship the jobs and credentials that enable us to live well. Molech may have lost his direct appeal; how can presumably well-meaning parents "heartlessly" sacrifice their children? Yet it's a question we would do well to put to ourselves. Social pressure is so strong that few, especially those without the foothold of God's word, are able to resist the drift. Our children are left to marinate in the secular broth of humanism, materialism, and unbelief.

There were numerous other deities in the region, all vying for people's attention.

Other Regional Gods

- Philistine *Dagon* (Judg 16:23-30; 1 Sam 5:2–7). A grain god, often depicted as half man/half fish. Son of Anu and father of Ba'al.
- Moabite *Chemosh* (1 Kings 11:7; 2 Kings 23:13).
- Sidonian *Ashtoreth*[63] (Judg 2:13; 10:6; 1 Sam 7:3–4; 12:10; 31:10; 1 Kings 11:5; 2 Kings 23:13).
- Household gods were also popular (Gen 31:19–35; Josh 24:14).

Divination

Part of the attraction of paganism, especially with respect to divination, was rooted in anxiety about the future. In the face of the uncertainties of life and a sense of powerlessness before the elements, it is hardly puzzling that the heavenly bodies were gods in Egypt, Syria, Babylon, and other neighboring lands. They were a source of constant temptation for the Israelites (2 Kings 21:3; Jer 8:2; Ezek 8:16).

If only we didn't have to worry! Yet Yahweh says we don't. He guided his people through Scripture, prayer, prophets, and priests using simple lots, Urim and Thummim (Ex 28:30; 1 Sam 14:41)—a "low-tech" method of discernment compared to pagan methods of divination. Among those methods were examination of animal entrails; analysis of patterns created by oil on water or smoke from incense; study of the movements of birds and other animals around city gates or in the temple precincts; and interpretation of celestial and meteorological phenomena. In contrast to leaving the interpretation of a god's message up to a priest's arbitrary verdict based on the ambiguities of "reading" animal entrails or oil on water, the biblical tradition of casting lots to discern Yahweh's revelation left no room for doubt.

The Slippery Slope

Wrong theology can lead us to bad places. Even though God's people in OT times had the patriarchs, the prophets, Torah, tabernacle, and the temple—where God's glorious presence was manifest—they assimilated the ambient culture, eventually absorbing the foreign gods into their religion.

A very useful biblical chapter summarizing the Israelite assimilation of heathen religious rites is 2 Kings 17. Numerous gods are explicitly named in the OT. National gods show up in 2 Kings 17:29 and Jer 2:28 and 11:13. For example, consider the Egyptian Amon (or Amun), god of the Thebes (hidden powers of nature, represented by a ram) in Jer 46:25, in addition to "all the [other] gods of Egypt" (Ex 12:12).

One Eye on the Text

The Mesopotamian gods squabble and jockey for position. They are depicted like human beings with competing desires. The Egyptian gods grow old and can die. They were produced by sexual unions between divine parents. Yet they are not powerful enough to protect the Egyptians from the forces of chaos. In contrast, the God of the Bible is God as defined by his power, wisdom, knowledge, and moral character. Yet not only is he holy; he also desires relationship with his creatures. This is why we read of the patriarchs in Genesis making altars to commemorate places where God revealed himself to them—a foreshadowing of the tabernacle and temple, where heaven and earth would meet in divine-human communion.

It is easy for us to underestimate the original impact of a text like Gen 1–11. On the nature of gods in the ancient Near East, Everett Fox comments,

> As has often been pointed out, Gen I is unmistakably reacting against prevailing New Eastern cosmogonies of the time. Most of the cultures surrounding ancient Israel have elaborate creation stories, highlighting the birth, sexuality, and violent uprisings of the gods… The concept of God presented here militates against such ideas, arguing chiefly out of omission and silence… The Genesis narrative has taken such old mythological motifs as battles with the primeval (female) waters or with sea monsters and eliminated or neutralized them. What remains is both utterly simple and radical in its time.[64]

So, when we read Genesis—as well as many other books of the Bible—it pays to keep one eye on the text and another on the cultural background. To prevent a plethora of details from clogging up the flow of this book, we have attempted to be concise. When we refer to the ancient accounts, we often simplify or combine details from *Enuma Elish*, *Gilgamesh*, and *Atrahasis* to shed maximum light on the cultural backdrop of Genesis.

Having briefly surveyed the background of the world in which the stories of Gen 1–11 are set, we are ready to dig in to the biblical text, beginning (of course) at the beginning. The effort to come to terms with contemporary pagan religions and deities will pay off, enhancing our reading of Scripture.[65]

---

48. Dennis R. Venema and Scot McKnight. *Adam and the Genome: Reading Scripture after Genetic Science* (Grand Rapids, MI: Brazos, 2017), 119.
49. Picture: Hadad, god of the storm, c. 2500 BC, Wikipedia, https://en.wikipedia.org/wiki/Hadad.

50. Ray Clendenen, "Idols and Idolatry in the Ancient Near East," http://www.academia.edu/4051333/Idols_and_Idolatry_in_the_Ancient_Near_East, accessed 11 October 2017.
51. An easy-to-read yet accurate source is Henrietta McCall, *Mesopotamian Myths* (London: British Museum, 1990).
52. Holland, *Religion in the Ancient World*, 64. See also Michael Jordan, *Encyclopedia of Gods: Over 2500 Deities of the World* (New York: Facts on File, 1993).
53. Holland, *Religion in the Ancient World*, 71.
54. In Mal 4:2 the Messiah is shown to be the true "sun," the sun of righteousness—imagery the early Christians seized upon.
55. In later times he was called *Bel* (Lord)—seemingly the Phoenician (and Canaanite) Ba'al.
56. Moreover, Egypt does not stop being important once we leave the pages of Genesis and Exodus. Egypt is mentioned over 800 times in the Bible.
57. The following section has been adapted from Douglas Jacoby, *Exodus: Night of Redemption* (Spring, TX: Illumination Publishers, 2017), 26–29.
58. The Hebrew word is simply "swarm." Most translators assume it means a swarm of flies. The Greek Septuagint (LXX) translates the term as *kunomuia*, dogfly. Philo seems to have thought this was a plague of multiple wild animals (*De Vita Mosis* I, xxiii, 130-132), possibly because Ps 78:45 says that the swarm of pests "ate" them. Yet it is easy to imagine the language of devouring: "The mosquitoes are eating me alive!"
59. Normally Thoth is depicted with the head of an ibis.
60. The Ras Shamra Tablets, discovered at Ugarit, contain writings about the Canaanite gods.

    > The most commonly accepted sequential arrangement and understanding of [the] six-tablet composition suggests that there were three main parts to the story. First, with the permission of El, Baal challenged Yam's kingship and won the ensuing battle. Second, since he was the victor, Baal obtained permission from El to have a palace built for himself as was fit for one with dominion among the gods. Third, Mot challenged Baal to a battle, which he won by defeating and killing Baal. In due course, however, Baal returned from the underworld, resumed his throne, and subdued Mot.

    Richard E. Averbeck, "Ancient Near Eastern Mythography as It Relates to Historiography in the Hebrew Bible: Genesis 3 and the Cosmic Battle," accessible at http://www.academia.edu/14523269/ANE_Mythography_and_the_Bible, 337–338.
61. Yahweh is God's personal name in the OT. In the Hebrew Bible, only its consonants were written (YHWH), ostensibly to avoid taking the Lord's name in vain by mispronouncing it. Yet it is unlikely such a practice was targeted in the third commandment (Ex 20:7). Rather, the command takes aim at (1) false oaths and (2) witchcraft, where the name would serve as a sort of talisman. This misuse of God's name in its ancient setting would have been understood as an attempt to manipulate him or harness his power for one's own selfish purposes. The "name" of a given pagan deity was frequently invoked as a technique—a magical incantation—to master supernatural forces to pursue earthly or material success. John H. Walton, "Interpreting the Bible as an Ancient Near Eastern Document," in Daniel I. Block, ed., *Israel: Ancient Kingdom or Late Invention?* (Nashville, TN: B&H Academic, 2008), 313–18.
62. See also 2 Kings 10:18ff; Num 25:1ff; Judg 2:10ff; 2 Kings 21:3, 9; Jer 2:8, 23–25; 7:9; 19:5; 23:13; 32:29, 35.
63. In the NIV; "Astarte" in the NRSV.
64. Everett Fox, *The Five Books of Moses*, The Schocken Bible, Volume 1 (New York: Random House, 2000), 12.
65. For more on the pagan background and its relation to God's people, see Douglas Jacoby, *A Quick Overview of the Bible* (Eugene, OR: Harvest House, 2013).

II

—

Creation: Chaos to Cosmos

We have finished our preparatory work—traveling through the world of early Genesis. Now we are ready to tackle the text: 276 verses from Genesis 1:1 to 11:9.

Genesis describes the primordial world as chaotic or, in the words of older translations, "without form and void"—or perhaps even "desolate and uninhabitable" (cf. Jer 4:23; Isa 34:11). The move from chaos (disorder) to cosmos (order) begins in the early verses of Genesis 1.

There are two creation accounts in Genesis 1–2, as well as a handful of additional creation passages in other parts of the Bible. Although the accounts are as simple as they are elegant, there's more going on than meets the (modern) eye. In the middle chapter of this section, we will ask why creation is depicted as occurring in a single week.

From here on, we will not only indicate points of contact between the Bible and the Mesopotamian background, but also highlight biblical truths and applications. For anyone tempted to consider the early chapters of Genesis to be primitive, out of date, or impractical, the best advice is, *Think again!*

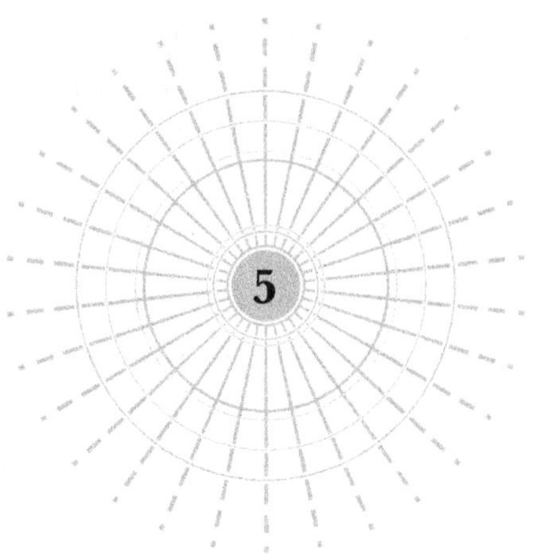

Panorama
First Account

Whereas the second creation account (Gen 2:4–25) is all about people, in chapter 1 humankind shows up only at the end of the final day of creation. The first account offers a sweep of cosmic creation—a panorama—in contrast to the entirely human-focused second account. Thus, we humans are the climax of the created world. Let us now proceed through the first account (Gen 1:1–2:3).

> *1:1 In the beginning when God created the heavens and the*
> *earth; 2the earth was a formless void and darkness covered the face*
> *of the deep, while a wind from God swept over the face of the waters.*
> *3Then God said, "Let there be light"; and there was light. 4And God*
> *saw that the light was good; and God separated the light from the*
> *darkness. 5God called the light Day, and the darkness he called*
> *Night. And there was evening and there was morning, the first day.*

In the beginning is the uncreated God. The Bible is a book whose central figure is our heavenly Father. He creates by his word; in essence, he thinks, and his will is executed.

Creation from Nothing?

Now, the Scriptures take for granted that God is the source of all reality outside of himself. This has been articulated as the doctrine of creation from nothing (Latin: *creatio ex nihilo*). The majority of biblical commentators take the Hebrew construction of Gen 1:1 as absolute ("In the beginning") rather than relative ("When God began to create"). This (for me, Paul) would be another example of the distinctiveness of the biblical God from the lesser ancient Near Eastern deities that typically created from preexisting materials. As Gordon Wenham wrote, it would be "going too far to argue that no material creation was involved."[66] *Creatio ex nihilo* is certainly evident in early Jewish theology. The NT likewise affirms that God created the visible, material world out of what is not visible (Jn 1:3; Heb 11:3). Through God's powerful word alone, the material creation comes into existence.[67]

Mesopotamian, Egyptian, and Hebrew origins accounts typically begin with a watery pre-creative state, without any mention of where it came from or who created it. Without denying the doctrine of creation out of nothing, others (like me, Douglas) would see Gen 1:1–2 simply presenting us with undifferentiated chaos that God puts into order. (Both of us would agree, though, that Gen 1 doesn't present primordial nothingness.) God works with the formless void, already present at the opening of Genesis. *Chaos* is the Greek word for disorder; *cosmos* refers to an ordered world. God transforms chaos (disorder) into cosmos. Chaos is brought under control—an odd notion, perhaps, to modern readers, but not to ancient ones.[68]

Means of Creation in Ancient Myths[69]

1. Making–Acting on undifferentiated matter. The primal chaos is usually depicted as a sea, since most countries in the Mediterranean area were not seagoing.
2. Conflict–Between creator god and chaos monster, usually a marine monster. The body of the slain monster is used in the creation.
3. Sexual generation–The god couples with the goddess, giving birth to the elemental gods.
4. Creation by word–Spoken word as a means of identifying, and thus controlling. The deity gives voice to an idea conceived in his mind. As breath, wind, and spirit are often conveyed by a single word in the ancient languages, when the god breathes, he or she imparts divine spirit, and thus substantial reality.

Unlike every other creation tradition, the OT does not describe God being created—a concept impossible by definition, since the necessarily existent God is neither created nor physical (part of the material world).[70]

The Babylonian creation story, *Enuma Elish*, begins with the sexual union of Tiamat (waters) with Apsu (the deep), generating the earliest gods. Of course, there are no other gods in the OT account. The Egyptian creation, too, begins with the watery abyss.[71]

In Canaanite and Babylonian accounts, the primeval dragon (Rahab or Tiamat[72]) is slain, cut in two. The top half becomes the heavens or sky, the bottom half becomes the earth.[73] We find no dragon slaying in the Genesis account. Where the dragon is mentioned in Scripture, the image is turned on its head and used to show the superiority of Yahweh (Job 9:13; 26:12; Ps 74:13; 89:10; Isa 27:1; 51:9; Ezek 29:3; 32:2; Rev 12:1–17).

The Watery Abyss

The watery abyss is the ordinary starting point for creation accounts in the ancient world. In Gen 1, we find sea and earth reduced to their true state: they are no longer feared, let alone worshiped, as primeval deities. Most ancient religions had a goddess of the earth as well as a goddess of the sea. Sea and earth are prepared for the benefit of humanity, not to rule over us, terrorize us, or prevent us from attaining happiness. Against the teaching of the pagan myths, the watery chaos of Gen 1 constitutes no ultimate threat.[74]

In ancient Hebrew thought, the sea was a dangerous place.[75] Among Israel's neighbors, Yam was the terrifying sea-god. Unlike their neighbors the Phoenicians (modern Lebanon), the Israelites were not especially fond of boats. The primeval waters of Gen 1 are frightening and chaotic. During "de-creation" (the flood), the primeval waters deluge the earth while Noah's family is rescued (1 Pet 3:20; Ex 14:22). The Red (or Reed) Sea is another scene of divine rescue, although the waters flood back once the Hebrews cross over to dry land, killing the pursuing Egyptians. Joshua, too, crosses the water (near Jericho), a similar miracle preparing the way for the Israelites to enter the promised land; and the parting of the waters takes place yet again in the lives of Elijah and Elisha (Josh 3:16; 2 Kings 2:8, 14).

Light

When God speaks, he proclaims, "Let there be light" (v. 3). In the Babylonian creation myth of *Enuma Elish*, it is not light that is created first.[76] Naturally (though unnaturally, in the ancient world) Genesis makes no mention of other gods. They are wholly absent. While that may not strike *us* as odd, it surely would have seemed unusual at the time, since all society was polytheistic (apart from Israel—at least in theory).

Note the *separation* of light and darkness (v. 4). We will return to this point in our next chapter. We observe also that day and night are established even before there is a sun—a hint that a woodenly literal approach to this creation account is unnecessary.

One more observation on these opening verses. Everything God creates is good. The world is not evil (as in Gnosticism, the heresy that second-century

Christians combatted), nor is it unreal (as in various schools of Hinduism or Buddhism). The physical creation is good, not evil. This means also that the opposite of spiritual is not *physical*, but *unspiritual*.[77]

> *6And God said, "Let there be a dome in the midst of the waters, and let it separate the waters from the waters." 7So God made the dome and separated the waters that were under the dome from the waters that were above the dome. And it was so. 8God called the dome Sky. And there was evening and there was morning, the second day.*

Firmament

God creates the firmament, a hard dome (vault) overarching the earth. Think of an inverted bowl—a hemisphere. One purpose of the dome or firmament is to separate the waters. This is difficult to visualize with a modern (Google Earth) view of ocean and sky. In ancient times, there were believed to be two bodies of water, one below and surrounding the earth, the other above it. Just as it sounds, the firmament is firm. There are openings (floodgates) in the firmament to allow water from above to water the earth.

In the ancient world, this was the standard model—and for God to have depicted a spherical earth in his word would have introduced an unnecessary complication into the simple and elegant power of the text. (Appendix A provides a diagram detailing this further.) Just as meteorologists appropriate the language of "sunrise" and "sunset," so God accommodates himself to this understanding of a flat and motionless earth at the center of the universe, which both the OT and NT appropriate throughout.

By separating the wild and dangerous waters, God brings everything under control—*not* like a referee separating two boxers in a clench, which would be a better image for the religions of the ancient Near East, where the powers of nature are deified and in conflict—but simply by his powerful word, which brings about the necessary shifts and separations.[78] Now there is room for dry land.

> *[9]And God said, "Let the waters under the sky be gathered together into one place, and let the dry land appear." And it was so. [10]God called the dry land Earth, and the waters that were gathered together he called Seas. And God saw that it was good. [11]Then God said, "Let the earth put forth vegetation: plants yielding seed, and fruit trees of every kind on earth that bear fruit with the seed in it." And it was so. [12]The earth brought forth vegetation: plants yielding seed of every kind, and trees of every kind bearing fruit with the seed in it. And God saw that it was good. [13]And there was evening and there was morning, the third day.*

The Plants from the Earth

God is finished with the water above the dome (the celestial ocean).[79] Now he works on the waters beneath, ordering them so that there is dry land. This is necessary if plants and trees are to grow.

However, note that this is not direct creating, but indirect (v. 11). The whole process of plants growing and bearing fruit takes place on this "day"—"And it was so." Now, plants come from seed, but here it is the earth that yields seed and trees and then fruits. In the ancient creation myths, plants and animals (including humans) spring forth from the ground, fully made. Genesis makes no attempt to correct such ancient suppositions. Yet it does emphasize that (1) all of this is by God's plan, and (2) the creation is good.

> *[14]And God said, "Let there be lights in the dome of the sky to separate the day from the night; and let them be for signs and for seasons and for days and years, [15]and let them be lights in the dome of the sky to give light upon the earth." And it was so. [16]God made the two great lights–the greater light to rule the day and the lesser light to rule the night–and the stars. [17]God set them in the dome of the sky to give light upon the earth, [18]to rule over the day and over the night, and to separate the light from the darkness. And God saw that it was good. [19]And there was evening and there was morning, the fourth day.*

The Lights

Light emanates from the gods in Babylonian stories, but in Genesis light is *created by* God. The sun and moon are not named, being called instead "the greater light" and "the lesser light." The Hebrew words *shemesh* (sun) and *yārēach* (moon) are avoided, for good reason. Shamash (the sun god) and Sin (the moon god) were widely worshiped in the Near East. In the OT we do find the Israelites occasionally struggling with worshiping the heavenly bodies.[80] In ancient times—as in modern superstitions like astrology—the sun, moon, and stars were thought to govern human destiny. Horoscopes, based on astrology, are equally silly. (Consider how twins, born on the same day, can be so different in their personalities. Also, why should a birthdate—instead of the date of conception—determine a person's "sign"? Or what about C-sections or induced labor, which are a departure from the natural delivery process and the alleged determinations of the stars?) There is no support for astrology in the Bible. Rather, this is shown to be vain and foolish, as God himself is the one who has set the stars in their courses.[81]

Instead of being divine, the status of the sun and moon is merely functional (v. 14). These lights serve to mark the seasons—not meteorological seasons like spring and autumn, but religious seasons (Ps 104:19).[82] The stars are mentioned too, almost in passing. This slight also nullifies astrology; revelation will come from Yahweh, not from stargazing.[83] It also counters the ancient belief that some gods and humans became stars, or constellations of stars.

One last comment on 1:14–19 is in order. We know the earth's rotation as it circles the sun regulates the cycles of night and day. However, if we try to press this text into the mold of modern science and ignore its literary nature, we run into trouble. After all, before day four, this day-and-night cycle would not have been possible. Again, we have here one of numerous pointers to the literary nature of the account. Some scholars would call Gen 1 poetry, as it bears many poetic qualities, while some view it as elevated prose. Others have called it "historico-poetic." Whichever the case, literalizing the account is problematic. While we don't always read the Bible *literally*, we should always read it *literarily*, keeping in mind the unique genre or type of literature we have before us.

> *[20]And God said, "Let the waters bring forth swarms of living*
> *creatures, and let birds fly above the earth across the dome of the*
> *sky." [21]So God created the great sea monsters and every living*
> *creature that moves, of every kind, with which the waters swarm,*
> *and every winged bird of every kind. And God saw that it was good.*
> *[22]God blessed them, saying, "Be fruitful and multiply and fill the*
> *waters in the seas, and let birds multiply on the earth." [23]And there*
> *was evening and there was morning, the fifth day.*

Sea and Sky

Again, we find indirect creating. God does not create marine life directly; rather, he commands the waters to bring forth various creatures, among them some large animals ("sea monsters," in v. 21), which are God's creatures too. This means that (1) for Yahweh, sea monsters aren't rivals to be defeated (Ps 148:7), and (2) we need not fear them, since they have no divine status or magic powers and, like all other creatures, are subject to God's laws.

Birds also are created on day five. There is a good reason that creatures of sky and sea come to exist on the same day—to be explained in our next chapter.

> *[24]And God said, "Let the earth bring forth living creatures of*
> *every kind: cattle and creeping things and wild animals of the earth*
> *of every kind." And it was so. [25]God made the wild animals of the*
> *earth of every kind, and the cattle of every kind, and everything that*
> *creeps upon the ground of every kind. And God saw that it was good.*

Animals from the Earth

Next, the land animals are created. Whereas we might scarcely notice God's command to the ground to put forth vegetation (1:11), we may miss entirely the wording of v. 24: "Let the earth bring forth… cattle…" You may have imagined that God would simply snap his fingers, so to speak, and the animals would appear. But the text has the *earth* bringing forth the animals. This was a common motif in ancient creation accounts. Of course, this could be read as an instantaneous creation (God says the word and at once the earth sprouts up cattle), yet it's not obvious why the earth would be involved unless this was a process of some sort. The point is that Yahweh caused them to exist—not any of the countless false gods.

Day six is not over yet, for the best is yet to come. This is not "speciesism"—the arbitrary bias or prejudice toward humans, as though the differences between us and the animals were minor. We will soon see that our relationship to nature is different from that of the plants and animals. Yet, as though to keep us humble, we don't get our own day, but must share it with other creatures.

> *26Then God said, "Let us make humankind in our image, according to our likeness; and let them have dominion over the fish of the sea, and over the birds of the air, and over the cattle, and over all the wild animals of the earth, and over every creeping thing that creeps upon the earth."*

Humans

To whom is God speaking when he says, "Let us…"? John Willis makes a good case that the audience is the heavenly council.[84] It appears to be divine self-deliberation (God alone creates) but in the midst of a heavenly angelic council or court; instances of such a council are found elsewhere in the Bible (e.g., Job 1:6; 2:1; 38:4, 7). Three biblically momentous facts appear in this passage. The first is that we are made in the divine image of the one true God. The heavenly council does not have this distinction, as none of its "members" possess sovereignty. The second is that we are to have dominion over the creation. A third is inherent in v. 26: *'ādām* (humankind, or Adam) includes both male and female. We will elaborate on these points in the next three sections.

Reading of the creation of humankind against the Mesopotamian background, in which humans were a mere postscript, we cannot help but be struck by the sensibility and credibility of Genesis. John Walton notes:

> In creation accounts from Mesopotamia an entire population of people is created, already civilized, using a mixture of clay and the blood of a slain rebel god. This creation comes about as the result of conflict among the gods, and the god organizing the cosmos had to overcome the forces of chaos to bring order to his created world. The Genesis account portrays God's creation not as part of a conflict with opposing forces but as a serene and controlled process.[85]

1. Image

Discussions on the meaning of "God's image" tend to cover possible physical, mental, emotional, and moral resemblances between humans and their Creator. The Bible does, after all, put us above the animals though "a little lower than God" (Ps 8:5), and the desire to discern our identity and know where we fit in is understandable. But maybe most such discussions aren't on the right track.

Jesus was the image of God even before the incarnation (Col 1:15), without a physical body. Nor does the image consist of some native capacity, such as artistic ability, mental dexterity, philosophical reasoning, or even conscience. Rather, image pertains to our *relationship* to God: both who we are and what he has entrusted us with.

When we consider ancient religions—and modern ones, like Hinduism and Buddhism—the matter of "image" comes into clearer focus.[86] In ancient times, the image of a god was his or her actual physical statue, which normally was housed in the deity's temple. Richard Averbeck shares about a fascinating discovery that sheds light on the connection between image and statue.

> As for Genesis 1, there has been a good deal of discussion in the scholarly literature about ancient Near Eastern texts, images, and monuments that bear on the meaning of "image" (*selem*) and "likeness" (*demut*) in Genesis 1:26-28. One such text stands out above the others. It is the bilingual (Aramaic and Akkadian) ninth century BC Tell Fekheriye inscription from northern Mesopotamia/Upper Syria. The reason this text is so important is that the Aramaic version uses the same two words for

> image and likeness as Genesis 1:26-27 and, more to the point, it uses them interchangeably to refer to the "image" or "statue" of the king on which the inscription itself is inscribed.[87]

The emptiness of the holy of holies of the tabernacle and temple of the Jews is thus striking. Fashioning an image of Yahweh was strictly forbidden—a violation of the second commandment. And yet making an image of God was not only prohibited, but superfluous. That is because humans *are* the image—or we may say that we *bear* the image (the point is the same either way we think of this).[88]

As God's image, or image-bearers, we occupy a position of tremendous honor and trust. When people see us, they are to see God. We are both his representatives (like ambassadors—2 Cor 5:20) and his lieutenants, carrying out his work (just as Christians, bearing the Spirit of Christ, are to *be* Christ to the world).[89]

In the ancient pagan world, the right of being God's image was exclusively reserved. The king is the image of God in the Mesopotamian and Egyptian texts.[90] Yet God's word tells us that *all* humans—king and commoner, male and female, citizen and alien—bear/are God's image.

Think how sensational this would have been for the recently liberated Israelites. They marched out of Egypt, where Pharaoh claimed to be the image of God. Everyone has heard of the boy pharaoh, King Tut. His full name, Tutankhamun, means "living image of Amon"; Amon/Amun was a god widely worshiped in Egypt. Yet the image of God is not the exclusive right of royalty.

There is another implication of the biblical doctrine of the divine image. Eastern religions and New Age teaching, which heavily stress our divine potential and even our divinity, are far from the mark. The Bible does not teach pantheism (everything is God), nor that spirits are recycled in a "circle of life." Nor does the universe magically adjust itself so that our every whim is honored, our every wish granted, as in Rhonda Byrne's bestseller *The Secret*. (In her view, the secret each of us must discover is, *"I am God."*)[91]

Not that we are insignificant. The sciences of cosmology, human origins, and biology can have the effect of making us feel like "zeroes." We may be tempted to think, "The cosmos is so large and so ancient. We are minuscule and ephemeral."[92] Yet in Genesis, God assures us that we are significant, we do have meaning, and our Creator cares for us. Even some naturalistic philosophers and scientists are catching on to this, as they acknowledge that humans are "different" in that they alone have "creeds"[93] and can "transcend their genetic imperatives"—indeed, "rebel against" them.[94]

None of us, of course, perfectly represents God in this world. Christ alone fulfilled the privileged human responsibility to be God's image here. As Christians, through the process of suffering and character building, we are increasingly conformed in Christ to his image (Rom 8:29). This requires keeping our eyes on Jesus (2 Cor 3:18; Heb 3:1; 12:2). One day we will become like him—image burnished—once we see him as he is, in all his perfection and glory (1 Jn 3:2).

2. Dominion

Adam (humankind) is to exercise dominion over all creation. This is what we would expect God, as King of the Universe to do—and so he does. Yet in a sense we begin to reign with him during this life, sharing in his rule as colaborers with God (1 Cor 3:9; 2 Tim 2:12; Rev 5:10). Three points must be made.

First, we are called to rule over creation, not over humankind.[95] Plants and animals and all the earth are ours. There is no mandate here to dominate, let alone oppress, fellow human beings. In eternity, if we have persevered and remained faithful to God, we will rule with God (2 Tim 2:12).

Second, "Let them have dominion over the fish… birds… cattle… wild animals… and over every creeping thing" (v. 26) implies responsible management and creation care. The planet is not at our disposal for unbridled greed or the pursuit of pleasure. It is a trust from God so that we may wisely manage it. A full-orbed biblical theology, in other words, includes stewardship of the natural resources God has entrusted to human care (Job 12:7–10; Ex 23:10–11).

Third, while all things exist for God's glory, animals can be brought into the service of humankind. Nothing that is created—including animals or even the earth—is to be worshiped by us. Rather, we are to exercise dominion over creation in a thoughtful and godly manner.

> *[27]So God created humankind in his image,*
> *in the image of God he created them;*
> *male and female he created them.*

3. Male and Female

Male and female constitute mankind; male is incomplete without female, and vice versa. Not only that, male and female alike are included in the image of God.

This does not mean that God is somehow both male and female (androgynous), since God is beyond sexuality—a sexless, though personal, being. Yet in his relationship with us, we experience him primarily as Father (a masculine image), just as we as the church relate to Christ as our bridegroom (another masculine image). That is, in relationship with God, his people are collectively and analogically feminine. Of course, that makes a human male no more sexually feminine than it makes God masculine; these are analogies.[96] Nor should we buy in to thinking that flattens out gender differences, as some "progressive" moderns wish to do.[97]

Furthermore, God is love (1 Jn 4:8). The physical love between man and woman is highlighted in Gen 2 as a manifestation in creation of the love that has eternally existed between the triune God. So that is why God declares about his image-bearers, "It is not good that the man should be alone; I will make him a helper as his partner" (Gen 2:18). Of course, the possibility for deep relationality for God's image-bearers extends beyond this (e.g., 2 Sam 1:26).

> *[28] God blessed them, and God said to them, "Be fruitful and multiply, and fill the earth and subdue it; and have dominion over the fish of the sea and over the birds of the air and over every living*

thing that moves upon the earth." [29]*God said, "See, I have given you every plant yielding seed that is upon the face of all the earth, and every tree with seed in its fruit; you shall have them for food.* [30]*And to every beast of the earth, and to every bird of the air, and to everything that creeps on the earth, everything that has the breath of life, I have given every green plant for food." And it was so.* [31]*God saw everything that he had made, and indeed, it was very good. And there was evening and there was morning, the sixth day.*

Be Fruitful and Multiply

God is not at odds with humans. He creates them and blesses them. Their dominion, exercised properly, constitutes an extension of the divine activity. To "fill the earth and subdue it" (v. 28) is not shameless exploitation of the environment, but responsible care. Note too that "subdue" (*kabāsh*) suggests that God's creation, though "very good," still requires taming, managing, keeping things in order. This will require human force and ingenuity to wisely engage with nature (think: weeds, pests, dangerous animals, etc.).

Next, notice that God provides food for humans (v. 29)—the exact opposite of the picture in the Mesopotamian myths, where the gods depend on humans for their sustenance.

Summing up the six creation days, everything God made is "very good." Six times in this chapter God has declared that his creation is good; on the seventh occasion, he underscores this point emphatically: it is *all* "very good."

- Since his creation is good, it stands to reason that God is good. In a time when the God of the Bible is negatively represented in academia, popular culture, and even within the church, the goodness of God is a precious reality. This is still axiomatic today, just as it was for Abraham (Gen 18:25). With evangelism, we invite the world to draw near to a good deity—not a sadistic, arbitrary, or even neutral one.
- False forms of spirituality are to be rejected, especially those that view the flesh and sexuality as evil, coerce others to treat their bodies harshly, or speak of the body as a temporary prison for the soul. These

are Greek philosophical ideas, not biblical ones. See Col 2:16–23 and 1 Tim 4:1–5.

- The current plight of the world is not God's fault. It got the way it is through creaturely rejection of God and his standards.

It may be asked, Is the climax of the creation day six or day seven? We will return to this question once we comment on 2:4, in Chapter 7. For now, it may be helpful to consider the biblical panoramic creation account—the first creation account of several—in light of the beliefs of the ancient Near East (chart below).

Order of Points of Contact Between *Enuma Elish* and Genesis 1

Enuma Elish	***Genesis 1***
1. Gods and matter coexistent and coeternal.	1. Yahweh creates matter, existing independently of it.
2. Primeval chaos. Tiamat surrounded by darkness.	2. The earth a waste. *Tᵉhôm* (the deep) is covered with darkness.
3. Light emanates from the gods.	3. Yahweh creates light.
4. The gods create the firmament.	4. Yahweh creates the firmament.
5. The gods create dry land.	5. Yahweh creates dry land.
6. The gods create the light-bearers.	6. Yahweh creates the light-bearers (sun, moon, stars).
7. The gods create man.	7. Yahweh creates man.
8. The gods rest and celebrate.	8. Yahweh rests and sanctifies the seventh day.

2:1Thus the heavens and the earth were finished, and all their multitude. 2And on the seventh day God [had] finished the work that

> *he had done, and he rested on the seventh day from all the work that he had done.* [3]*So God blessed the seventh day and hallowed it, because on it God rested from all the work that he had done in creation.*

Rest

The seventh day marks the end of the creation week. God "rests" from his work, not because he is fatigued and needs the rest as we do (Isa 40:28). Rather, he "rests" in the sense of pausing.

The wording is a clue that Genesis was written in the time of the Israelites, and not necessarily earlier, since the references to the Sabbath would have likely meant little during the time of the patriarchs—but much more as Israel was a young, wandering nation (Ex 16:23–35) and then especially after the giving of the Law at Sinai (Ex 20:8–11; 31:12–17). This is also in contrast to pagan religions. The gods of Mesopotamia long for rest—hence they enlist people to become their servants. The creator god of Egypt, Ptah, is tired out after doing his work of creating. Yahweh was not challenged in digging creeks and rivers or in building mountains. The God of the Bible does not need sleep, as the pagan gods do (Ps 121:4).

God made everything not with his hands but with his words. He rested not out of fatigue but because his work was finished. God's rest (2:2) cannot be literal, since the Bible states that God never rests. So why does the day on which God "rested" have to be a literal day?

God's "resting" is an anthropomorphism[98]—a portrayal of deity in human form. His cessation from creating was a rest from a human perspective. In the same way, the seven days are not literal days. They are described as they are to convey *theological* truths—not *chronological* truths.

Days

The ancients did not always think of time in the way we moderns do. They thought more in terms of quality (the kind of day), whereas we think more in terms of quantity (twenty-four hours). Still, we grasp the principle because we use "days" in a qualitative sense when we speak of "glory days," or when we say, "In my day, a Big Mac cost a quarter." It would be inappropriate to ask, "Exactly which day are you talking about?" or "How many 'glory days' were there?"

Furthermore, day seven is unclosed. Notice that the six creation days all close with the same formula: And there was evening, and there was morning—the nth day. In fact, Heb 4 insists that there remains a Sabbath rest for God's people because the day is still open. It was never closed out. Jesus' reasoning in Jn 5:17, in stating that God is "always at work to this very day" (NIV), presumes that God is working on the Sabbath. This is yet another instance where it is problematic to construe "day" literally.

Interestingly, in Mesopotamian thought, the seventh, fourteenth, twenty-first, and twenty-eighth days of the month were considered unlucky.[99] Yet the OT makes the seventh day the special day. Not only is the Sabbath motif strong in Genesis—as it is in the rest of the Law—but God is even said to "bless" the seventh day (2:3).

Sevens

Shābath, "rested" (2:2–3) is cognate with *shabbāth*, "Sabbath." They are not the same word, yet they are closely related etymologically. The schema of a creation week—the topic of our next chapter—suggests the Sabbath. Judaism had a New Moon Celebration, and the months of the year were tied in to the lunar cycle.

In Egypt, it is doubtful that the taskmasters gave the Hebrews the weekend off. Day seven would have reminded the Jews of the good news that they were no longer slaves.[100]

In the Bible "day" (*yôm*) can refer to a twenty-four-hour period, or the daylight portion of that same period. In Gen 2:4, it refers to the entire time of creation. The word is even compared to "a thousand years." It suggests "an indefinite period of time," as is the case also in Gen 2:17 (cf. 3:5); Ex 6:28; 32:34; Jer 11:5; etc. Thus, it is not possible to show from the meaning of the word "day" that it must mean a twenty-four-hour period in Gen 1.[101] Moreover, the evidence against the days of creation being literal days is substantial.[102] So, exactly what is going on in the first creation account? What are we supposed to conclude? This will be our investigation in the next chapter.

RECAP

To facilitate remembering the material, Chapters 5 to 15 all end with a "Recap" section. Here the principal *biblical truths* of the text will be listed, followed by *points of contact with pagan culture and mythology, connections with the NT*, and then *application*.

Biblical Truths

- God is the Creator.
- The creation–not just the spiritual, but the physical–is good.
- Yet this does not mean that nature should be worshiped. Yahweh alone is divine.
- Humans, at the apex of creation, have a special relationship to God.
- The divine image is reflected in both male and female, peasant and prince–in all humans.
- As God's image, we represent him and join him in his kingdom work.
- Humankind has been placed over creation to exercise dominion. In our time, dominion implies responsibility and requires stewardship of the earth's resources.

Points of Contact with Pagan Culture

- The initial watery chaos
- Firmament, oceans above and beneath, earth center of universe
- Plants and animals brought forth from the ground
- Rest after creation

NT Connections

- Compare 1:1 with Jn 1:1 and 1 Jn 1:1. These passages are not primarily about human creation. They are panoramic, taking in the whole sweep of the cosmos.

- Note Christ's role in creation in Col 1:15–17.
- With Christ's bodily resurrection on the first Easter, a new creation has already begun (2 Cor 5:17). The church fathers called this "the eighth day of creation."[103] The Sabbath of the first creation finds its completion in Christ (Col 2:17), who is the second Adam, the "new man," and the founder of a renewed, redeemed humanity (1 Cor 15:45; Eph 2:15; Col 3:9–11).
- Various days of creation have connection points to Christ and the new creation: light (Jn 8:12); water (Jn 4:14); land/earth (2 Pet 3:13); trees (Rev 22:14); fruit (Rev 22:2; Heb 13:14–15); animals (Jn 1:29; Rev 5:5); humanity (Eph 2:15; Phil 2:6–7); and the Sabbath (Heb 4:9–10).

Application

- Since humans are intended to be the Lord's representatives, we should strive to cultivate a constant consciousness of Christ's presence. We are being groomed to reign with Christ–a reign which has begun (Eph 2:6; Rev 3:21) but that will culminate in the new heavens and earth (Rev 5:10).
- Men and women should regard each other as equals, as they are co-rulers with God over creation.
- Although the NT exempts us from following the complete OT Sabbath system (Col 2:16), we still benefit from Sabbath wisdom.[104] It is not God's will that we burn ourselves out, but rather that our bodies be refreshed for useful service to God and humankind (Ps 127:1–2; Mt 11:28–30; 1 Jn 5:3–4).[105]

---

66. Wenham, *Rethinking Genesis* 1–11, 13.
67. See Paul Copan and William Lane Craig, *Creation ex Nihilo: A Biblical, Philosophical, and Scientific Exploration* (Grand Rapids, MI: Baker, 2004).
68. As Hyers points out:

    > Gen 1:2 begins in a way very puzzling to modern interpreters, yet natural to ancient cosmogonies: with a picture of primordial chaos. This chaos—consisting of darkness, watery deep and formless earth—is then formed, ordered, assigned its proper place and function… [It] is brought under control, and its positive features are made part of the cosmic totality…. If one is determined to interpret the account as a scientific statement, then one would need—to be consistent—to affirm several undesirable things. There is no scientific evidence whatsoever, whether from geology or astronomy, that the initial state of the universe was characterized by a great watery expanse, filling the universe.

    Hyers, "Narrative Form," 209b.
69. Adapted from Holland, *Religion in the Ancient World*, lesson 6.

70. Some ask, "Who created God?" Yet God is by definition uncreated. Further, God is unlike material objects, which come into existence and thus require a cause, according to the second law of thermodynamics. Indeed, the entire universe came into existence, according to cosmologists and astrophysicists. Finally, there is nothing metaphysically problematic with an eternally existent entity. Since it is impossible that something could pop into existence uncaused out of nothing, the only alternative is that something must have always existed. See Paul Copan, "If God Made the Universe, Who Made God?" which answers the question, "Is it philosophically incoherent to say that something could be eternally existent and uncaused?" Accessible at http:/enrichmentjournal.ag.org/201202/201202_122_who_made_God.cfm.
71. Averbeck states:

    The deep dark watery abyss is also one of the standard starting points for creation in the Egyptian world. For example, in one Coffin Text we read: "…on the day that Atum evolved—out of the Flood, out of the Waters, out of darkness, out of lostness..." There is also the wind or breath of the god Amun moving over the waters, similar to Genesis 1:2c, "and the S/spirit (or breath or wind) of God was hovering over the waters." This clause seems to anticipate God's creation decrees in Genesis (i.e., God just spoke and things happened; that is, by his "breath"). Note that darkness is also particularly highlighted in Egypt. This is probably because of the importance of the sun god in Egyptian religion. And it seems that here, as in Genesis 1, light preceded the creation of the sun. (See COS 1.22–23 with Gordon H. Johnston, "Genesis 1 and Ancient Egyptian Creation Myths," *Bibliotheca Sacra* 165 [2008]: 183–84, 186–87.)

    Richard E. Averbeck, "Ancient Near Eastern Creation and Cosmos Texts Related to Genesis 1–4," Templeton Foundation consultation (Ft. Lauderdale, FL; February 21–22, 2013), 2–3.
72. Note that here "Rahab" is the name of the primeval monster, not the harlot of Jericho (Josh 2) and ancestor of Jesus (Mt 1:5). Among the Canaanites the serpent was also called Leviathan (Lotan), and is equivalent to Yam, the sea serpent *and* god of the sea. Averbeck explains:

    The association of Leviathan with "the dragon" (Heb. *tnnyn*) who is in the "sea" (Heb. *ym*; cf. the Ugaritic god Yam) in Isa. 27:1 makes perfectly good sense against the backdrop of the world of the Ugaritic Baal myth.… In the biblical text we have clear allusions to an ancient Near Eastern myth about an evil serpent with whom Yahweh does battle.

    "Ancient Near Eastern Mythography," 341.
73. When Marduk slays Tiamat, she splits like a seashell; both the earth and the firmament are *hard*.
74. The Bible "demythologizes" ancient myths. Please listen to "Dragons and the Bible" at https://www.douglasjacoby.com/dragons-and-the-bible/. This study explains the mythology in the King James Version (unicorns, satyrs, cockatrices, and dragons) as well as the "mythology" in the Bible (including Leviathan and Rahab). Col 2:15 makes a similar point. Whether or not these powers are real (there are reasons to believe they are), it is the credence we give them that enables them to frighten or affect us.
75. One source states:

    The massive power and unpredictability of the sea is why ancient peoples saw it as a symbol of evil. The inhabitants of ancient Israel, who were not a seafaring people, viewed the ocean as a realm of chaos, destruction, and darkness. Rather than a delightful place for recreation, to them the sea was a dark abyss to be feared. In their literature, including the biblical narrative, the sea became a metaphor for the forces of evil and disorder that stood in opposition to their God of order and beauty.

    Skye Jethani, *With: Reimagining the Way You Relate to God* (Nashville, TN: Thomas Nelson, 2011), 136. Referring to the next world, Philip Graham Ryken adds:

> The sea represents everything that chafes and frets under the dominion of God; everything that is out of our control. But there is nothing like that in the new heaven and the new earth. Everything there is under the orderly blessing of God.

In D. A. Carson and Jeff Robinson Sr., eds., *Coming Home: Essays on the New Heaven and New Earth* (Wheaton, IL: Crossway, 2017), 125.

76. *When on high the heavens had not yet been named / and below the firm ground had not yet been given a name / when primæval Apsu, their better / and mother Tiamat, who gave them all birth / still mingled their waters / the reed had not yet sprung forth nor had / the marsh appeared / none of the gods had been brought into being / they were still unnamed and their fortunes were not determined / then the gods were created in their midst…* (tr. Hartmut Schmökel). Cited in John C. L. Gibson, *Genesis, Volume 1*, in The Daily Study Bible Series (Louisville, KY: Westminster John Knox Press, 1981), 16. For another (substantively identical) translation, see James B. Pritchard, ed., *Ancient Near Eastern Texts Relating to the Old Testament*, 3rd ed. (Princeton, NJ: Princeton University Press, 1969), 60–61. In other words, in ancient times the origins of the gods were to be accounted for: a theogony. Since God is spirit (Jn 4:24) and stands in a wholly different relationship to his creation (transcendent and yet immanent), he never *came into* being. He simply *is* (and was, and shall be).
77. This distinction is central to the Apostle Paul's argument about the resurrection in 1 Cor 15. There Paul isn't contrasting a physical body to a spirit "body." No, the "natural" (lit. "soul-animated"), corruptible, physical body gives way to a renovated, immortal, still-physical "spiritual" (lit. "[S]pirit-animated") body—a transformed physicality (cf. Rom 1:4).
78. Ps 77:16–20 alludes to this primeval separation, although this passage refers directly to the Exodus, when Yahweh led his people through the sea.
79. Gen 1:9 LXX (the OT, which is the version nearly always quoted from in the NT) has a *synagogē* (gathering) of waters—the same word used for the congregation (OT) and the assembly of the church (Jas 2:2).
80. Ezek 8:16; Am 5:25 LXX.
81. Deut 4:19; Isa 47:13; Jer 10:2; Dan 2:2, 4, 5, 10, 27; 4:7, 5:7.
82. David J. Rudolph, "Festivals in Genesis 1:14," *Tyndale Bulletin* 54.2 (2003), 23–40. Paul reminds the Galatians that they are no longer obligated to observe the Jewish religious calendar (with New Moon celebrations, Sabbath years, and so on—see Gal 4:10–11).
83. Since the stars are much smaller than the sun, they may be described as falling like figs (Rev 6:13; Isa 34:4; see also Mk 13:25–30). Even today we speak of meteors as "shooting stars"—which do indeed look like stars, except in fast motion. The notion that the sun is simply a star (and an average one, at that) would have not only struck the ancient Hebrews as incorrect, but also would have caused an unnecessary obstacle to faith.
84. He writes:

> The OT often depicts God as a king seated on his throne with his angels or heavenly council gathered about him (see 1 Ki 22:19–22; Ps 82:1; Job 1:6; 2:1). Isaiah 6 describes him as "sitting upon a throne" (v. 1) with angelic beings called "seraphim" gathered about him (vv. 2, 3, 6), and as saying, "Whom shall *I* send, and who will go for *us*?" (v. 8). Apparently, the first-person plural ("us") here refers to the Lord and his heavenly council. This may be what the author of Gen 1:26 has in mind (see also Gen 3:22; 11:7).

John T. Willis, *Genesis,* in The Living Word Commentary on the Old Testament (Abilene, TX: Abilene Christian University, 1984), 87.

85. John H. Walton, *The Lost World of Adam and Eve: Genesis 2–3 and the Human Origins Debate* (Downers Grove, IL: IVP Academic, 2015), 29.
86. The Hebrew words are *tselem* (image or idol), *pesel* (idol), and *temûnāh* (likeness).
87. Averbeck, "Ancient Near Eastern Creation and Cosmos."

88. The Hebrew preposition *bᵉ*, meaning "in," seems to be synonymous with *kᵉ*, meaning "as," in Gen 5:3. God is making man as his image. See also Ex 6:3, where God appears "as God Almighty" (*kᵉ 'el shaddai*). Hence Paul (oddly from the perspective of most English translations) can say man "is the image… of God" in 1 Cor 11:7. Whether made *in* God's image, or *as* God's image, the essential theological point remains the same. The spirit conferred on humankind does not emanate from us, as if it were a portion of the Spirit of God.
89. A similar thought is expressed in 2 Cor 2:14–16.
90. For example:

    > Amenhotep II (1427–1400 B.C.E.) is described variously as "image of Re," "image of Horus," "image of Atum," "holy image of the lord of the gods," "foremost image of Re," "holy image of Re," "holy image of Amon, image of Amon like Re," and so on. Amenhotep III (1390–1352 B.C.E.) is addressed by Amon as "my living image, creation of my members, whom Mut bore to me." Amenhotep III is also addressed by Amon-Re: "You are my beloved son, who came forth from my members, my image, whom I have put on earth. I have given to you to rule the earth in peace."

    J. Richard Middleton, *The Liberating Image: The* Imago Dei *in Genesis 1* (Grand Rapids, MI: Brazos, 2005), 55–60.
91. Byrne elaborates:

    > You are God in a physical body. You are spirit in the flesh. You are Eternal Life expressing itself as you. You are a cosmic being. You are all power. You are all wisdom. You are all intelligence. You are perfection. You are magnificence. You are the creator, and you are creating the creation of You on this planet.

    Rhonda Byrne, *The Secret* (New York: Atria Books, 2006), 164.
92. We will return to this point in the endnotes to Appendix D. In short, the universe has to be as large as it is for human life to be feasible.
93. Daniel Dennett, *Breaking the Spell: Religion as a Natural Phenomenon* (New York: Viking, 2006), 4.
94. Richard Dawkins, *The Selfish Gene*, 2nd ed. (New York: Houghton Mifflin, 2006), 200–201.
95. Noted by Venema and McKnight, *Adam and the Genome*, 131.
96. Listen to the podcast "The Gender of God" at https://www.douglasjacoby.com/godgendermp3/.
97. In the view of Henri Blocher,

    > There is a kind of subtle balance. In all earthly relationships, the man represents God more obviously than does the woman: in active transcendence, in keeping an objective distance, in leadership and in work. But we realize at once that it is the woman who best represents humanity in relationship with God: in the face-to-face relationship with the Lord, every human being, male or female, must accept a feminine position, existing from him and for him, receiving and bearing the seed of his word, receiving and bearing the name he gives.

    Henri Blocher, *In the Beginning,* trans. David G. Preston (Downers Grove, IL: InterVarsity, 1984), 82.
98. For more anthropomorphisms of God, see the table in Chapter 8.
99. Religious ritual was governed by a lunar cycle. At times, the 19th too was considered inauspicious.
100. Wenham, *Genesis 1–15*, xlix–l.
101. Willis, *Genesis*, 101.
102. Problems with interpreting Gen 1:1–2:3 literally are legion: (1) There is no evidence of an ancient celestial ocean. (2) Fish fossils are older than plant fossils (400 million years before the appearance of fruit trees). (3) Birds did not precede land animals, which were on earth some 200 million years previously. (4) Plants and trees depend on sunlight, seeding, and fruit

bearing, so they could not have lived before the creation of the sun. (This sticky problem has led to many ingenious speculations: perhaps the sun was created but not visible—but no hint of this in the text; or God created the sunlight [like starlight] before he created the sun [!].) (5–12) There are several archaeological problems vis-à-vis the order of appearance of the following: plant and animal domestication (about 9000 BC), permanent settlements (about 7000 BC), flutes (30,000 BC), lyres (3000 BC), bronze (3200 BC), and iron (1200 BC). (13) If Gen 1 is strictly sequential, Gen 2:5 must refer to Day 3, because dry land did not exist before Day 3, and rich vegetation existed by the end of Day 3. Land inundated with water only yesterday (Day 2) does not dry out in a few hours, especially without the sun, which was not created until Day 4. (14) While God could have preserved plants without rain, man, or the sun, that is not how Gen 2:5 explains the delay of the creation of plants. Rather, it was because of the lack of water, a secondary means of preservation. Therefore, the six days in Gen 1 appear to be topical, not sequential.

Consider what it means if the sixth day is a literal 24 hours. After all the animals are made, Adam is created. He then receives commands from God (2:15–17). Then he is apparently lonely (2:18)—so fast? Then he names "every animal of the field and every bird of the air" (2:19)—all except the fish. Even at the rate of one per second, Adam wouldn't have had time to name even 75,000 species, much less the *millions* of species that have lived on earth (over 99% of which are now extinct). Then Adam is put into a deep sleep for the operation (2:21). After Eve has been formed, he is brought back to consciousness, he and Eve meet, and he recites his poem about her (2:23). They become man and wife. (What did you accomplish on *your* wedding day?) If someone adopts literalism for the sixth day, this will demand the interpretation we have outlined here.

103. *Epistle of Barnabas* xv; Justin Martyr, *Dialogue with Trypho* xxiv; xli; Cyprian, *Epistles* lviii.4.
104. For a podcast and notes on this topic, see https://www.douglasjacoby.com/sabbathmp3/.
105. How may we implement the wisdom of the Sabbath, applying the OT principle to NT times? Rhythms—daily, weekly, monthly, annually—are important to mark the passage of time and to keep life from becoming murky and unfocused. Also, God designed us to sleep—not all day, of course! (See Prov 6:9–11; 19:15; 20:13; 24:30–34). And yet, on the other hand, it is not "spiritual" to deprive ourselves for deprivation's sake (Col 2:20–23). We are not superior to others just because we sleep fewer hours.

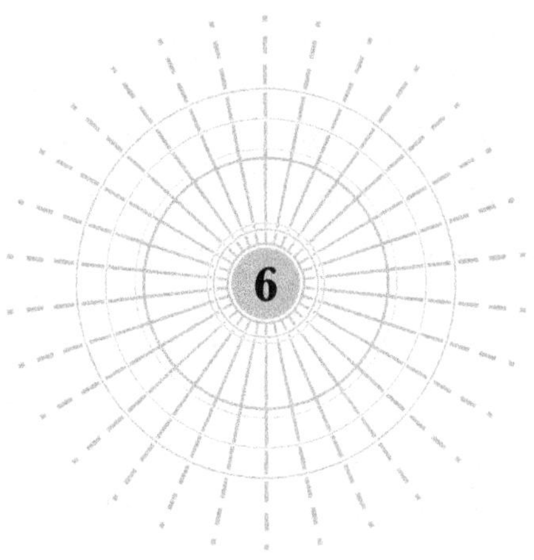

Schema
Creation Week

Scheme: A diagrammatic presentation; broadly: a structured framework or plan.
–Merriam Webster's Collegiate Dictionary

The purpose of this chapter is to take a closer look at the creation week, and particularly how the narrative is structured.

To appreciate the logic and elegance of the account, it helps if we read the account slowly. Notice any key terms, parallelism, and repeated words or phrases.

Following are the passages (abbreviated) for each of the seven days.

{DAY 1} *[1:3]Then God said, "Let there be light"; and there was light. [4]And God saw that the light was good; and God separated the light from the darkness.... [5]And there was evening and there was morning, the first day.*

{DAY 2} *[6]And God said, "Let there be a dome in the midst of the waters, and let it separate the waters from the waters." [8]... And there was evening and there was morning, the second day.*

{DAY 3} *[9]And God said, "Let the waters under the sky be gathered together into one place, and let the dry land appear."... [11]Then God said, "Let the earth put forth vegetation."... [12]The earth brought forth vegetation.... And God saw that it was good. [13]And there was evening and there was morning, the third day.*

{DAY 4} *[14]And God said, "Let there be lights in the dome of the sky to separate the day from the night; and let them be for signs and for seasons and for days and years, [15]and let them be lights in the dome of the sky."... [19]And there was evening and there was morning, the fourth day.*

{DAY 5} *[20]And God said, "Let the waters bring forth swarms of living creatures, and let birds fly above the earth across the dome of the sky."... [23]And there was evening and there was morning, the fifth day.*

{DAY 6} *[24]And God said, "Let the earth bring forth living creatures."... [26]Then God said, "Let us make humankind in our image."... [31]And there was evening and there was morning, the sixth day.*

{DAY 7} *[2:1]Thus the heavens and the earth were finished, and all their multitude. [2]And on the seventh day God [had] finished the work that he had done, and he rested on the seventh day.*

Views on the Meaning of "Day"

What are we to make of these days? In the previous chapter we observed several points telling against a strictly literal interpretation of the seven days.

For example, the days—consisting of evening and morning, in accordance with the Jewish custom of reckoning days—begin even before there is sunlight. (The common explanation that God must have created the sunlight before making the sun is not convincing.) The literal approach to the days is problematic.[106]

There are five approaches to the "days" of Gen 1: the Literal Theory, the Gap Theory, the Day-Age Theory, the Revelatory Day Theory, and the Literary Theory. The first four views (with their strengths and weaknesses) will not be reviewed in the body of this chapter.[107] Of all these views, we find the literary view far and away the most convincing.

In this interpretation, the days are a literary device for communicating the truth about creation. The account is construed as poetic, semipoetic, or (at the least) highly elevated literature. For another, even more poetic, version of the Creation, see Prov 8:22–31. Further poetic or semipoetic accounts and descriptions of creation may be found in Job 36–41; Pss 8; 19; 33; 104; 148. Consider also the highly theological creation accounts of Jn 1:1–5 and Col 1:15–17. Thus, there are many ways in which Yahweh conveys the basic truths about the creation. *Every* account is true, and each conveys something important about the Creator and his creation. The original readers of Genesis, sharing the author's culture, probably understood exactly what he meant. In brief, the scheme of Gen 1 is logical, not chronological.[108]

A Literary Approach to the Creation Week

Most important, the Literary Theory recognizes divine providence. God was preparing the world for habitation. He did this with care, not haste. His wisdom is boundless, even if occasionally his ways are inscrutable (Rom 11:33–36). Next, this theory recognizes a definite structure to the creation account, a definite schema. Notice how God's providence and forethought are portrayed, as the first three days correspond to the following three.

Conrad Hyers has convincingly analyzed the symmetrical division of the first creation account into three movements: Problem, Preparation, Population—each with three elements.[109]

Outline of Genesis 1[110]

Problem (v. 2)	*Preparation (days 1–3)*	*Population (days 4–6)*
Darkness	1a Creation of Light (Day) 1b Separation from Darkness (Night)	4a Creation of Sun 4b Creation of Moon, Stars
Watery Abyss	2a Creation of Firmament 2b Separation of Waters Above from Waters Below	5a Creation of Birds 5b Creation of Fish
Formless Earth	3a Separation of Earth from Sea 3b Creation of Vegetation	6a Creation of Land Animals 6b Creation of Humans

Each of the problems is remedied by a corresponding separation (vv. 4, 7, 9—although the word "separate" is only implied in the third instance). Once the barriers are removed, the earth will return to its primordial state. This is precisely what will happen in the flood (Gen 6–8).

The days serve as a framework for the truth God intends to communicate to his people. The literary view doesn't claim that God *couldn't* have created everything in six twenty-four-hour days, or in one second, or in many eons. That's because this view is not tied to any presuppositions about biology or the age of the earth. The Genesis writer isn't presenting a strict cosmological or biological sequence, but is showing how God prepared the world for human habitation.

This view also appreciates God as a God of order (1 Cor 14:33). It also teaches that the universe is not the result of chance, but of careful planning.

There is a specific historical and literary context to the book of Genesis as a whole.

A Structured Account

Genesis never purports to be a scientific study of "what happened," yet it does contain a carefully constructed account based on the calculated use of symbolic numbers, especially three, seven, and ten. Biblical scholars, studying the text of Genesis as a whole, and its first literary section (Gen 1:1–2:4a) in particular, have discovered a masterful inner structure. Various words and phrases appear a *theologically* determined number of times. The chances are low that these are all coincidental.

- "God said" occurs ten times: three times in reference to man and seven times for all other creatures.
- The verb "to be" ("let there be") occurs three times for creatures in the heavens, and seven times for the world below.
- The verb "to make" occurs ten times, and so does "according to their kinds."
- There are three blessings.
- The verb "to create" is used on three occasions, three times on the third occasion.
- "And it was so" occurs seven times.
- "And God saw that it was good" occurs seven times.
- God either names or blesses seven times.
- Gen 1:1 has seven words, 1:2 has two x seven words, and 2:1–3 (the seventh paragraph) has five x seven words.
- The word "earth" occurs three x seven times, and "God" (*'Elohim*) five x seven times.
- The names of God occur seventy (seven x ten) times in Gen 1–4. Ten times it is Yahweh (God's personal name; see Ex 6:3), two x ten times *Yahweh 'Elohim* ("Yahweh God"), and four x ten times *'Elohim* ("God").

And this is only the beginning. Special numbers and patterns occur throughout Genesis, and the numbers three, seven, and ten themselves express *fullness* or *completeness* here and in many other places in Scripture. These verbal arrangements are carefully constructed, literarily complex, and numerologically rich.[111]

Rejecting the Pagan Narrative

The literary view takes stock of the historical situation, recognizing the rejection of rival stories circulating in Egypt, Mesopotamia, and the rest of the contemporary Mediterranean world. The Genesis material stands in stark contrast to, and in judgment on, the ancient Near Eastern creation accounts, in which humankind is little more than an afterthought, or a source of irritation to the gods. How different the Genesis account is from the Sumerian, Babylonian, Assyrian, and Egyptian stories!

Theology of the Sabbath

The literary view recognizes that Gen 1 provides a theology of the Sabbath, which would have been highly relevant to the ancient Israelites, who as a nation had just come into a covenant relationship with God.

Poetry and Hymn

While some say that they "take the Bible literally," they very often don't (e.g., the trees of the field clapping their hands [Isa 55:12] obviously isn't literal). Most leading scholars of the OT recognize Gen 1 as a magnificent hymn attesting to the oneness and omnipotence of God. Once we get past any fear of moving away from the mistakenly labeled "literal" interpretation, we recognize a "clearly poetic dimension to this creational prologue."[112] The rules for reading poetry differ from those for reading prose. Some thirty percent of the Bible is poetry (Psalms, Proverbs, most of Job, much of the Prophets, sections interspersed among the narratives of both testaments). Learning to think poetically is a valuable asset for biblical interpretation.[113]

Unfortunately, in attempting to interpret Gen 1 and 2 "scientifically," many miss the richness of the descriptions, symbolism, numerology, poetry, and careful construction of the account.

RECAP

Biblical Truths

- God is a God of order. The sevenfold creation schema reemphasizes this fact.
- When he explains himself and his ways to us, God must come down to our level. Given his immense might, intellect, and energy, we expect language accommodated to our culture and mental capacity. (More on this in Appendix D.) The creation week was an excellent device for teaching the Hebrews about the created world and its Creator.
- Humans bear/are the image of God.
- Rest follows work. Although in God's case he did not rest for refreshment–he simply rests from (ceases) his work–the pattern he sets for us humans is important for our flourishing.

Points of Contact with Pagan Culture

- Whereas in pagan culture the world results from conflict between gods, in the Bible there is no struggle at all. God, who is omnipotent and infinitely wise, creates effortlessly.
- In Mesopotamian religion, the waters Apsu and Tiamat are separated. Apsu is the subterranean abyss of fresh water, undulating in purposeless motion. Tiamat is the bitter sea waters, a chaos monster, above. In Genesis, God separates the waters–yet there is no killing, no "gods," no mythology.
- Nothing God created in Gen 1:1–2:3 is divine. Even the sun and moon, both important deities in ancient religions, are simply implements. God uses them to illuminate the earth, fix the Sabbath days (and years), and connect his people to the festival calendar of Judaism.

NT Connections

- God speaks the world into existence. That is, he creates through his Word (Jn 1:1–3).
- All of creation prefigures Christ's nature, identities, and purpose.
- The seventh day is still open, according to the Hebrew writer (Heb 4:9), although as we noted in the last chapter, Christ brings the Sabbath to fulfillment in the new creation, which began with his bodily resurrection.

Application

- Sometimes we need to slow down when we read Scripture. Unless we do, we will miss many of the details that alert us to the structure, emphases, and theology of the text. Reading through the Bible quickly is fine—may we all complete the entire Bible multiple times in the course of our lives!—but there are times when nothing substitutes for careful, methodical, observant, meditative study of Scripture.
- Since God is a God of order, and the Bible urges us to live disciplined lives, we shouldn't make excuses for disorganization, slovenly habits, or even sloppy thinking.

---

106. Conrad Hyers explains:

> In this case, one of the obvious interests of the Genesis account is to correlate the grand theme of the divine work in creation with the six days of work and seventh day of rest in the Jewish week. If the Hebrews had had a five-day or a seven-day work week, the account would have read differently in a corresponding manner. Seven was a basic unit of time among West Semitic peoples, and goes back to the division of the lunar month into 4 periods of 7 days each. By the time Genesis was written, the seven-day week and the Sabbath observance had been long established. Since what is being affirmed in the text is the *creative work* of God, it was quite natural to use the imagery of 6 days of work, with a 7th day of rest. It would have seemed inappropriate and jarring to have depicted the divine creative effort in a schema of, say, 5 days or 11 days.

Hyers, "Narrative Form," 213a.

107. The four theories are laid out at https://www.douglasjacoby.com/interpretations-genesis-days-origins-note-107/. See also https://www.douglasjacoby.com/qa-1502-long-days-genesis-1/.

108. For more, see Paul Copan, "The Days of Genesis: An Old-Earth View" (written in dialogue with John MacArthur, who takes the young-earth view), *Areopagus Journal* 5/2 (March–April 2005): 15, 17, 19. Accessible at http://www.paulcopan.com/articles/pdf/revised-genesis-science.pdf.

109. Hyers's insight into the text points up a strange irony:

> This triadic structure of three sets of three points up another problem with a literal reading of the account. Literalism presumes that the numbering of days is to be understood in an arithmetical sense, whether as actual days or as epochs. This is certainly the way in which numbers are used in science, history and mathematics—and in practically all areas of modern life. But the use of numbers in ancient religious texts was often numerological rather than numerical. That is, their symbolic value was the basis and purpose for their use, not their secular value as counters. While the conversion of numerology to arithmetic was essential for the rise of modern science, historiography and mathematics, the result is that numerological symbols are reduced to signs. Numbers had to be neutralized and secularized, and completely stripped of any symbolic suggestion, in order to be utilized as digits.... In the literal treatment of the six days of creation, a modern, arithmetical reading is substituted for the original symbolic one. This results, unwittingly, in a secular rather than religious interpretation. Not only are the symbolic associations and meanings of the text lost in the process, but the text is needlessly placed in conflict with scientific and historical readings of origins.

Hyers, "Narrative Form," 212b–c.

110. Hyers, "Narrative Form," 211b.
111. We will further examine numbers, in particular symbolic and sacred numbers, in our commentary on Gen 5. For an introduction to biblical numbers, see John J. Davis, *Biblical Numerology: A Basic Study of the Use of Numbers in the Bible* (Grand Rapids, MI: Baker, 1968). Of course, the numbers in the Bible are not ciphers to be manipulated to prophesy current events—wars, weather, or politics.
112. Fee and Stuart, *How to Read the Bible Book by Book*, 27.
113. Hyers writes that "in order to interpret its meaning properly, and to understand why its materials are organized in this particular way, one has to learn to think *cosmogonically*, not scientifically or, historically—just as in interpreting the parables of Jesus one has to learn to think parabolically." Hyers, "Narrative Form," 209b.

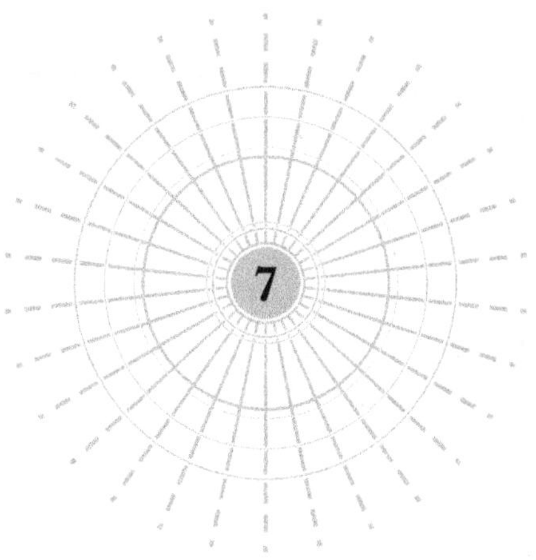

Humankind
Second Account

The panoramic creation story moves from primordial darkness through divine preparations during the first three days to the inhabitation of the spaces now created during the next three days, all followed by Sabbath rest. When we come to the second account, the subject of this chapter, we observe many differences from the first. Humans, absent until late on day six, are not simply the crown of creation. Rather, nearly the entire account focuses on *Adam*, which is the Hebrew word for humankind. The order of events is different. Furthermore, no longer is there a sabbatical (seven-day) framework.

> *2:4 These are the generations of the heavens and the earth when*
> *they were created. In the day that YAHWEH God made the earth and*
> *the heavens, 5 when no plant of the field was yet in the earth and no*
> *herb of the field had yet sprung up—for YAHWEH God had not caused*
> *it to rain upon the earth, and there was no one to till the ground;*

> [6]*but a stream would rise from the earth, and water the whole face of the ground–*[7]*then* YAHWEH *God formed man from the dust of the ground, and breathed into his nostrils the breath of life; and the man became a living being.*
>
> * Note that the phrase in v. 7, "living being" (*nephesh chayyāh*–"living being or creature"), is used of various animals in Gen 1:20-30, as well as of beasts and birds in 2:19.

The word "generations" (*toledoth*) informs us that the next origins account is beginning.

Whereas many versions read "…when they were created" (v. 4), a more literal translation would be, "This is the account of the heavens and the earth *in the day God* created them."[114] The point: in 2:4 the word "day" is used in a nonliteral sense, summing up six days.

In v. 4 is the first time God is called Yahweh—the first of nearly 7000 mentions in the OT.

In v. 5 we note that there are not yet any plants—or possibly there is no agriculture, given the references to field and tilling.

This creation story begins with a lot of water. Everything is wet, although nothing is growing. The first account also begins with water, yet the second is nowhere near as threatening.

Humans are created from earth. We are used to thinking of the soul as the eternal part of humans. Yet in the Bible there is no "eternal" part at all. Unless we receive the gift of salvation through Jesus Christ, we will not possess eternal life. Humans were not created with immortal resurrection bodies. Like the other animals, they were created with perishable bodies that God sustained in existence, but God withdrew that sustaining grace when they rebelled, and natural mortality took effect (see Eccl 12:7).[115] This ties in with the separation of the first couple from the tree of life, as we will see in the next chapter.

In the *Atrahasis Epic*, people are created out of clay and the blood of a dead god—with the spit of the gods mixed in. Egyptian myth had humans come into being through a mixture of dust and the tears of the gods. In ancient

Near Eastern religion, humans are created to give rest to the gods. But in Genesis it is Yahweh who works until he has provided for the earth, and especially for humankind. Humans are more than drones; they are created for relationship, both with one another and with God.

Adam: A Better Translation?

The first few times the Hebrew *'ādām* occurs, it refers to the human race, not to any individual. Thereafter it morphs into a handy name for the first human. One theological implication appears to be this: because we are human, we are Adam—or Adam and Eve. (In light of 1:27, Adam and Eve are both *'Ādām*—though she is not named Eve until the end of Gen 3.) Adam's story of being created to relate to God but (eventually) turning from God is the story of our own individual lives.

The point is that there is an obvious wordplay in the Hebrew (v. 7). *'Ādām* is a masculine form of the feminine noun *'adāmāh.* The man is called *'Ādām* because he was taken from the *'adāmāh,* which is the earth. This wordplay is entirely lost in translation. There are some pretty good alternate names for the human—no disrespect intended toward any readers who may be Adams (or Adamses). Let's do some of our own wordplay.

Personal name:	**Dusty** (from dust)
	Clay (from Clay)
	Adam (loses the wordplay)
Species focus:	**Human** (from the humus)
Terrestrial focus:	**Earthling** (from the earth)

We are aware that "Dusty" and "Clay" are actual names—Dirty (from dirt) and Earthy (which has a somewhat different meaning in our time) are not. "Human" and "Earthling" cannot but elicit thoughts of space travel. Earthling, however, is a nice rendering, for several reasons. It is an accurate translation. It is a helpful reminder of our humble origins. It reminds us, too, that God is in heaven—and that at the consummation of all things, we will no longer be separated.

The fact that a name is symbolic doesn't necessarily mean the individual is unhistorical. Douglas and Paul (our names) come from the Gaelic *dubglas* ("dark stream") and the Latin *paulus* ("small"). Yet Douglas is not a flow of water, nor is Paul small (he's tall)—and neither is a fictional character. Christians through the ages have had different interpretations of Adam. Rather than insist there is only one way to look at this, ought we not to admit that determining what is literal and what is symbolic is a challenge facing all interpreters of Gen 1–11—just as it is for Rev 1–22?

> *8And YAHWEH God planted a garden in Eden, in the east; and there he put the man whom he had formed. 9Out of the ground YAHWEH God made to grow every tree that is pleasant to the sight and good for food, the tree of life also in the midst of the garden, and the tree of the knowledge of good and evil.*

Though we often speak of Eden *as* the garden, Yahweh plants the garden *in* Eden (v. 8), which is a region. It's the Garden in Eden (v. 8), or the Garden of Eden (v. 15).[116] It is "in the east." East of what? Undoubtedly the referent is Israel. Notice the location of Babylon on the map below. Later we will discuss the significance of "east" in the book of Genesis.

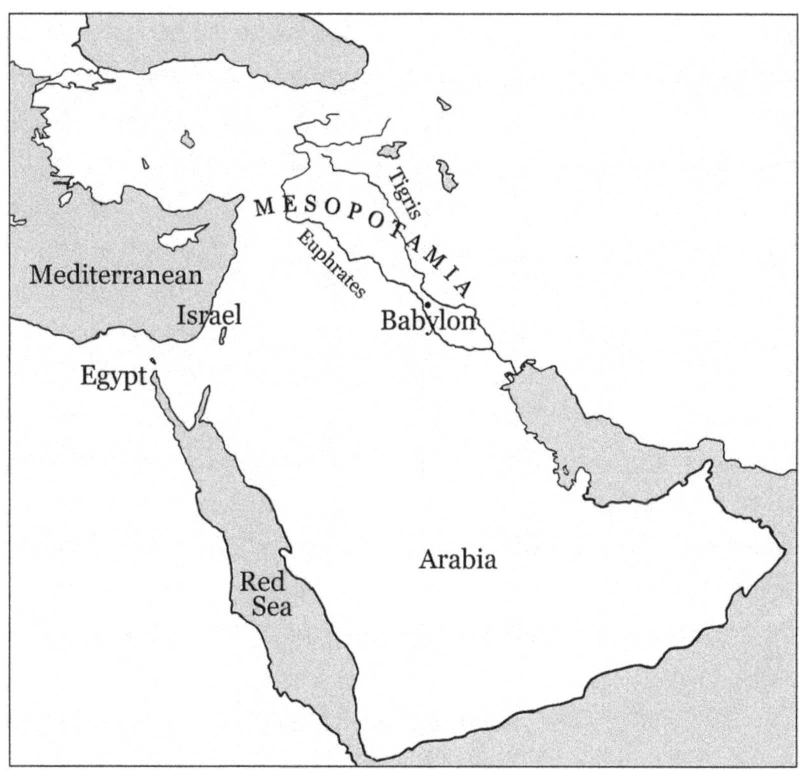

The World of Genesis 1-11

Among the many delightful plants and trees in the garden are two of special significance: the tree of life (which conferred immortality) and the tree of knowledge.[117]

> [10]*A river flows out of Eden to water the garden, and from there it divides and becomes four branches.* [11]*The name of the first is Pishon; it is the one that flows around the whole land of Havilah, where there is gold;* [12]*and the gold of that land is good; bdellium and onyx stone are there.* [13]*The name of the second river is Gihon; it is the one that flows around the whole land of Cush.* [14]*The name of the third river is Tigris, which flows east of Assyria. And the fourth river is the Euphrates.*

The next passage brings us back to water—essential for the existence of life, and laden with literal and symbolic meaning. Two of the four rivers are well known, two are obscure. In Mesopotamia, the floodwaters of the Tigris and Euphrates were vital—agriculture depended on these great rivers, just as the Egyptians depended on the annual flooding of the Nile. The locations of the Pishon and the Gihon are unknown.[118] Notice also the mention of Assyria. We assume the first readers of Genesis were familiar with the regional history and geography.[119] (That's a strong reason for us to strive for the same.)

The passage also mentions precious stones and metal. The entire garden depiction, in fact, contains numerous elements found in the Jewish tabernacle/temple, just as the fine artistic work of the tabernacle and temple includes themes from the creation account of Gen 2. Scholars have recognized various correspondences between the tabernacle, the Edenic garden, and the universe. "But will God indeed dwell on the earth?" Solomon asked. "Even heaven and the highest heaven cannot contain you, much less this house that I have built!" (1 Kings 8:27). The universe is Yahweh's dwelling place, his temple (1 Kings 8:13), which itself is coursing with Edenic themes. It took Solomon seven years to build his temple (1 Kings 6:38), just as it took God seven days to make the world. Although we cannot go into detail, these parallels are worth pursuing.[120]

How Literal Is Eden?

Many readers of Genesis, understandably, regard Eden as a literal place. Yet when it comes to "paradise" at the other end of the Bible (Rev 21–22), most of us take the details as symbolic. Perhaps we should consider that symbolic elements can be found in early Genesis as well. Ezek 28:13–14 interprets Eden in a nonliteral fashion: the "garden" of God has become the "mountain" of God. Even the apostle John, in the final chapters of the Apocalypse, fuses the imagery of Gen 2 with the imagery of Ezek 47.

The entire Eden account is couched in symbolic language. Rev 12 is an apt parallel, where the woman clothed with the sun is the people of God, Satan is the dragon, and after the birth of a male child (Christ) the woman is protected in the wilderness—symbolizing God's faithfulness to his persecuted saints.[121]

John utilizes symbols to describe important first-century realities. Whatever the case, we ought not to be overly dogmatic.

Many theologians hold that the Eden account gives us *historical realities in symbolic language.*[122] Biblically, we find human history is framed between two paradises: paradise lost (early in Genesis) and paradise regained (late in Revelation). Between the indefinite past and the indefinite future lies the definite present, the temporal space we occupy and the time in which it is our responsibility as image-bearers to influence this world for Jesus Christ (Heb 9:27).

> *15YAHWEH God took the man and put him in the garden of Eden to till it and keep it. 16And God YAHWEH commanded the man, "You may freely eat of every tree of the garden; 17but of the tree of the knowledge of good and evil you shall not eat, for in the day that you eat of it you shall die."*

Yahweh does not create Adam to lounge in the garden, but to work it. Yahweh is the landlord, Adam the gardener. Work is not a punishment, but a privilege (2:15). Jesus taught the same (Lk 19:15–19, 26). Notice also the single prohibition: to avoid the tree of the knowledge of good and evil.[123] Otherwise, there is nothing ominous or undesirable about the garden. There are Mesopotamian parallels. For example, the *Epic of Enki and Ninhursag* tells of a primeval paradise, an idyllic age.

> *18Then YAHWEH God said, "It is not good that the man should be alone; I will make him a helper as his partner." 19So out of the ground YAHWEH God formed every animal of the field and every bird of the air, and brought them to the man to see what he would call them; and whatever the man called every living creature, that was its name. 20The man gave names to all cattle, and to the birds of the air, and to every animal of the field; but for the man there was not found a helper as his partner.*

The animals are unsuitable helpers—as much as we may delight in our pets. God creates many animals—none up to the task of being Adam's soulmate.[124] That role can only be filled by his equal and counterpart, the woman. "Helper" (*'ēzer*) doesn't imply that the helper is weaker than the one being helped. The case is frequently the opposite (for example, where God is a help/helper to Israel [e.g., Ps 121:1–2]). Note that Adam names the animals. Naming is connected with ruling and leadership.

> *[21]So YAHWEH God caused a deep sleep to fall upon the man, and he slept; then he took one of his ribs and closed up its place with flesh. [22]And the rib that YAHWEH God had taken from the man he made into a woman and brought her to the man. [23]Then the man said,*
> *"This at last is bone of my bones*
> *and flesh of my flesh;*
> *this one shall be called Woman*
> *for out of Man this one was taken."*

Surgery is performed. Yahweh did not create two women for the man (Lamech), or four (Islam), or hundreds (Solomon), but just one.[125] The Bible consistently holds up the high ideal of monogamy and illustrates narratively the problems occurring when the primordial norm is ignored.

There is wordplay here. She is called *'ishshāh* (woman) because she is taken from *'īsh* (man). This works fairly well in English (man/wo-man), except that etymologically "man" is a person, not necessarily a male. In Middle Eastern culture, when one person is very close to another it is said: "He is my rib." The rib protects the heart. Matthew Henry put it well:

> Not made out of his head to top him, nor out of his feet to be trampled upon by him, but out of his side to be equal with him, under his arm to be protected, and near his heart to be beloved.[126]

The woman is created by and has her own relationship with Yahweh, even though she is the man's helper and closely connected to her mate. Adam is ecstatic, as his outpouring of poetry (or song) indicates.

> [24]*Therefore a man leaves his father and his mother and clings to his wife, and they become one flesh.* [25]*And the man and his wife were both naked, and were not ashamed.*

Gen 2:24 affirms that sexual relations belong in—and only in—the context of marriage. Scripture doesn't treat sexuality as something shameful—otherwise it wouldn't show up on page two of the Bible or be celebrated in the Song of Songs. This text assumes that marriage involves one man and one woman in a one-flesh relationship for one lifetime.[127]

Review: Why Two Accounts?

There are two creation stories in Genesis because each conveys different theological truths. The first affords a panoramic and orderly view of God's creative activity, which culminates in humankind. There we also learn that we bear (or *are*) God's image, representing him to the world. Moreover, we learn that men and women equally share in the divine image. The second story focuses entirely on humanity: our humble, earthy origins; our being created not as slaves, but as sharers in God's divine activity—our work sanctified as we serve in God's temple; our relationship to the zoological and botanical worlds; our emotional need for companionship; and the ideal of marriage. In Gen 2 woman is created after man, while in Gen 1 they seem to come to exist together. In Gen 2 the animals are created after man, while in Gen 1 they come into existence beforehand.

In short, the focus of Genesis is humanity more than the other parts of creation. Gen 1 gives us the panorama, then chapter 2 zooms in on the human world in relation to God.[128] The focus will narrow further as Genesis moves from Abraham to his descendants through Isaac and to Isaac's descendants through Jacob.

The Details

Understood literally, the details do not neatly mesh together—an indication that such an approach is misguided. For a rough parallel, consider the parables of Jesus. While many details are realistic, others are not. In the Parable of the Workers in the Vineyard, the workers received the same wage whether they worked for one hour or twelve (Mt 20:9–10)! Another monetary example is found in the Parable of the Merciless Servant. The ungrateful servant owes 10,000 talents ("10,000 bags of gold," NIV), or four billion dollars![129] The details paint a picture and heighten the impact of the parable. But if the details are taken literally, the reader is quickly sidetracked—missing the point, the reason Jesus is telling the story in the first place.

Biblical Creation Passages

There are multiple "creation stories" and images in Scripture.

- **Gen 1:1–2:3**—God separates the watery abyss into two oceans, terrestrial and celestial. He prepares the world for the light-bearers (day 1, for day 4), the birds and fish (day 2, for day 5), and for plants and animals (day 3, for day 6). Humans are the climax of creation, and God's work is followed by Sabbath rest.
- **Gen 2:4–25**—God creates Adam, then the garden, then the other animals, then the woman as man's "helper." The entire chapter is concerned with humans in relationship to God, and the garden itself is a kind of sacred space—with multiple similarities to both the tabernacle and temple of later times.
- **Ps 89:9–12**—God crushed Rahab (the cosmic serpent, in this case a cipher for Egypt).[130] He created the north and the south, and the mountains (Hermon and Tabor, in northern Israel) sing for joy at his name.
- **Prov 8:22–31**—God creates the world through Wisdom. The details of the earth conform with those of Gen 1. (See also Appendix A.) Furthermore, Christians benefit from the insight that Christ is the Word of God and the Wisdom of God (1 Cor 1:30).

- **Isa 40:21–28**—God stretches out the heavens like a curtain (referring to the hemispherical dome), brings out the heavenly host and numbers them, and sits above the circle (disc) of the earth.
- **Ezek 28:12–15**—For context, the broader passage stretches from v. 12 to v. 19. Ezek 28 features precious jewels, like Gen 2. Yet the accounts are similar and dissimilar. Eden is a holy mountain (unlike in Gen 2). In Ezek 28, expulsion from Eden isn't because of illicit consumption of fruit, but because of economic greed and violence. While the passage applies directly to the King of Tyre (a city-state north of Israel), the language also refers to primordial paradise.
- **Jn 1:1–3**—God creates through his Word alone. True, in Gen 1 God says, "Let there be…," and yet creation is indirect. The *ground* produces plants and animals. Something already exists when God begins to shape chaos into cosmos.
- **Col 1:15–17**—Once more, God creates through Christ. Yet there is no mention of a creation week, or a garden, nor is there any detail about plants and animals. The passage highlights "things visible and invisible, whether thrones or dominions or rulers or powers." As we see, most of the material on the theology of creation is found in the OT, not the NT. (But then the OT *is* three quarters of the Bible.)

See also Pss 8; 19; 33; 104; 148.

Alas, the perfection of Eden will not endure. It cannot endure, on account of a simple reality: sin. Paradise will be lost.

RECAP

Biblical Truths

- Humans are made of earth–organic material–a feature we share with all other earthly creatures. Yet we are uniquely human by God's decision. Our very life depends on him (Job 33:4; 34:14–15; Ps 104:29–30).

- Although we *are* animals, we are also superior to them—placed over them to responsibly manage them.
- God created humanity for relationship: with him and with one another (spouses, in Gen 2, but the circle will widen in succeeding chapters). The Garden of Eden is a sort of temple for Yahweh.
- There are multiple creation stories and images in the Bible. Although, in general, they are rich in symbolism and contain different (and sometimes discordant) details, *all are true.*
- God created humans as mortals; their access to immortality was conditional.
- Marriage meets an emotional and social need. When man and woman unite, they are one flesh. Although not all humans will marry, marriage is the norm—*monogamous* marriage.
- The proper context of sexual activity is marriage. This means there is not to be sex before or outside of marriage.

Points of Contact with Pagan Culture

- Whereas the pagan accounts have humans being created from physical and divine components (earth and the blood of a dead god), Genesis does not teach that humans are divine. We are not demigods. The image is not a divine substance but a reflection of God's will as we represent him on this earth.
- Mesopotamian stories, like the *Epic of Enki and Ninhursag*, depict a primeval paradise. But the relationship of humans to the gods is qualitatively different from the human relationship with Yahweh that we find in Genesis and the rest of the OT.

NT Connections

- The NT creation passages offer a more theological (and Christocentric) outlook on creation than the OT presents.
- We are to work in order to eat (2 Thess 3:10).
- Monogamous marriage is the ideal for Christian leaders (1 Tim 3:2; Ti 1:6).
- Just as the OT begins with a paradise, so the NT ends with one (Rev 2:7).

Application

- If we marry, we are to strive for the ideal: a monogamous, heterosexual, and joyful relationship.
- Since God has created us for productive activity (2:15), we should embrace it. It was part of the first paradise, and indications are it will be part of the second one too (Lk 19:17, 19, 26; 2 Tim 2:12; Rev 22:5).
- The Scriptures come alive–and make sense–when we read with literary and historical sensitivity. Such sensitivity must be cultivated through disciplined study habits and openness to input from others who know the territory.

---

114. The literal meaning of Hebrew *b^{e}yôm* is "in [the] day," not "when"—although "when" is perfectly acceptable in a free translation or paraphrase.
115. What about conditional immortality, the doctrine that immortality is only available to those who believe in Christ? Even if (for some?) hell lasts thousands of years, the implication of Mt 10:28; 1 Cor 15:28; and Rev 2:11; 20:6, 14; 21:8 is that eventually it comes to an end. (The first death may destroy the body, but the second destroys the soul. Ultimately there will be only one kingdom [God's], not two, and it will fill the universe, with no room for any other kingdom.) For more on the terminal view of punishment, see https://www.douglasjacoby.com/heaven-hell-terminal-punishment/. Though I (Paul) feel the weight of the argument, I am not as convinced of it as Douglas is (cf. Rev 14:11; 20:10).
116. *Eden* sounds like the Hebrew word for pleasure or delight, as in Ps 36:8. The Greek of 2:15 has "garden of delight," whereas the Hebrew has "garden of Eden." The Greek version of Eccl says Solomon planted *paradeisous* ("paradises"), or gardens (NRSV) (Eccl 2:5 LXX).
117. Islam mistakenly has the two trees combined into one (*Qur'an* 20:120). Its frequent errors when it refers to the OT and NT probably arose from Muhammad's limited knowledge of Christianity and Judaism.
118. According to James Hoffmeier, the Pishon is unknown in ancient geography, though it may be the "Fossil River" that once ran through Kuwait but dried up before 2000 BC (see his comments in *Genesis: History, Fiction, or Neither? The Bible's Earliest Chapters*, ed. Charles Halton [Grand Rapids, MI: Zondervan, 2015]). The Gihon is the stream that brings fresh water to Jerusalem; but it is called *Geon* in the LXX, so perhaps it is not intended to allude to Jerusalem. The Tigris and the Euphrates are well known, and flow today. Cush is either a region in East Africa (modern Sudan/Ethiopia) or a land in Palestine south of the Dead Sea.
119. The Tigris and Euphrates are both mentioned at the beginning of the *Atrahasis Epic* (1:25), another parallel between the biblical and Mesopotamian accounts.
120. See Walton, *Lost World of Adam and Eve,* 48.
121. More precisely, national Israel gives birth to the Messiah, whose people become the New Israel/the church (see Mt 21:43).
122. For an excellent work promoting this view, see Henri Blocher, *In the Beginning: The Opening Chapters of Genesis*; see also James Hoffmeier's and also Gordon Wenham's chapters in *Genesis: History, Fiction, or Neither?*
123. Concerning the knowledge of good and evil, see 2 Sam 14:17, 20, which raises the possibility that good and evil do not refer to morality at all, but to breadth of knowledge. "Like the

angels" (or "like God") suggests a vast knowledge. In striving after human autonomy, then, the first couple sought comprehensive knowledge—something allowed only to God, and (to a lesser extent) to the angels.

124. Note that in this account the animals are made after Adam, not before, as in Gen 1.
125. Gen 4:19; *Qur'an* 4:3; 1 Kings 11:3.
126. Matthew Henry, "Genesis 2," *Commentary on the Whole Bible* (London: Marshall, Morgan and Scott, 1961).
127. This succinct summary comes from our friend Greg Koukl.
128. What Gen 1–2 tell us about God is nicely fleshed out in Isa 40–48.
129. A talent is twenty years of wages—now multiply by 10,000! In today's terms, if a common laborer earning $20,000 a year were the character in the parable, his debt would be $4,000,000,000 (four billion dollars)—200,000 years' wages. Such a thing has never happened and never will.
130. The psalmist is not affirming pagan mythology, but appropriating and adjusting the story in order to assert Yahweh's supremacy. For a fuller explanation, listen to "Dragons and the Bible" at https://www.douglasjacoby.com/dragons-and-the-bible/.

III

Cycles: Eden to Deluge

The third section of *Origins* moves from the earthly paradise to the outbreak of sin to its pandemic level prior to Noah's preparations for the flood. This cleansing of the earth is, biblically speaking, a "de-creation."

Along the way, we will address some vexing questions—for example, the identity of the Nephilim and the extreme longevities in Genesis 5.

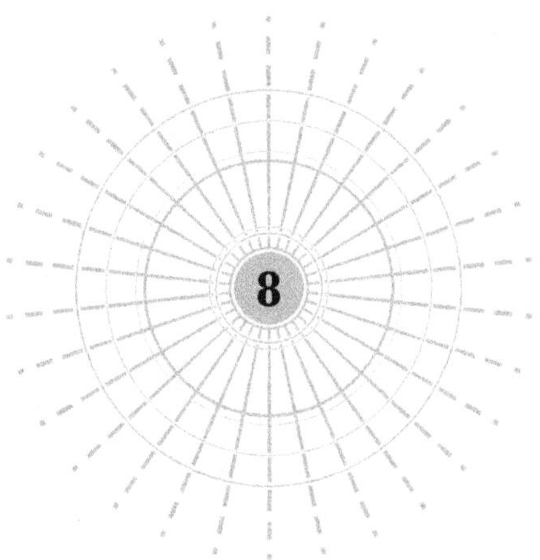

Paradise Lost

ADAM & EVE

Life is good for the man and the woman. They enjoy a beautiful garden paradise, plenty of water and food, a relationship with Yahweh, and a fresh and blissful marriage, and they are subject to only a few simple mandates: exercise dominion, till the garden, be fruitful, and avoid the tree of knowledge. In addition, they have no need for clothing or any other material necessity; there is no conflict or tension; and they are trusted by the Lord to be/bear his image.

As wonderful as the garden is, things will soon change. The story is moving along at a fast clip.

> [3:1]*Now the serpent was more crafty than any other wild animal that* YAHWEH *God had made. He said to the woman, "Did God say, 'You shall not eat from any tree in the garden'?"* [2]*The woman said to the serpent, "We may eat of the fruit of the trees in the garden;* [3]*but God said, 'You shall not eat of the fruit of the tree that is in the*

> *middle of the garden, nor shall you touch it, or you shall die.'" [4]But the serpent said to the woman, "You will not die; [5]for God knows that when you eat of it your eyes will be opened, and you will be like God, knowing good and evil."*

A walking, talking snake was a symbol of evil in the ancient Near East. "The serpent would have been viewed as a chaos creature from the nonordered realm, promoting disorder."[131] In Canaanite and ancient Near Eastern mythology, the cosmic serpent bore various names: Yam, Leviathan, Lotan, Rahab, Tannin, and Behemoth. The serpent was also a giver of power and secret knowledge, and it represents the attraction of pagan religion and its magic. It is also an emblem of the fertility cults, which engaged in ritual prostitution (both male and female) to ensure success in agriculture. There are multiple OT references to fertility cult prostitution or promiscuity in the temple (e.g., 1 Sam 7:3–4; Deut 23:17–18; 1 Kings 11:4–8; 14:23–24; 1 Kings 15:12; 22:26; 23:7; Gen 38:15, 21).

Just as its body slithers and twists, the serpent twists the word of God. It tempts the woman (she has not yet become "Eve") with prospects of becoming like God or like the gods (v. 5)—both translations are valid—which in context would mean angels or other heavenly beings.

Note that Eve informs the serpent that she is not permitted to take from the tree of the knowledge of good and evil—presumably having heard this instruction through Adam (2:16–17). She goes further than the divine command, adding "nor shall you touch it." Perhaps Adam had added that to keep Eve from temptation (unless she did it on her own). In either case, this addition would serve to make Yahweh seem more restrictive and less reasonable. As one scholar puts it, God had focused on blessing and freedom ("you may eat") while this sinister presence now highlights prohibition and restriction.

> *[6]So when the woman saw that the tree was good for food, and that it was a delight to the eyes, and that the tree was to be desired to make one wise, she took of its fruit and ate; and she also gave some to her husband, who was with her, and he ate. [7]Then the eyes*

of both were opened, and they knew that they were naked; and they sewed fig leaves together and made aprons for themselves.*

* Loincloths in the NRSV. There is no need to assume such skimpy covering; the Hebrew suggests something more ample.

The serpent succeeds. The woman eats, as does the man, who is with her. (There is no indication here as to whether Adam chose to disobey God in order not to be separated from his wife.[132]) They fashion aprons of fig leaves—not the skimpy single leaves of European paintings.

What has been lost? They forfeit not only the security of the garden but immortality itself—as we shall soon see. Recall that in the *Gilgamesh Epic*, the snake devours the plant of rejuvenation.[133] In the *Atrahasis Epic*, the bread of immortality is offered to Atrahasis, but he refuses it, unaware of its properties. In the Sumerian myth of Dilmun, Enki mischievously enters a garden and eats illicitly—and ends up in intense agony.[134] It is noteworthy that nowhere does the biblical text say that either Adam or Eve ate of the tree of life. Both trees were in the middle of the garden (2:9), so perhaps in making sure that they obeyed God's command, they avoided both trees. That would make God's removal of access to it from them (3:22) a merciful act of love by limiting their life span, rather than punishment for disobedience. On the other hand, there is no reason they wouldn't have enjoyed the fruit of the tree of life, since there was no prohibition.

The irony is deep. Eve seeks to become a goddess, Adam to become a god. Yet for all their grasping,[135] they become *less* godlike. Fruit will soon be the cause of trouble again later on in the primeval narrative.

About the "Fall"

Traditional Christianity (from the early Middle Ages on) speaks of the "fall"—the moral lapse of humankind, beginning in the garden and somehow affecting the nature of the entire world.

There is no doubting that sin is real, or that all humans have sinned and fall short of the glory of God (Rom 3:23). From Genesis to Revelation, Scripture doesn't sugarcoat the awful truth about sin. Nor are humans demonized. Nature, nurture, choice—there is sufficient freedom of will that everyone is rendered responsible (Rom 2:12; 3:19). Like all other books in the Bible, Genesis portrays humans as *sinners*:

- "Yahweh saw that the wickedness of humankind was great in the earth, and that every inclination of the thoughts of their hearts was only evil continually" (6:5).
- "The inclination of the human heart is evil from youth" (8:21b).
- "How great is the outcry against Sodom and Gomorrah and how very grave their sin!" (18:20).

Yet the existential reality of sin in our world—and in our lives—does not mean the divine image was defaced, or that humans, though depraved, had lost all vestiges of created goodness. No, we still bear the image of God (5:3; 9:6). The idea that Adam's sin resulted in his guilt being imputed to us did not arise until around AD 400 with Augustine and goes beyond what apostolic teaching affirms: terrible consequences, yes; Adam's own guilt, no.[136]

In addition to the consequence of now having a self-oriented disposition, all of us recapitulate the original cycle of sin in our behavior; we ourselves would have done what our ancestors did. Even so, there has been no change in our fundamental human nature;[137] after all, philosophically speaking, our "nature"—which Christ and unfallen Adam and Eve shared—is what makes us human. Sin is not essential to our human identity. We could say that our created nature remains unchanged, but we have become different sorts of persons through behavioral and attitudinal changes that are now *second* nature.[138] The important thing is that we are still divine image-bearers, and we still possess free will, which renders us accountable for our actions (4:7; 39:9).[139] Furthermore, "Nature disappears as a ruling factor in human affairs, replaced by a principle of morality which is unshakable precisely because it comes from a God who is beyond the rules of nature."[140]

Gen 3 never offers any suggestions on the origin of evil.[141] The narrative is not a treatise on philosophy or theology, but a recounting of human rebellion and darkness, projected back to the dawn of civilization. Today's sunny optimism when it comes to the human condition (and denial of sin) makes for a stark contrast with the biblical account. Yet the rejection of God's diagnosis of the human condition isn't anything particularly "modern." In the second century AD, some Gnostics made Eve out to be heroic, in antithesis to Yahweh, a bad god.

> [8]*They heard the sound of YAHWEH God walking in the garden at the time of the evening breeze, and the man and his wife hid themselves from the presence of YAHWEH God among the trees of the garden.* [9]*But YAHWEH God called to the man, and said to him, "Where are you?"*

Yahweh reveals himself to the couple as landlord or owner of the garden. Notice the anthropomorphism—God appearing as a man, even expressing ignorance of their location ("Where are you?" cf. Ps 139:1–12). As a parent might call out to a child hiding behind a piece of furniture, or even its own hands, God interacts on their level. He asks one of the two most important questions in the entire Bible.

The first of these questions is "Where are you?" (3:9). The second will be asked (of Cain), "Where is your brother?" (4:9). At this time, it may help to read the passage less as a Bible student and more as a man or woman in the presence of God. We cannot run away. Eventually our sin will find us out (Num 32:23). But before we can answer God's question, Where are you? and take stock of how we are doing, we must make sure we have a biblical concept of sin.

Where Are You?

Disobeying God's law (1 Jn 3:4) has consequences, knock-on effects. Moral choices affect everyone: Virtue has a leavening effect through society (Mt 5:13). Vice, like pollution, diminishes the quality of life for us all.

Further, while all sins are not equal (e.g., intentional vs. unintentional sins [Num 15]), all are serious, from the "little ones" to "big sins." We may be horrified by murder, but what about premarital sex? How about slander or disrespect? As sin is a violation of God's will, it is destructive. We can develop this idea further.

Is littering harmless? We all pay: collectively by higher taxes, or aesthetically by being forced to behold ugliness in place of natural beauty. Gluttony—are there any victims besides the gourmand? For those living in Western democracies, higher health premiums affect everyone. All crimes, from tax evasion to bank robbery, drive up the cost of living—even if it wasn't my bank that was robbed. Indulging in porn assures the victimization of a steady stream of young women (and men and even children). Even if the drunk isn't driving, his poor judgment still affects others: absenteeism has the effect of lowering our wages (we have to work harder to cover him); he probably hogs more than his fair share of health care too. Gossip may seem trivial, but it unfairly affects how we view and interact with third parties. Academic cheating lowers educational standards, raises the curve and thus lowers grades for others, and confirms the cheater in patterns that may continue in the workplace. Materialism—which the Bible calls greed—feeds consumerism, which often furthers the exploitation of workers in the developing world.

> Sin twists character, saps moral strength (virtue) and integrity, and weakens love for others. Sin affects the individual (guilt), but it also has social consequences (alienation). The most serious effect of sin is separation from God (Isa 59:1–3; Col 1:21).[142]

In our day, the supposed separation between private life and the public sphere is too facile. It is naively imagined that one's private behavior is not relevant to one's public life. Yet surely someone who's made thousands of little compromises is more likely, given some big task (like running a company or leading a nation), to make a few big compromises. Further, a man who betrays his wife (adultery) may think little of selling out those who trust him to do what is right. He may defend any of his actions as long as they "aren't hurting anyone."

Ultimately, all sin is between us and God (Gen 39:9; Ps 51:4). And yet most sin affects others, directly or indirectly. It's simply not true that our poor moral choices don't hurt others.[143]

In Scripture and conscience, the Lord asks *all* of us, "Where are you?" He isn't seeking geographical information, but, rather, spiritual self-examination and personal confession. It is a classic question we must answer before we can get help.

Seven Consequences of Sin

1. Guilt
2. Alienation from others
3. Difficulty trusting
4. Alienation from God
5. Dishonesty about where we are
6. Excuse making
7. Loss of access to immortality

> *10He said, "I heard the sound of you in the garden, and I was afraid, because I was naked; and I hid myself." 11He said, "Who told you that you were naked? Have you eaten from the tree of which I commanded you not to eat?" 12The man said, "The woman whom you gave to be with me, she gave me fruit from the tree, and I ate." 13Then YAHWEH God said to the woman, "What is this that you have done?" The woman said, "The serpent tricked me, and I ate."*

Adam hears the sound of Yahweh in the garden, and this deeply concerns him. Here and elsewhere in Genesis we find anthropomorphism. Adam is now set against his Creator as well as his wife. Everyone is making excuses. The consequences of his sin ripple outward.

Anthropomorphism

God alarms the man and woman because they are guilty. But isn't God an omnipresent spirit, not a local landlord? Of course. God's late afternoon stroll through the garden is an instance of anthropomorphism (from Greek: *anthrōpos*, human, and *morphē*, form); it is a depiction of deity in human terms. The Bible is full of such descriptions. God has an arm—and it isn't too short for him to reach and save us (Isa 59:1–2). The train of his robe fills the temple courts, in the prophet's vision (Isa 6:1). Yet we realize that God, who is spirit, does not require a robe any more than he needs to exert himself to try to reach us or see through our excuses.

Anthropomorphisms of God

In Genesis 1–11

Potter (2:7)[144]
Surgeon (2:21)
Landlord or **Gardener** (2:8)
Tailor (3:21)

Outside Genesis 1–11 (selected)

Bridegroom (Isa 62:5)
Husband (Isa 54:5)
King (Ps 45:6)
Warrior (Ex 15:3)
Counselor (Isa 9:6)
Judge (Isa 3:13)
Shepherd (Ps 23:1)
Wrestler (Gen 32:24)

Other biblical metaphors for God (selected)

Bird (Ruth 2:12)
Fortress (Ps 18:2)
Rock (1 Sam 2:2)
Fire (Deut 4:24)
Light (Ps 27:1)
Shield (Ps 28:7)

> [14]*Yahweh God said to the serpent,*
> *"Because you have done this,*
> *cursed are you among all animals*
> *and among all wild creatures;*
> *upon your belly you shall go,*
> *and dust you shall eat*
> *all the days of your life.*
> [15]*I will put enmity between you and the woman,*
> *and between your offspring and hers;*
> *he will strike your head,*
> *and you will strike his heel."*

God does not curse Adam or Eve, but only the earth and the serpent. In the next chapter, in contrast, he curses Cain directly (4:11).

Many have weighed in on how to interpret Gen 3:15. It is easy for us to see in this the birth of Christ, since we are looking at the OT backward (from our understanding of the Gospels), while we read the NT forward (from our understanding of the OT).[145]

Further, there is a tie-in with Ps 74:14, where Yahweh crushes the heads of the serpent.[146] As Richard Averbeck explains,

> The serpent was the first to raise an explicit challenge to God in the Bible, and this happened in Genesis 3. The challenge, and so also the battle between God and the serpent, is actually over mankind. People are the battleground–the "territory" under dispute–and the central concern of this battle of the ages has as much to do with people as with the great serpent. Both mankind and serpent "fell" out of favor with God here, so the battle rages between all three. We stand right in the middle of a ferocious cosmic fray. Ancient Israel's preservation–and ours, believe it or not–depends on Yahweh's willingness to redeem us in the midst of this brawl. The apocalyptic vision is that there will come a day when God will bring all this to final resolution by making an end of the "twisted serpent" of old.[147]

Next come God's words to the woman:

[16]To the woman he said,
"I will greatly increase your pangs in childbearing;
in pain you shall bring forth children,
yet your desire shall be for your husband,
and he shall rule over you."

For the woman, the pain of childbirth will increase. Whether this implies previous pregnancies or refers to her future the text leaves open (see 5:4).[148] It at least suggests that although humans were created with a capacity to feel pain—which is a good thing for getting along in the world—this pain would intensify as a consequence of the fall. Childbirth was perilous in ancient times and remains so in some parts of the world today. We may recall Rachel, who exclaimed, "Give me children, or I shall die!" (Gen 30:1). The birth of Joseph seems to have occurred without complication (30:22–24), but her second pregnancy (with Benjamin) resulted in her death (35:16–18).

In any event, as for the husband's domination of his wife, the passage is considered by various scholars to be a description, rather than a prescription.[149] Walter Brueggemann notes: "In God's garden, as God wills it, there is *mutuality and equity*. In God's garden now, permeated by distrust, there is *control and distortion.* But that distortion is not for one moment accepted as the will of the Gardener."[150] Her desire for independence (promised by the serpent) will conflict with her husband's demands for submission, as Wenham points out.[151] Whatever the case, disturbances in domestic felicity are among the consequences of sin.

[17]And to the man he said,
"Because you have listened to the voice of your wife,
and have eaten of the tree
about which I commanded you,
'You shall not eat of it,'
cursed is the ground because of you;

in toil you shall eat of it all the days of your life;
18thorns and thistles it shall bring forth for you;
and you shall eat the plants of the field.
19By the sweat of your face
you shall eat bread
until you return to the ground,
for out of it you were taken;
you are dust,
and to dust you shall return."

For the man, the punishment isn't having to work—that was already his responsibility (2:15). Yet his labor will now become arduous.

20The man named his wife Eve, because she was the mother of all living. 21And YAHWEH God made garments of skins for the man and for his wife, and clothed them.

Up to this point, the woman has remained unnamed. Here Adam gives to his significant other the name "Eve." There is wordplay here. Her name, *Chawwāh*, is related to the word for "live," *chayyāh.* To convey it fully in English, we might select a name like "Livia."[152] As for the term "the mother of all the living," this title[153] was given to the Sumerian fertility goddess Ninhursag—and later to the Hurrian goddess Kheba. But there is no mother goddess in the Bible.[154]

After the man had named his wife, the Lord made garments of skin for them both. God was protecting them from the elements to which they would soon be exposed. Skins (v. 21) replace leaves (v. 7). Perhaps this clothing cost the lives of the animals from which they came. If so, it was not only an act of grace; it may also have been a reminder of sinfulness,[155] just as the OT sacrifices reminded the Israelites that the guilt of sin affects the innocent—and only the blood of the innocent can take it away (Gen 22:13; Heb 9:22).

22Then YAHWEH God said, "See, the man has become like one of us, knowing good and evil; and now, he might reach out his

> *hand and take also from the tree of life, and eat, and live forever"–*
> *[23]therefore the* LORD YAHWEH *God sent him forth from the garden of*
> *Eden, to till the ground from which he was taken. [24]He drove out the*
> *man; and at the east of the garden of Eden he placed the Cherubim,*
> *and a sword flaming and turning to guard the way to the tree of life.*

One of Us?

God says that Adam and Eve had "become like one of us." Who are these others? Some have suggested that this is a royal plural, a plural of majesty. Yet that is not a Hebrew idiom. The first-century AD *Epistle of Barnabas* and the second-century *First Apology* of Justin Martyr construed the plural as specifically Trinitarian, though this may be reading too much into the text. Might the divine council, which would have included angels, explain the "us"? We find similar language in 1:26 ("Let us make…"). Is it credible that the Lord made angels and humans in his image? Perhaps angels, sharing in the divine work, are in some derivative way bearers of his image. Yet Heb 1:4–14 seem to militate against this possibility.

On the other hand, Peter says that believers, through divine power and knowledge of him who called us "may become participants of the divine nature" (2 Pet 1:3–4)—that is, sharing in the life of the triune God. This is another mystery of God in the Scriptures; we may not know how to resolve it, but just accept it for what it is—a mystery.

The couple is driven out of the garden. They are driven "east"—which, after the fall, often has negative associations in the book of Genesis (3:24; 4:16; 10:30; 11:2; 13:11; 16:12 [NASB]; 25:6, 18). Like the Northern Israelites exiled by the Assyrians in 722 BC and the Southern Judeans led into captivity by the Babylonians (in three waves) in 605, 597, and 587 BC, they are forcibly removed from the land. Land is a major theme in Genesis, as it is in the rest of the OT. Loss of land is too—God's ultimate punishment for his wayward people Israel (Deut 28:63–64).

Immortality

Adam has forfeited access to the means of immortality—apparently the Lord's original intention for humans, since the tree of life was not forbidden. As noted earlier, this means that we are not innately immortal; human immortality is a doctrine in quite a few pagan religions, but not of the Bible. Only through Jesus Christ is immortality, via bodily resurrection, regained (Jn 3:36; 6:40; Rom 6:23; 1 Jn 5:11). In this sense, immortality in the OT is conditional, depending upon redemption—as in the NT (1 Tim 1:16–17; 6:16).

There is a connection with the *Gilgamesh Epic.* Leaving the plant that confers immortality at his side, the heedless Gilgamesh takes a nap—during which time the snake swallows the plant. Gilgamesh loses immortality through bad luck (or stupidity); in the Genesis account, it is forfeited through moral failure, rebellion against God. But note the common elements: snake, plant, (im)mortality. In pagan as well as biblical accounts, humans are mortals.

Assyrian Cherub
Metropolitan Museum of Art, New York

Cherubim

Cherubim block the way back into Eden. A familiar element in ancient Near Eastern culture, cherubim are composite creatures occasionally mentioned in the Bible, with bodies of lions or oxen, feathered wings, and human faces—and sometimes with the head of a hawk or a ram (singular: *cherub*; plural: *cherubim*).[156] They frequently serve in the capacity of guardian spirits. Cherubim featured prominently in the furnishings of the tabernacle (Ex 25–26).

Are these creatures real? They are not classed with the angels, who in Scripture are created beings and who appear on earth as men—*without* wings.[157] Hundreds of ancient sculptures of cherubim have survived: you can view them in the museums of the world, like the British Museum (London), the Louvre (Paris), and the Metropolitan Museum of Art (New York). Cherubim may well have been an invention of the ancient Near East, appropriated by God from pagan religion and "converted" for symbolic use in his word, just as Paul borrowed from familiar pagan writers to help people to come to terms with Jesus' message.[158]

Humbling Things in Genesis 2-3

- We did not create ourselves, nor are we "self-made."
- Man is incomplete without his partner, the woman.
- We are made from dirt.
- We were formed on the same "day" as lots of other animals.
- We disobeyed a really simple command, losing our access to the tree of life.
- We do not participate in immortality unless we receive the gift of eternal life in Jesus Christ.
- Even after receiving grace, we tend to get caught in the cycle of complacency–sin–repentance–grace–comfortable rest.

Mercy and Grace

God had to block the couple from reentering the Garden, eating of the tree of life, and living forever. Why? A rebellious, immortal being bent on selfishness could wreak havoc in the universe. Imagine what the world would be like if Hitler, Stalin, and Genghis Khan had been immortal! God does not offer eternal life to those who have rejected him. This is not to say that Adam and Eve are depicted as having lost their relationship with God. Grace was extended to the first couple after their rebellion. They did not die immediately. Nor were they heartlessly turned out of Eden. The Lord took care that they would be able to cope with their new, rugged environment. Such a scenario will be repeated four more times in Genesis. Thus, there are five key events in which mercy and grace are extended:

- After the rebellion in Eden, God spares Adam and Eve (Gen 3).
- After the murder of Abel, God spares Cain, giving him a fresh start (Gen 4).
- In the deluge, God spares Noah and his family (Gen 6–9).
- At Babel, God again protects man from himself and extends grace (Gen 11).
- Grace is extended through God's call of Abram, as the patriarch is called out of a world of idolatry into a covenant relationship with Yahweh (Gen 12).

Of course, grace can be abused. It can, has, and will always be taken advantage of. That is an inherent danger with any gracious act.[159]

Adam and Israel

Adam's story mirrors Israel's story from the Exodus to the Exile. This is not only the story of humankind in general, but also of Israel in particular. Scott McKnight, too, sees multiple connections (and these are all the more striking when we read the OT in Hebrew or in one of the more literal translations):

- Genesis 1:1 speaks of the creation of the "heavens and *earth*," where "earth" is the Hebrew word usually used for the "land" of Israel (*hā-'ārets*).
- Genesis 1:2 speaks of "formless and empty," terms used in Jeremiah for the condition of the land of Israel after exile (Jer 4:23). This suggests that the phrase is probably better rendered "desolate and uninhabitable."
- Genesis 1:14 refers to the greater and lesser lights as signs determining days, years, and seasons (*mô'ēd*)—the word used in Leviticus for "appointed times" for feasts and other holy events (e.g., Lev 23:2, 4, 37, 44).
- Genesis 1:28 speaks of *subduing* the earth, and this is the same term (*kābash*) used in Numbers 32:22, 39 for conquering the land.
- Genesis 2:17 announces a death sentence for the one who eats of the tree, and in Ezekiel 37 exile is described as a valley of dead bones.[160]

If the first couple had not had offspring, sin would have ended with them. Alas, sin cycles on through their children and grandchildren to all the world because everyone chooses to sin (Rom 5:12 ["because all have sinned"]; Ex 20:5; Deut 5:9). Imagine this: if they hadn't sinned at all, as one preacher put it, the Bible would be wafer thin—just four chapters, Gen 1–2 and Rev 21–22.

RECAP

Biblical Truths

- Sin has consequences which affect both ourselves (quality of life) and others.
- Immortality is a gift from God, not an innate human quality.
- God mercifully and graciously offers protection and may intervene to keep us from self-destruction.
- God frequently presents himself in anthropomorphic terms, accommodating his presence and messages to our limited, human state.

Points of Contact with Pagan Culture

- Like Gilgamesh, Adam and Eve forfeit immortality–Gilgamesh by carelessness, they by disobedience. For the pagans, humans are mortal by no fault of their own. Yet followers of Yahweh know that death is the penalty for sin.
- Cherubim were common guardians in the religion and sculpture of the ancient Near East.

NT Connections

- The possibility of immortality forfeited in Gen 3 once again becomes available in Jesus Christ (Rom 5:15; 6:23; 1 Cor 15:45).
- Paul refers to Gen 3 in 2 Cor 11:2-4, where compromise on the basics of Christianity is compared to sexual seduction. The Enemy may be attempting to woo us away from a pure faith.

Application

- In making humanity the center and measure of all things–in striving to make of ourselves gods and goddesses–we lose. As the Apostle Paul urged us, let us be completely humble (Eph 4:2), following the example of our Lord and Savior, Jesus Christ (Phil 2:5-8).
- When we find ourselves getting confused about what God *really* says in his word (about the gospel, or the Spirit, or who Jesus really is), this may be a danger sign.

---

131. For Walton, this is "Proposition 14," in *Lost World of Adam and Eve*, 128–139. To be fair to the snake, however, it should be acknowledged that in ancient religions it was not necessarily the abhorrent reptile we think of today, but often something more attractive, even beneficial. It represented life, healing, and health, as in the Greek Asklepios cult. Even today, the caduceus, the staff of the American Medical Association as well as the British Medical Association, has a snake coiled around it—inspired by the biblical healing incident of Num 21:6–9.

132. In John Milton's famous poem, *Paradise Los*t, Adam knows exactly what he is doing. Even though Eve wins him over with charm, he is still aware of the consequences of a single act of disobedience. He would choose even death if this meant he could retain Eve. "She gave him of that fair enticing fruit / With liberal hand: he scrupled not to eat / Against his better knowledge; not deceived." *Paradise Lost* IX.996–998. The Bible seems to agree (1 Tim 2:14).

133. Interestingly, in the Sumerian *Adapa* myth, Adapa *obeys* Ea and does *not* eat the forbidden fruit. *The Myth of Adapa* (also called *Adapa and the Food of Life*) is a Mesopotamian story that explains why human beings are mortal.
134. As a result of his illicit act, Enki's entire body hurts (head, teeth, stomach…). Therefore, Ninhursag creates a god for each pain. Ninhursag is also called "Lady of the Rib."
135. See Phil 2:6.
136. Augustine's articulation of "original sin" served as an apologetic for infant baptism, which was becoming more common in his day.
137. See John F. Kilner, *Dignity and Destiny: Humanity in the Image of God* (Grand Rapids, MI: Eerdmans, 2015).
138. This is our understanding of Eph 2:3. See also https://www.douglasjacoby.com/q-a-0587-romans-9-10-24-predestination-calvinism/.
139. The patristic writers seem to be unanimous about the reality of free will—nor do they assume that God's foreknowledge limits free will.
140. Fox, *The Five Books of Moses*, 4.
141. Sometimes Isa 45:7 is referenced as a scripture asserting that Yahweh created evil. In Hebrew the word for evil, *rā'*, is also used for any loss or misfortune. This verse reads, "I form light and create darkness / I make weal and create woe / I the Lord do all these things" NRSV. Weal and woe (prosperity and disaster, NIV) make perfect sense in context: turns of events, not moral right or wrong. For more, see Paul Copan, "If God's Creation Was 'Very Good,' How Could Evil Arise?" *The Enrichment Journal*, http://enrichmentjournal.ag.org/201301/201301_024_good_creation.cfm.
142. Any sin can be forgiven (except for the one we refuse to repent from), but divine forgiveness doesn't obliterate sin's psychological, social, and spiritual consequences. The Bible tells us that our true problem isn't intellectual, but moral. Embracing "values" in lieu of the biblical diagnosis needs to be exposed for what it is. Only then will people recognize their true need and realize that the gospel is good news.
143. This discussion has been adapted from Douglas Jacoby's weekly newsletter, specifically http://us7.campaign-archive1.com/?u=4a5682d4bc6d3a2ee49519a21&id=3de6fb87b4 (3 June 2015).
144. God is portrayed as potter not only here (2:7), but also in Isa 29:16; 45:9; 64:8; Jer 18:6, 11; Rom 9:21.
145. See http://www.patheos.com/blogs/jesuscreed/2014/11/03/reading-the-bible-backwards/, where Scott McKnight comments on the work of Richard Hays.
146. Averbeck comments:

    The "heads" of Leviathan referred to in Ps. 74:14 (cf. also v. 13) are of particular interest here. Genesis 3:15 refers to the seed of the woman crushing the "head" of the serpent. The same word for "serpent" (Heb. *nāchaš*; Gen. 3:14) is used as in Isa. 27:1. More than that, Ps. 74:14 has God crushing (*rss*, admittedly not *swp* as in Gen. 3:15) "the *heads* of Leviathan." The "crushing" of the serpent's head in Gen. 3:15 is conspicuous in light of these parallels.

    "Ancient Near Eastern Mythography," 352.
147. Averbeck, "Ancient Near Eastern Mythography," 354. Averbeck's article mentions ANE parallels, like "the serpent that stole the plant that rejuvenates life from Gilgamesh at the end of the flood story in the Gilgamesh Epic tablet 11." He continues, "From Anatolia we have Iluyanka, the evil serpent in Hittite myth, and from Egypt the story of the repulsing of the dragon, in which Seth binds the serpent 'who goes on his belly' and then runs off with his strength." Ibid, 355.
148. Duke University's Carol Meyers argues that the passage should be translated "I will make great your toil and your many pregnancies"—referring to the necessity of women laboring in the subsistence economy, as opposed to the luxury of staying home and taking care of the

children. Carol Meyers, *Rediscovering Eve: Ancient Israelite Women in Context* (New York: Oxford University Press, 2013), 102.

149. As McKnight notes in Venema and McKnight, *Adam and the Genome,* 141.
150. Walter Brueggemann, *Genesis,* in Interpretation: A Bible Commentary for Teaching and Preaching (Louisville, KY: Westminster John Knox Press, 2010), 48.
151. Wenham, *Rethinking Genesis* 1–15, 89.
152. In Greek, *Chawwāh* is *Zōē*. This is the word chosen by the Greek translators of the Hebrew Scriptures (who produced the Septuagint).
153. The Sumerian title was *Nintu*.
154. The demand for a mother goddess was strong. In OT times, some Jews worshiped the Queen of Heaven, believed to be an Assyrian and Babylonian goddess, aka Ashtoreth, the wife of Baal, aka Molech (Jer 7:18; 44:17–19, 25). A few centuries into the new covenant, Mary was promoted to be "mother of God" (at the Council of Ephesus in AD 431).
155. Now that man had fallen, the law would later prohibit priests from approaching God with their private parts exposed (Ex 20:26; 28:42). This was in contrast to pagan priesthoods, which not only lacked such modesties, but occasionally required priests to officiate unclothed.
156. In Ezek 1:10 they have four "faces" of the four highest in created beings: man, the highest in creation; the lion, greatest in the animal kingdom; the eagle, most magnificent of birds; and the ox, the strongest of domesticated animals. And as they stand with lowered wings in the sapphire throne room of God, Ezekiel hits the floor in reverence, only rising when the Spirit enters him and a voice tells him to get up so he can talk to him (1:25–2:2). These beings represent the most magnificent of created guards to worship and protect God.
157. See Gen 18:1–2; 19:1 (cf. Heb 13:2); Judg 13:3–6; Dan 3:24–28; and the resurrection narratives (Mt 28:1–5: "angel"; Jn 20:12: "angels"; Mk 16:5: "young man"; Lk 24:4: "two men"); Acts 10:3, 30 ("angel," "man in dazzling clothes").
158. Did God appropriate them from pagan writers, or did they get visions of them from God first? Either is conceivable.
159. God's grace may be seen in his kind treatment of Adam and Eve—for whose names ours could easily be substituted! There are three ways in which God's grace is poured out: he clothes us, he protects us against ourselves, and he forgives us. First, God clothes us with Christ, calling us sons and daughters (Gal 3:26–27). Lk 15 is a beautiful NT chapter revealing the heart of God, while Genesis 3 is a beautiful OT passage with the same message. Next, now that we have experiential knowledge of sin, God keeps danger at arm's length, protecting us against ourselves. Finally, he forgives us. Sin has consequences, yet redemption is full.
160. Venema and McKnight, *Adam and the Genome*, 143 (some Heb. vowels corrected).

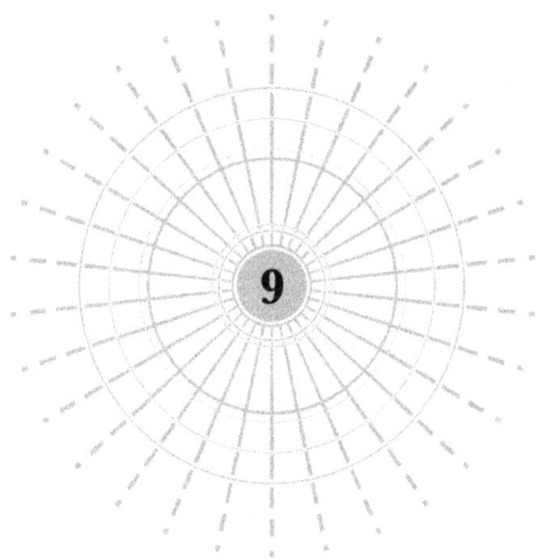

Pandemic

Cain & Descendants

When I was seven years old, I (Paul) remember getting angry with a neighborhood boy, Michael, because he had been wrestling with my brother Vic (then nine years of age) and had cheated by pulling Vic's hair. When I saw him riding by on his bicycle later that day, I happened to have my metal cap gun, and I ran alongside him and repeatedly hit him on the back with it. My sister Helen (age eleven) heard the commotion, came to the window while I was trying to hide the evidence in a nearby garbage can, and promptly told my mother. I was not only disciplined, but was marched down to Michael's house to apologize to him and his parents—while his mother was washing his bleeding back.

As a seven-year-old, I (Douglas) got into a fight with my brother Steve (then only five). A toad had crawled for shelter into our woodpile, and both of us wanted to hold it. We began to quarrel, and when Steve threatened me with his toy pistol, I struck him on the head with a piece of firewood. He bled profusely. I can still feel the heat of panic, the denial and the shame. I fled into the house, trying to hide from my parents and grandparents. My brother recovered quickly, but I would never forget my action or the burning guilt. Being a fugitive is no fun. A year or two later, I read Genesis for the first time—including the story of Cain and Abel. The story was about me.[161] There was no confusion about which of the brothers I was.

> *4:1 Now the man knew his wife Eve, and she conceived and bore*
> *Cain, saying, "I have produced a man with the help of YAHWEH."*
> *2 Next she bore his brother Abel. Now Abel was a keeper of sheep,*
> *and Cain a tiller of the ground. 3 In the course of time Cain brought to*
> *YAHWEH an offering of the fruit of the ground, 4 and Abel for his part*
> *brought of the firstlings of his flock, their fat portions.*

Cain and Abel are born. Like scores of the personal names in Genesis, theirs have symbolic overtones. Cain (Hebrew *Qāyin*) sounds like the word for spear, or possessed, or smith (keep in mind that Cain's descendants were metalworkers). Abel (*Hābel* or *Hebel*) sounds like the word for mist or vapor (*hebel*).[162] His name sounds like his short life, which extends only from Gen 4:2 to 4:8.

Both brothers present offerings to God, yet Cain's are not presented according to God's will (Heb 11:4). It is evident from the text that Cain's "sacrifice" was an offering in name only. He approached God in a pagan way: attempting to use God, instead of being willing to be used by him. He felt that his religious acts ought to earn him something. All they earned was a challenge. Adam's second son brought firstlings of the flock, while his first son offered neither firstlings nor firstfruits.[163]

> *4 And YAHWEH had regard for Abel and his offering, 5 but for Cain*
> *and his offering he had no regard. So Cain was very angry, and his*
> *countenance fell. 6 YAHWEH said to Cain, "Why are you angry, and*
> *why has your countenance fallen? 7 If you do well, *can you not hold*
> *your head high? And if you do not do well, sin is lurking at the door;*
> *its desire is for you, but you must master it."*

* The translation "can you not hold your head high?" (NEB footnote) is a reasonable rendering of the Hebrew.[164]

Inversion

Inherent in the interaction is a strong countercultural inversion. The normal order, when it comes to children, is to provide for the firstborn son abundantly beyond the provision made for other children. When it comes to inheritance, he receives the double portion of the firstborn. Culturally, society favored the eldest son, just as it favored the birth of boys over that of girls. Yet with God there is no favoritism—which means that God's word sometimes condemns, and at other times seeks to moderate, attitudes and practices that smack of favoritism. Think how many times the younger is the more important (historically or theologically)—like Moses, younger brother of Aaron and Miriam; and Jacob, younger brother of Esau, who ended up as Israel, patriarch of the Twelve Tribes.[165]

Cain is rejected—through his own disobedience, as we will see; Abel is chosen. And so, a common biblical theme is introduced: the election of the younger son over the elder son. Along with this comes another pattern: the persecution of the younger son by the elder. The rejection of the assumption that the elder child should always be the favorite and dominant one is nearly as radical an idea today (in most of the world) as it was in OT times.

Angry and Depressed

Sin crouches at the door; vigilance is required.[166] In this Cain fails. Instead of responding humbly before the Lord, Cain is angry and crestfallen (4:6). The Lord challenges Cain's self-pitying attitude. Rather than take responsibility and repent, he gives in to sin. His unrighteousness is mirrored in his facial expression.[167] So, God's rejection of Cain was the result of Cain's rejecting God and his ways.

8Cain said to his brother Abel, "Let us go out to the field." And
when they were in the field, Cain rose up against his brother Abel,
and killed him. 9Then YAHWEH said to Cain, "Where is your brother

Abel?" He said, "I do not know; am I my brother's keeper?" [10]*And* YAHWEH *said, "What have you done? Listen; your brother's blood is crying out to me from the ground!* [11]*And now you are cursed from the ground, which has opened its mouth to receive your brother's blood from your hand.* [12]*When you till the ground, it will no longer yield to you its strength; you will be a fugitive and a wanderer on the earth."*

The Fugitive

Instead of mastering his selfish desires, Cain allows them to master him. Satan crouches, ready to pounce (see 1 Pet 5:8). Cain, totally focused on himself, is overcome by sin. His simmering resentment comes to a boil in murder. He slays his own brother—the definition of fratricide.[168] The murder takes place in an open field. According to Deut 22:25–27, murder in the open field proved that the crime was premeditated.[169]

God now opposes Cain; he is under a curse. Once again, the cycle of sin is repeated. His successive four sins—an unacceptable offering 4:5, unrepented anger 4:6, murder of his brother 4:8, and lying 4:9—are evidence that sin was now ruling over him. Abel's blood cried out "from the ground" for judgment and punishment on Cain, while Jesus' blood cries out from heaven for mercy and forgiveness for those who accept his offer of grace.

The cycle of sin is repeated. Cain is banished to the land of Nod, where he will be a "restless wanderer" (NIV), because only in God do our souls find rest (Ps 62). What do we see in Cain's life? Not only separation from God, but also excuse making. Life becomes oppressive, and he is restless—and possibly a touch paranoid (4:14).

Where Is Your Brother?

As Davis Atkinson puts it, "The individual question to Adam becomes the social question to Cain."[170] We should ask ourselves—and others—God's penetrating first question (to Adam and Eve), "Where are you?" along with his second question (to Cain), "Where is your brother?" Of course, in superficial fellowship such queries will never be made. But asking the tough questions needn't be a mark of meanness or judgmentalism. Rather, they may be signs of genuine love.

Cain displays the hardness of his heart and a bit of sardonic wordplay before God, as Abel was a keeper of sheep, in asking his own famous question, "Am I my brother's keeper?" God's tacit response: "Yes, you are." God's children need to look after each other (Gal 6:2; Heb 3:12–14). Our needs will never be fully met until we are totally committed to one another, just as the early Christians were devoted to fellowship (Acts 2:42).

The death of righteous Abel is a theme picked up in the NT and even connected with the death of Christ (Mt 23:35; Heb 11:4; 12:24).

Like Father, Like Son

The parallels between Cain and Adam are striking. Compare Gen 4 with Gen 3: Cain sins too (3:1–7), evades responsibility (3:8–10), and is affected by a divine curse (3:11–19), after which God provides a fresh start (3:20–26).

The destructive momentum of sin is ramping up. It would be hyperbole to call it an epidemic at this early stage—but it will become one.

> *13Cain said to YAHWEH, "My punishment is greater than I can bear! 14Today you have driven me away from the soil, and I shall be hidden from your face; I shall be a fugitive and a wanderer on the earth, and anyone who meets me may kill me." 15Then YAHWEH said to him, "Not so! Whoever kills Cain will suffer a sevenfold vengeance." And YAHWEH put a mark on Cain, so that no one who came upon him would kill him. 16Then Cain went away from the presence of YAHWEH, and settled in the land of Nod, east of Eden.*

Although Yahweh will offer a fresh start, both Adam and Cain had to leave after God confronted them. But Cain was a fugitive, not just an exile: "If someone is burdened with the blood of another, let that killer be a fugitive until death; let no one offer assistance" (Prov 28:17).[171] Further thoughts on the fugitive:

- We hear no word of regret from Cain, no plea for forgiveness—so he cannot be pardoned.
- He also cannot truly be rehabilitated, because he refuses to see the wrong he has done.
- His dominant emotion is fear. He settles for a lamentable life, separated from God and family, prisoner to his own "heart of darkness."
- In the Sumerian account, the gods rescue man from wandering. In Genesis, wandering is a judgment placed on the murderer. Mesopotamian accounts are generally optimistic about human progress, while Genesis depicts the advance of sin.

God's gracious treatment of the seemingly unbroken fugitive is stunning. Protection is offered, including the mysterious mark God put on Cain kept anyone from killing him. The mark isn't a stigma, but rather something like the mark of protection in Ezek 9:4–6. The nonsensical idea that the mark involved Cain's skin turning dark as a punishment is both racist and ridiculous.[172]

Last, Cain settles in the land of Nod, which signifies "wandering." Many names and places in this part of Genesis have symbolic meaning, and the significance of this one is thinly veiled.

> *17Cain knew his wife, and she conceived and bore Enoch; and*
> *he built a city, and named it Enoch after his son Enoch. 18To Enoch*
> *was born Irad; and Irad was the father of Mehujael, and Mehujael*
> *the father of Methushael, and Methushael the father of Lamech.*
> *19Lamech took two wives; the name of the one was Adah, and the*
> *name of the other Zillah. 20Adah bore Jabal; he was the ancestor of*
> *those who live in tents and have livestock. 21His brother's name was*
> *Jubal; he was the ancestor of all those who play the lyre and pipe.*
> *22Zillah bore Tubal-cain, who made all kinds of bronze and iron tools.*
> *The sister of Tubal-cain was Naamah.*

Cain Marries and Builds

Cain feared he might become the target in an honor killing (v. 14). But who would hunt him down? His parents? Equally odd to the modern reader, whom did Cain marry if there were now only three humans on the earth?[173] And why build a city for such a small number of people? It is difficult to escape the implication of the Scriptures that civilization already exists *outside* the area of the "first family." In short, this can be interpreted in at least two different ways, both of which seem to rest on Scripture.

Cain's building a city corresponds with the beginning of urbanization[174]—and a whole host of ills to follow. We see also in 4:17 his concern about carrying on his name—to achieve immortality in the only way he could conceive: by forcing his memory on posterity, naming the city after his son.

Cain's Progeny

Lamech marries Adah and Zillah, whose names are worth commenting on. *'Adāh* in Hebrew means "ornament." It has been suggested that Zillah (*Tsillāh*) means "shade" or "tinkling," as in the sound of a bell. If this is the case, the women's names highlight appearance and voice—underscoring the shallowness of Lamech's attraction.[175] Lamech, like Samson later, falls for sensuality. Not only that, but in marrying Adah and Zillah, Lamech has the distinction of being the first polygamist (technically, bigamist) in the Bible.[176]

The line of Lamech raised livestock. They had time for music, achieving some degree of sophistication. In the OT, as in many ancient religious writings, music is often associated with idolatry and debauchery. His family also had a business: metalwork. The *Adapa* myth speaks of seven sages living before the flood. They brought the arts of civilization to humankind: animal husbandry, agriculture, music, and metallurgy.[177] In contrast, in Genesis these are merely areas of human achievement, unremarkable in light of the biblical doctrine of humans as the image of God.

> *23 Lamech said to his wives:*
> *"Adah and Zillah, hear my voice;*
> *you wives of Lamech, listen to what I say:*

I have killed a man for wounding me,
a young man for striking me.
[24]If Cain is avenged sevenfold,
truly Lamech seventy-sevenfold."

Song of the Sword

Next, we come to the so-called "Song of the Sword," which Lamech sings to his wives. Lamech takes revenge, much in the spirit of his spiritual father, Cain. The punishment he inflicted definitely did not fit the crime: death for personal injury. Lamech cares little for God's righteous decree (v. 15). We see in him a strong-willed and self-centered individual, quick to rationalize his heinous crime. Sevenfold vengeance may suggest the escalatory nature of violence.

Despite their similar psychological profiles, Lamech was much more "civilized" than his ancestor Cain. He had technology: the ability to forge the perfect weapon to deliver all seventy-seven blows. Whereas Cain succumbed to sin, Lamech celebrated it. And he has the refinement of words—poetry—to express his brutality. How modern this sounds.

[25]Adam knew his wife again, and she bore a son and named him Seth, for she said, "God has appointed for me another child instead of Abel, because Cain killed him." [26]To Seth also a son was born, and he named him Enosh. At that time people began to invoke the name of YAHWEH.

The line of Cain has little concern for Yahweh. Their accomplishments were focused elsewhere: construction, music, metalwork, and murder. Throughout those generations, their minds were "on things that are on earth" (Col 3:2). Sin has reached epidemic proportions. Gregory Koukl sums up:

> Death spreads like plague through all mankind. Brother slays brother in cold blood and calm arrogance. Men, proud of their violence, boast of their killings. With each generation, man's

> rebellion becomes more dramatic. The darkness spreads. One thoughtless act of sin and self-will changed the world forever.[178]

With Seth, there is hope. His name is a play on the Hebrew word for "granted"; he is "granted" in the place of Abel. At last Adam and Eve have a son (again) who is spiritually minded. The line of Seth will be God-focused (Gen 5:2–32). Beginning with Seth and his son Enosh,[179] people begin to call on the name of Yahweh (Gen 4:26). A new day is dawning.

In the Next Two Chapters

Gen 5 presents the lineage of Seth. We will examine it in our next chapter, principally to determine the meaning of the unusually large numbers there. In the following chapter we will again pick up the theme of the epidemic of sin, soon to reach pandemic proportions.

RECAP

Biblical Truths

- When we give to God, we are to give our best–whether called upon to sacrifice or on our own initiative.
- Resisting sin requires resolve–character and determination. We have a choice, and we cultivate character through the actions we take and the patterns we set.
- Although we celebrate developments in civilization and technology, nothing is more valuable than godliness.

Points of Contact with Pagan Culture

- Whereas the ancients celebrated craftsmanship, agriculture, and music, Genesis values them far less than fearing and walking with God.
- Vengeance and warfare were admired in the ancient world, but Genesis exposes them as violent and selfish.

NT Connections

- Abel is remembered in Mt 23:35/Lk 11:51; Heb 11:4; 12:24.
- Jesus alludes to the seventy-sevenfold vengeance of the "Song of the Sword." In his Parable of the Unforgiving Servant, we are encouraged to forgive seventy-seven times[180]–another way of telling us to always be ready to forgive–and in abundant measure (Mt 18:22).

Application

- Without being busybodies, do we truly care about others?
- Are we prouder of our family members for their temporal achievements, or for their spiritual achievements? (Are we more pleased that our daughter was accepted to Oxford, or that she is a woman of character and faith?)
- We can be like the line of Cain, or the line of Seth–putting ourselves first, or calling on the name of Yahweh. Which shall it be?

---

161. Lest anyone give me (Douglas) more credit than due, you should know that my foray into Scripture was extremely short lived. I got bogged down in the Table of Nations (Gen 10). It wasn't until age seventeen that I developed the habit of daily reading, and not until age eighteen that I felt emboldened to follow Scripture.
162. *Chebel* appears in Job 7:16; Ps 39:5; Eccl 1:2. *Chebel*—vanity, emptiness, meaninglessness, vapor, puff—is a common word throughout Ecclesiastes.
163. Wenham, *Genesis 1–15*, 103.
164. See also Job 11:15 ("you will lift up your face without blemish").
165. Esau too generated his own genealogy (Gen 36:1–43), and Ishmael, in the previous generation, was the patriarch of Twelve Tribes (Gen 17:20; 25:12–16).
166. The original text would appropriately describe a demon or evil spirit attempting to invade a home and overpower the occupant.
167. See Prov 15:13; Isa 3:9; Mk 10:22 (NIV); Ps 34:5.
168. There is a textual consideration with 4:8. All surviving Hebrew manuscripts of Genesis 4 are missing the phrase "Let us go out to the field." As these words are found in translations from Hebrew into Greek and other languages, we can be fairly confident that they are original. The number of surviving copies, and in various languages, is thus an important factor in establishing the biblical text.
169. In addition, as brother to Abel, Cain would have naturally become his "avenger of blood" (Num 35:12–28). See the similar scenario in 2 Sam 14:6–7. It makes sense to read the narratives of Genesis in light of the laws to be given in Ex–Num, for Genesis was in the first instance a book for the Jewish people.
170. Davis Atkinson, *The Message of Genesis 1–11: The Dawn of Creation,* The Bible Speaks Today (Downers Grove, IL: InterVarsity, 1990), 109.
171. Prov 28 seems especially crafted for Cain and those who resemble him spiritually (Prov 28:1, 5, 9, 13, 14, 17, 24 [in that Cain deprived his parents of a son]). It was the duty of the

"avenger of blood" to take the life of the murderer (Num 35:19; Deut 19:6; Josh 20:3; 2 Sam 14:11). This custom is still practiced in many countries today. This is not to say that vengeance for bloodguilt is endorsed by God. Rather, this is the social reality with which Cain has to deal.

172. For example, the Book of Mormon reflects 19th-cent. white supremacist prejudice. See discussion at https://www.douglasjacoby.com/qa-1517-dark-skin-divine-curse/.
173. Some early Christians taught that Cain married a sister. (Recall that the daughters of Adam and Eve are mentioned, though not named, in Gen 5.) The apocalyptic and pseudonymous 2 Enoch teaches that he married Luluwa, his twin sister. In later Jewish tradition, Cain marries her after the stipulated period of mourning for Abel has run out (2 Enoch 1:74:5; 2:1:6). Abel also has a twin sister, Aklia (2 Enoch 1:75:11), whom Seth marries (2 Enoch 11:7:5). Another opinion was that Cain was already married, and that his wife fled with him (Josephus, *Antiquities* II.1). At any rate, she is not an important figure in the story.
174. Longman and Walton note that:

    The early chapters of Genesis contain a number of obvious anachronisms to everyone but to those who refuse to pay any attention to the evidence we have from the ancient world. An illustrative but not exhaustive list includes:

    1. the care of domesticated animals occurring in the second generation of humanity (Gen 4:2–5)
    2. the construction of the first city in the second generation of humanity (Gen 4:17)
    3. musical instruments in the eighth generation (Gen 4:21)
    4. bronze and iron making in the eighth generation (Gen 4:22)

    We point out these anachronisms because they suggest that we must remember that real events are being rhetorically shaped for theological reasons.

    Lost World of the Flood, 28–29.

    "Permanent settlements begin to appear in the ancient Near East as early as the ninth and eighth millennia BC. Jericho and Nahal Oren in Palestine, Mureybet in Syria, Çatal Hüyük in Anatolia and Ganj Dareh in Iran are probably the best known." *The Times Atlas of the Bible* (London: Times Books Ltd, 1987), 26.
175. Cassuto finds a parallel in Song of Songs 2:14: "Your voice is sweet, and your face is lovely." Umberto Cassuto, *A Commentary on Genesis 1–11*, trans. I. Abrahams (Jerusalem: Hebrew University Magnes Press, 1964), 1:234.
176. Bigamy is not recommended here, only recorded. If the OT shows us anything about polygamy, it is that whoever practiced it paid a heavy price. Consider, for example, the constant rivalry and bickering between Sarah and Hagar (Gen 16), or Rachel and Leah (Gen 29 and 30).
177. Gone are the simpler, olden days of the Neolithic Age. We are now anticipating the Early Bronze Age.
178. Gregory Koukl, *The Story of Reality: How the World Began, How It Ends, and Everything Important That Happens in Between* (Grand Rapids, MI: Zondervan, 2017), 84–85.
179. Like *'ādām, 'enosh* is another generic word, meaning "human."
180. If the number is interpreted as 70 x 7 (490), the point is the same, although the obvious connection with Lamech is lost.

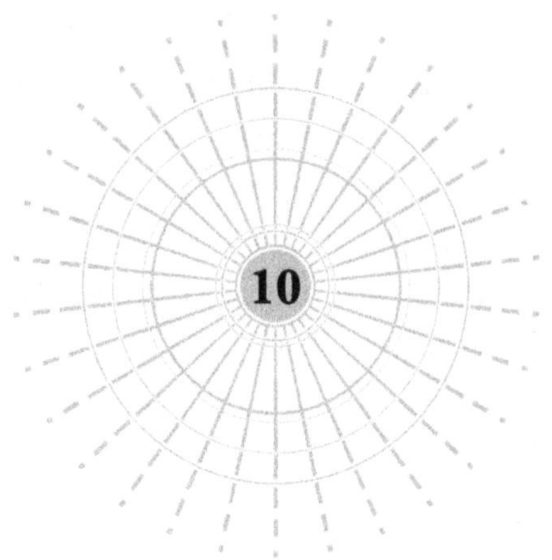

Numbers

Literal or Symbolic?

When we as youngsters read Genesis, we came across those genealogies that left us with plenty of questions. For example, when I (Douglas) came to Gen 5, I was at a loss what to think. The numbers seemed way too big—Adam lived to 930, and Methuselah even longer! I remember a momentary excitement when I figured that the years were months. I began dividing everything by 12, yielding life spans of 77, 76, 75… until I got to Enoch: 365 was an suspicious total (the solar year). On my lunar assumption, that would mean that the fellow lived to 30—but became a father (v. 21) at the age of five (65 ÷ 12)! "That can't be right," I thought, and continued to be nonplussed—for another forty or fifty years (years, not months!).

In this chapter we approach the enormous longevities of Genesis from a more promising angle. If you aren't a "math person," you might want to skim down to the section on the Sumerian King Lists, read the section called "Comparison," and skim through to the Recap section of the chapter.

5:1This is the list of the descendants of Adam. When God created humankind, he made them in the likeness of God. 2Male and female he created them, and he blessed them and named them "Humankind" when they were created.

3When Adam had lived 130 years, he became the father of a son in his likeness, according to his image, and named him Seth. 4The days of Adam after he became the father of Seth were 800 years; and he had other sons and daughters. 5Thus all the days that Adam lived were 930 years; and he died.

6When Seth had lived 105 years, he became the father of Enosh. 7Seth lived after the birth of Enosh 807 years, and had other sons and daughters. 8Thus all the days of Seth were 912 years; and he died.

9When Enosh had lived 90 years, he became the father of Kenan. 10Enosh lived after the birth of Kenan 815 years, and had other sons and daughters. 11Thus all the days of Enosh were 905 years; and he died.

12When Kenan had lived 70 years, he became the father of Mahalalel. 13Kenan lived after the birth of Mahalalel 840 years, and had other sons and daughters. 14Thus all the days of Kenan were 910 years; and he died.

15When Mahalalel had lived 65 years, he became the father of Jared. 16Mahalalel lived after the birth of Jared 830 years, and had other sons and daughters. 17Thus all the days of Mahalalel were 895 years; and he died.

18When Jared had lived 162 years he became the father of Enoch. 19Jared lived after the birth of Enoch 800 years, and had other sons and daughters. 20Thus all the days of Jared were 962 years; and he died.

21When Enoch had lived 65 years, he became the father of Methuselah. 22Enoch walked with God after the birth of Methuselah 300 years, and had other sons and daughters. 23Thus all the days of

Enoch were 365 years. [24]Enoch walked with God; then he was no more, because God took him.

[25]When Methuselah had lived one 187 years, he became the father of Lamech. [26]Methuselah lived after the birth of Lamech 782 years, and had other sons and daughters. [27]Thus all the days of Methuselah were 969 years; and he died.

[28]When Lamech had lived 182 years, he became the father of a son; [29]he named him Noah, saying, "Out of the ground that YAHWEH has cursed this one shall bring us relief from our work and from the toil of our hands." [30]Lamech lived after the birth of Noah 595 years, and had other sons and daughters. [31]Thus all the days of Lamech were 777 years; and he died.

[32]After Noah was 500 years old, Noah became the father of Shem, Ham, and Japheth.

Notes

- The list begins with Adam and ends with Noah and his sons. The chapter stops short of the flood, though the reader knows it is coming.
- In each generation a son is mentioned first, not a daughter. This is probably a culturally stylized way of doing genealogy.
- There is also a Mesopotamian list of pre-flood figures—all sages. The seventh, Utuabzu, ascends to heaven.[181] In the Hebrew lists, Lamech—not the second Lamech, father of Noah (5:28), but the first—comes seventh in the first genealogy (4:18), as does Enoch in the second (5:21), but with a difference. Lamech is an ungodly fellow, while Enoch is so spiritual in his walk with Yahweh that God "took him" (5:24). It seems that Lamech and Utuabzu are being connected. Lamech followed the ways of the world (the Sumerians and others in Mesopotamia), while Enoch pleased God because he walked with him—in obedience to God's commands, like Noah (6:9; see also Deut 8:6; Josh 22:5; 1 Kings 9:4; 1 Jn 2:3, 6). Note that Enoch is seventh and Noah tenth from Adam, both of whom "walked with God." This is not an accidental arrangement, given that these numbers are used

to signify completeness or fullness in early Genesis and elsewhere in Scripture. The numerical order in the genealogy is being used here to highlight the faithful obedience of these two men.

- Some claim that these ages have Methuselah, Noah's grandfather, drowning in the deluge. When we do the math, however, he seems to die immediately before the cataclysm.
- Unless Noah's sons were triplets, or contained a set of twins, they were not all born in the same year (when Noah was 500). Their names are given as Shem, Ham, and Japheth, possibly because this sounded better in Hebrew, or perhaps Shem was mentioned first since he was the ancestor of the Israelites. The actual order of birth was Japheth, Shem, Ham. (Ham is called Noah's youngest in 9:24.) Note also that if the flood came in Noah's 600th year, his first son being born when he was 500, then all three sons were close to being centenarians. This passage also highlights the faith of Noah (cf. Heb 11:7), who is portrayed as building the ark (at age 480) before his sons had even been born (after he was 500).
- Although there are gaps in some biblical genealogies, none appears in Adam-Seth-Enosh… Noah-Shem (cf. 1 Chr 1)—as often suggested by those seeking a concordist solution between Adam and paleoanthropology. We would expect gaps here, if that were the case.

See Anything Unusual?

Do you notice something unusual about the antediluvian (before flood) ages—apart from their magnitude?[182] Each of the ten men has three numbers associated with him (age at son's birth, years lived after son's birth, age at death), 30 digits in all. Look at the final digits: 000 (Adam)—572 (Seth)—055 (Enosh)—000 (Kenan)—505 (Mahalalel)—202 (Jared)—505 (Enoch)—729 (Methuselah)—257 (Lamech)—000 (Noah).[183] However, since the third number is determined by the final digit in the sum of the first two, for the purposes of analyzing probability, we need only pay attention to the first two digits. Surprisingly, not a single one ends with a 1, 3, 4, 6, or 8.[184] The odds that this would be the case are less than a million to one—and a billion to one when we continue the lineage through Noah's son Shem all the way to Abraham with the names supplied in 11:10–32.[185] This is not even including the low probability that in both sets of ten, male children would always be born first.

Not Decimal—But Sexagesimal

Depending on when and where you attended grade school, you may remember being taught how to count in base 8, base 12, and so forth. It can be done, even if we haven't had to use these systems since we were eleven years old. (Of course, base 2 is far more common in our binary, digital age.) We think decimally, and that is useful when it comes to noticing anomalies (as in Gen 5). But the ancient Hebrews were not using the decimal system—since it was only developed by Indian mathematicians long after the time of the OT.[186]

The ages in the hundreds of years in Gen 5 may be *idealized* numbers based on a modified sexagesimal (base 60) system. In this system, 60 is a perfect number, and multiples of 60 take on special significance. (Noah's age is 10 x 60, Moses' age is 2 x 60, and so on.) Ages tend to be multiples of 60 months (5 years) or multiples of 5 plus 7 (or 2 x 7, in the case of Methuselah). All numbers end in a base-60 number,[187] augmented by 2, 4, or 7. When we consider that these may not be base-10 numbers, but base-60, the odds change drastically—a thousandfold difference for the first ten generations. That is, from Adam to Noah, all of the ages end in 0, 5, 7, 2 (5 + 7 = 12), or 9 (5 + 7 + 7 = 19)—a probability of one in a billion!

In the two tables below, based on the lists in Gen 5 and 11, it becomes plausible that the Genesis writer is using the sexagesimal numbers of the Sumerians/Babylonians. At least it's a possibility worth considering.

	Age at Son's Birth	Years Lived after Son's Birth	'60 Times X' Formula	
	A	**B**	**A X 12 =**	**B X 12 =**
1. Adam	**130**	**800**	60 X 26	60 X 160
2. Seth	**105**	807	60 X 21	60 X 160*
3. Enosh	**90**	**815**	60 X 18	60 X 163
4. Kenan	**70**	**840**	60 X 14	60 X 168
5. Mahalael	65	830	60 X 13	60 X 166
6. Jared	162	**800**	60 X 31*	60 X 160
7. Enoch	**65**	**300**	60 X 13	60 X 60
8. Methuselah	187	782	60 X 36*	60 X 155*
9. Lamech	182	**595**	60 X 35*	60 X 119
10. Noah	**500**	**[450]**	60 X 100	60 X 90

Genesis 5: Adam-Seth Genealogy and Ancient Stylistic Numbers
Bold numbers are multiples of five (0 or 5). * Mystical number 7 is subtracted from a nonmultiple of five and then multiplied by 12 in order to fit '60 Times X' formula. [450] derives from Gen 9:29.

	Age at Son's Birth	Years Lived after Son's Birth	Age at Death	'60 Times X' Formula	
	A	**B**	**A + B**	**A X 12 =**	**B X 12 =**
1. Shem	**100**	**500**	**[600]**	60 X 20	60 X 100
2. Arphaxad	**35**	403	[438]	60 X 7	–
3. Shelah	**30**	403	[433]	60 X 6	–
4. Eber	34	**430**	[464]	–	60 X 86
5. Peleg	**30**	209	[239]	60 X 6	–
6. Reu	32	207	[239]	60 X 5*	60 X 40*
7. Serug	**30**	**200**	**[230]**	60 X 6	60 X 40
8. Nahor	29	119	[148]	–	–
9. Terah	**70**	**[135]**	**[205]**	60 X 14	60 X 27
10. Abram	**100**	**[75]**	**[175]**	60 X 20	60 X 15

Genesis 11: Shemite Genealogy and Ancient Stylistic Numbers
Bold numbers are multiples of five (0 or 5). * Mystical number 7 is subtracted from a nonmultiple of five and then multiplied by 12 in order to fit '60 Times X' formula. Dashes (–) denote numbers that do not conform to mathematical formula. Figures in brackets [ ] derive from Gen 11:32 (Terah); Gen 21:5; 25:7 (Abram).[188]

Sexagesimal Mathematics Today?

The sexagesimal system was used in Uruk as early as 3000 BC. "At least from the late third millennium BC onward, 'sacred numbers' were used in religious affairs for gods, kings, or persons of high standing."[189] Examples of the Mesopotamian sexagesimal system are still with us today in the form of the 360° circle, with 60-minute degrees and 60-second minutes, and with respect to time, the 60-minute hour and 60-second minute.[190] Since we have retained only a vestige of sexagesimal mathematics, in our timekeeping and geographical coordinates, it is hardly startling that we stumble at Gen 5.

The Sumerian King Lists

In addition to the sexagesimal nature of the large numbers in Gen 5 (and 11), there is another reason to approach the genealogy as a less-than-literal record. There is a parallel in the background culture: the Sumerian King Lists.[191]

Sumerian Kings (some persons mythological)

Antediluvian	
Alulim	8 sars (28,800 years)
Alalngar	10 sars (36,000 years)
En-men-lu-ana	12 sars (43,200 years)
En-men-gal-ana	8 sars (28,800 years)
Dumuzid	10 sars (36,000 years)
En-sipad-zid-ana	8 sars (28,800 years)
En-men-dur-ana[192]	5 sars and 5 ners (21,000 years)
Ubara-Tutu	5 sars and 1 ner (18,600 years)
Later rulers (selected)	
First Dynasty of Kish	1200, 960... 625 years

First Rulers of Uruk	324, 420, 1200... 126 (Gilgamesh)
Then:	30, 15, 9...[193]
	Key: 1 sar = 3600 years; 1 ner = 600 years

Such tables were justification for claims of kingship in Mesopotamia. The numbers were unlikely to have been understood literally, especially once the kings were contemporary with those who created the records. All the earlier Sumerian royal ages are unmodified sexagesimals. Let's compare the Sumerian system with the biblical numbers.

Comparison

There does not seem to be any direct literary dependence of Gen 5 on the Sumerian King Lists—no rewriting of sources. Yet there are sufficient parallels that Gen 5 would have struck a chord in the ancient Near East, and we should take notice:

- Both Sumerians and Hebrews were familiar with sexagesimal numbers.
- None of the ages is realistic—presumably the ancients appreciated this fact.
- The genealogies have different starting points: the Sumerians with a king, the Hebrews with the first earthling (Adam).
- In the OT lists, the figures are neither royal nor divine.
- The Sumerians focused on length of reign, not length of life.
- Not only does the Hebrew genealogy of Gen 5 terminate with Noah (and sons), but the terminal figure is righteous.

It seems probable the Genesis writer is making a deliberate comparison with the Sumerian King Lists, and the original readers of Genesis were expected to notice. Think of it this way:

The way of the world:

- Venerates royalty
- Respects power (not only rule, but length of rule)
- Claims divine access and unique spirituality
- Moral behavior is secondary

The way of Yahweh:

- Worships God
- Respects equality for all persons
- Rejects human claims of divinity; all bear image of God
- Righteousness is primary

Our discussion of ancient numbers isn't over. Besides the base-60, Sumerian-Babylonian approach to mathematics, we should also recognize that some ages were *actual* (literal), while others were *idealized*.

Long Live the King!

For a simple example of symbolic age—or, in this case, length of reign—we were watching a play set in the court of an Asian monarch. The chorus hymned the emperor: "May you live 10,000 years!" This variation on the familiar "Long live the king!" is surely not an indication that the emperor's courtiers believed their sovereign might live for actual millennia.

Now imagine for a moment that the chorus had chanted, "May you live 9000 years!" The immediate question would have been, "Why not (the full) 10,000?" The number is culturally conditioned, and so it should be culturally appreciated and interpreted.

One Hundred and Ten…

In ancient Egypt, one did not have to be a centenarian to be accorded the honor of a **110**-year-old. The Egyptians considered 110 to be the *ideal* age—not the ideal age at which to die, but the age to be credited to the ideal man. For example, Imhotep, vizier under the pharaoh starting in the third dynasty (2686–2613 BC), "lived to 110."[194] In other words, he lived a perfect life. Joseph lived a full and *exemplary* life in Egypt too; thus, we aren't taken aback to find his age given as 110 years (Gen 50:26). This was not necessarily Joseph's *actual* age.[195] The notion of having two ages, an actual age and a symbolic one, sounds strange in our day. And yet it is well evidenced in ancient times. Please note that idealized ages do not have to be sexagesimal.

Neither of us would mind living past 100. Five of my (Douglas's) great-aunts and uncles did, one reaching the ripe old age of 108. One of my (Paul's) Lithuanian-born great-aunts—we called her Tante Vody—lived to be 100. And she experienced a lot in her lifetime, including listening with bated breath to one of her sisters (my grandmother) as she reported her encounter with the Czarina of Russia, being in Moscow during the outbreak of the Russian Revolution, having her house searched by the NKVD (the Soviet secret police), helping Jewish refugees find safety, fleeing the country just ahead of an invading Soviet army, and living through the bombing of Dresden.

Though our lives are fairly tame in comparison, most of us would probably want to live for a century, assuming quantity of years doesn't mean lack of health and mental function. Perhaps medicine will dramatically lengthen our lives, although in North America, longevity is currently *declining* due to poor exercise and eating habits. Of course, the issue with the Genesis ages is not whether God is able to extend our lives beyond what is medically probable, since he is omnipotent. Yet historical and biblical evidence points us toward a figurative interpretation. The question is what these figures meant to the original recipients of these accounts.

One Hundred and Twenty…

A wisdom text from Emar, an ancient town near Aleppo (Syria) that flourished in the fourteenth through twelfth centuries BC, cites 120 years as the maximum given to humans by the gods.[196] Syria, like Egypt, is next door to Israel. Among the Israelites it was 120 that was considered the ideal age. And yet the OT considers 70 years a full life, though there was an outside chance of 80 for those who were especially vigorous (Ps 90:10). Moses, the writer of Ps 90, seems not to even consider the possibility of a 120-year lifespan.

Moses' own lifespan is recorded as **120**; the great lawgiver was apparently in excellent health (Deut 34:7). Is this an idealized age? Could it be that he lived only to 79 or 88? The impression of an idealized age is plausible when we consider that his life is presented in three periods of 40 years each. His actual age at death is not a matter of theological significance. Yet the 120 and the three 40s would have elicited responses among the ancient Hebrews quite different from those it does among us. And consider Job: his terminal age was *double* that of Moses (4 x 60).[197]

One more thing to consider: The Apostle Paul tells us that we have *every* spiritual blessing in Christ, while Jesus came to bring us life to the full (Eph 1:3; Jn 10:10).[198] Yet no one has lived an extra century by becoming a Christian, and quite a few have met early deaths.

Two Hundred and Forty?

While it may be easy to accept the explanation for the extreme ages of Gen 5 and 11, it may not be so easy to accept the final section of this chapter. Apart from the ages of early Genesis, ranging from 365 to 969, there are many other long ages that, while seemingly not as implausible, are still past the limits of what seems medically feasible. For example, the godly priest Jehoiada lived to 130 (2 Chr 24:15), Abraham's eldest son Ishmael to 137 (Gen 25:17), and his grandson Jacob to 147 (Gen 47:28). Abraham's younger son Isaac's age at death is given as 180 (Gen 35:29),[199] and Abraham's own age at death as 175 (Gen 25:7). (Consider this: if we take the genealogies in Gen 11 as strict, literal chronologies, then Noah would still have been alive when Abraham was born. Yet the Genesis text presents a picture that these two saints inhabited very distinct eras.) *Since in recent times one or two people have reached 120, an age of 130 doesn't sound too farfetched. But 175? 180? Or 240 (in the case of Job)? Could it be that symbolic sexagesimal conventions explain these ages, as they do those in Gen 5 and 11?*

Notice the 60s and 12s in the chart below, and the way that many of the ages dance around numbers that are multiples of 60.

Ages of Various OT Figures (listed chronologically)

	Age	Sexagesimal and Symbolic Analysis	
Job	**240**	(4 x 60)	(12 x 20)
Abraham	175	(3 x 60) - 5	(12 x 14) + 7
Ishmael	137	(2 x 60) + 12 + 5	(12 x 11) + 5
Isaac	**180**	(3 x 60)	(12 x 15)
Jacob	147	(2 x 60) + 12 + 5	(12 x 12) + 3
Esau*	**120**	(2 x 60)	(12 x 10)
Miriam**	127	(2 x 60) + 7	(12 x 10) + 7
Aaron	123	(2 x 60) + 3	(12 x 10) + 3
Moses	**120**	(2 x 60)	(12 x 10)
Jehoiada	130	(2 x 60) + 10	(12 x 10) + 10

* Working backward from Isaac's age at death, Esau's last *known* age is 120. Gen 35:28 / 25:26 (180–60) = 120.

** Figure from Jewish tradition. See http://www.chabad.org/library/article_cdo/aid/112396/jewish/Miriam.htm.

Yet even if the sexagesimal element in the table above is coincidental, consider the four generations from Abraham to Joseph. Abraham lived to 175 = 7×5^2; Isaac lived to 180 = 5×6^2; Jacob lived to 147 = 3×7^2. Joseph lived to $5^2 + 6^2 + 7^2$—in a sense, summing up his predecessors' lives.

Conclusion

For further study, you might want to dig into a meaty article by Carol Hill, originally posted at the website of the American Scientific Affiliation.[200] A mathematical analysis of sexagesimal counting may be found in "Time and Tide: Babylonian Mathematics and Sexagesimal Notation."[201] Of course, not every scholar agrees with a symbolic interpretation of the numbers of Gen 5 and 11, and there are other ways of approaching these texts.[202] We simply did not find them as convincing.

Taking into account the Babylonian sexagesimal system along with the Mesopotamian notion of sacred numbers moves us toward clarity regarding the extreme longevities in antediluvian times. Conrad Hyers is on target:

> In the literal treatment of the six days of creation, a modern, arithmetical reading is substituted for the original symbolic one. This results, unwittingly, in a secular rather than religious interpretation. Not only are the symbolic associations and meanings of the text lost in the process, but the text is needlessly placed in conflict with scientific and historical readings of origins.[203]

Heroes

In the next chapters we will compare two types of hero and realize how differences in attitude and behavior between the polytheists and the Hebrews connect to the flood of Noah.

RECAP

Biblical Truths

- The Hebrew concept of time is linear, not cyclical. There are no endless cycles, all without ultimate meaning, but rather clear beginnings, middles, and ends.
- While people tend to glorify power and powerful people, God accepts the righteous person. This truth is emphasized strongly in the antediluvian genealogy, which seems to stand in judgment on the Sumerian (ancient Babylonian) tradition.
- For more on the genealogies, see Appendix C.

Points of Contact with Pagan Culture

- As in ancient culture, religious texts could be numerological rather than numerical.
- The humanistic king lists of the ancient Sumerians are downplayed by the creation of the list in Genesis of righteous descendants of Adam through Seth. Yahweh values godliness, not pretensions of godhood.

NT Connections

- By NT times, idealized ages were no longer common.
- The genealogy of Gen 5 shows up in Lk 3. Whereas Matthew's genealogy of Christ moves *forward* from Abraham to Jesus (Mt 1:1–16), Luke's moves *back* from Jesus to Adam, the son of God (Lk 3:23–38). Matthew emphasizes Jesus' Jewishness and messiahship, Luke his humanity and divinity.

Application

- Some biblical passages are difficult. Yet just because a passage may not make sense to us now doesn't mean that it never will in days to come. Trust him, and trust his word.
- To the extent that we have our own lineage (children, grandchildren…), let us reject the glory of the world–and embrace godliness. As with the "Hall of Fame of Faith" in Heb 11, may our descendants be known not for their wealth or power, but for their righteousness and allegiance to Christ.

---

181. See https://en.wikipedia.org/wiki/Apkallu.

182. Seekers of truth in the Bible should honestly admit the lack of evidence for any ancient humans reaching ages in the centuries. There is no palaeoanthropological evidence (the bones and the teeth do not lie)—though one could argue that the bones of the centenarians may one day be discovered (a weak argument). The challenges to a literalistic interpretation are theological, mathematical, and biological:
    - Biological, because given the nature of our telomeres, humans are not "programmed" to live a thousand years, even under the best of conditions. Worse for any literal interpretation of the extremely long ages, ancient humans died considerably younger than we do.
    - Mathematical, because the numbers of Gen 5 and 11 make sense under a sexagesimal reckoning.
    - Theological, because the Genesis writer is not teaching science, but is making a statement about the pagan world—what it values.

183. For Noah, the second and third numbers are found in 9:28.
184. Let us take into account these two distinct sets: {1, 3, 4, 5, 8} and {0, 2, 5, 7, 9}. The chances that the 20 first two digits would be exclusively in the second set are 1 in 2^n, where n = 20. For a single instance the chances would be = 1 in 2^1 = ½. For ten numbers, the odds would be 1 in 2^{10} = 1 in 1024. For 20 numerals (1024^2), the odds are approximately 1 in 2^{20} = less than one in a million.
Full disclosure: The ages differ in the Masoretic (MT), Greek Septuagint (LXX), and Samaritan Pentateuch (SP). By the time of the LXX, which began to be translated in the 3rd cent. BC, it is likely that no one remembered the original significance of the numbers.
185. Calculations based on the numbers in 11:10–32, which are 100/500/600, 35/403/438, 30/403/433, 34/430/464, 39/209/248, 32/207/239, 30/200/230, 19/119/138, 70/135/205.
186. The Chinese were thinking decimally, possibly in the mid–second millennium BC, but there does not seem to have been any direct influence from the Middle Kingdom at this early date.
187. 1, 2, 3, 4, 5, 6, 10, 12, 15, 20, 30, and 60, of which 2, 3, and 5 are prime.
188. Tables of sexagesimals used with permission from Denis O. Lamoureux. The tables appear in his *Evolutionary Creation: A Christian Approach to Evolution* (Eugene, OR: Wipf & Stock, 2008), 211, 235.
189. Carol A. Hill, "Making Sense of the Numbers of Genesis," in *Perspectives on Science and Christian Faith* (the Journal of the American Scientific Affiliation) 55, no. 4 (December 2003): 248.
190. See https://www.scientificamerican.com/article/experts-time-division-days-hours-minutes/.
191. There is a version with eight sage-kings, another with ten. See http://www.livius.org/sources/content/anet/266-the-sumerian-king-list/.
192. Also known as *Enmeduranki*.
193. Modest lengths, with a few exceptions (after 2500 BC). One version of this list even contains three kings who reigned 72,000 years each (20 sars).
194. Although 110 seems an unlikely age for an ancient, the pharaoh Rameses II (c.1303-1213 BC) may have reached 90, and a millennium earlier, Pepi II (2278–2184 BC) managed to live into his mid-nineties. Still, the odds of reaching 110 (from the age of 90), even in the era of modern medicine, are negligible. A 90-year-old male in excellent health has only a 20% chance of reaching 100, and a near 0% chance of reaching 105—let alone 110. See http://www.longevityillustrator.org/.
195. Recall that, apart from Benjamin, Joseph was the youngest of Jacob's sons—age 39 at the time of their reunion in Gen 46:29. He was 17 when was sold as a slave (37:2), entering Pharaoh's service at the age of 30 (41:46)—unless 30 is an approximation. After 7 years of plenty, the 7 years of famine began (41:54). Joseph met his brothers two years into the famine (45:6)—9 years after commencing royal service. And yet his older brothers bury him.
196. John H. Walton, Victor H. Matthews, and Mark W. Chavalas, *The IVP Bible Background Commentary: Old Testament* (Downers Grove, IL: InterVarsity, 2000), 36.
197. The number is supplied by the Greek OT (Job 42:16 LXX). The Hebrew text does not mention his total lifespan. Not all scholars consider Job to be a historical figure. For further discussion of this perspective, see Tremper Longman III, *Job*, Baker Commentary on the Old Testament (Grand Rapids, MI: Baker, 2012); John Walton, *Job*, NIV Application Commentaries (Grand Rapids, MI: Zondervan, 2012).
198. Further, Eccl 6:6 speaks *hyperbolically* of an age of 1000 years.
199. Isaac fathered Jacob and Esau when he was 60 (Gen 25:26). He is said to be feeble and blind (Gen 27:1) when Jacob deceives him in order to appropriate Esau's blessing of the firstborn, soon after which Jacob heads to Paddan Aram (28:2, 10) to escape his brother and to take a wife. Did Isaac live for another (nearly) 120 years after this time?

200. Accessible at https://www.douglasjacoby.com/wp-content/uploads/Numbers%20in%20Genesis.pdf.
201. Accessible at http://www.spirasolaris.ca/sbb1sup1.html.
202. See http://www.biblearchaeology.org/post/2017/04/26/From-Adam-to-Abraham-An-Update-on-the-Genesis-5-and-11-Research-Project.aspx#Article and http://www.biblearchaeology.org/about/pdf/29-2-3BAS_PrimevalChronologyRestored.pdf.
203. Hyers, "Narrative Form," 212c. Hill also put it well: "The important question to ask is: Is Genesis, and the record of the patriarchs from Adam to Abraham, to be considered mythological or historical? Ironically, by interpreting the numbers of Genesis 'literally' Christians have created a mythological world that does not fit with the historical or scientific record." Hill, "Making Sense," 250.

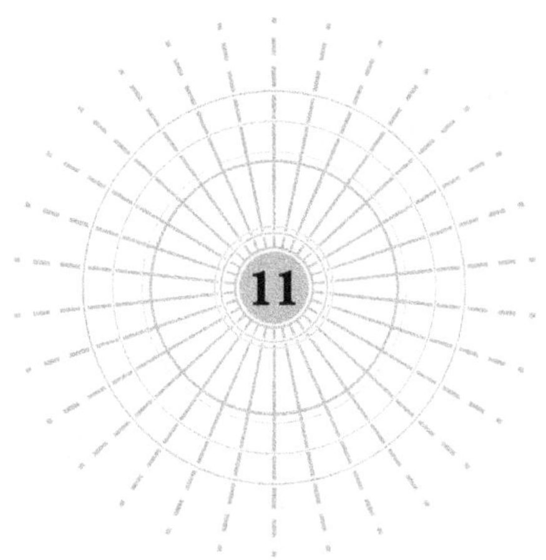

Heroes

Nephilim, Nimrod & Noah

One winter, I (Douglas) took a trip to Iceland. During my visit, a friend, knowing of my interest in history, made me a gift of two Icelandic classics, *Edda* and *Njáls Saga*, both dating to the thirteenth century AD. I read repeatedly of strength, honor, family loyalty, and vengeance. Through the generations, men would sit around the fire, exchanging tales of courage and prowess. Like their Nordic cousins on the mainland of Scandinavia, these men dreamed of Valhalla, the massive dining hall where warriors would eat, drink, and boast of the day's feats. After sleep, they would begin a new day of exploits and battle. The scenario would be repeated every day: fighting, then feasting.

Needless to say, this is not the image of heroism held up in Genesis. Heroic men women are those who obey God, and they are frequently called to reject what is celebrated by society. This should not astound us, since the sin that began in the garden gained traction in Nod and gathered momentum through the line of Cain.

Yet not everyone on the face of the earth has become wicked; members of the godly line of Seth call upon Yahweh. Unfortunately, sin continues to infect the human race, until God has but one option—but let's not get ahead of ourselves. We begin with one of the most puzzling passages in the Bible—frequently popping up in our emails and online Q&As.

> *6:1 When people began to multiply on the face of the ground, and daughters were born to them, 2 the sons of God saw that they were fair; and they took wives for themselves of all that they chose. 3 Then YAHWEH said, "My spirit shall not abide in mortals forever, for they are flesh; their days shall be one hundred twenty years." 4 The Nephilim were on the earth in those days–and also afterward–when the sons of God went in to the daughters of humans, who bore children to them. These were the heroes that were of old, warriors of renown.*

Humans are being fruitful and multiplying. The "sons of God" are marrying beautiful women. This is displeasing to Yahweh.

Sons of God?

Just who are the sons of God? There are at least four possibilities.

1. They are angels. This is the majority view.[204] Even though Jesus seems to teach that the angels do not marry or procreate (Mt 22:30; Lk 20:35), some scholars note that *fallen* angels are in view, as angels can take on human appearance and characteristics (see Gen 18:1–8). It was thought that the offspring of angelic-human relations were giants. [205]
2. They are aristocrats, whereas the "daughters of men" come from humbler families. This is a medieval Jewish interpretation.
3. They are kings exercising the practice of "first night."[206] This is a variation on Theory 2.

4. They are those who call upon the name of Yahweh (4:26)—the descendants of Seth (4:25–5:32), as opposed to the descendants of Cain (4:17–24).[207]

If we are scandalized by the taint of mythology in the Bible, we might well prefer (4) to be true: unspiritual marriages (between unequally yoked partners). The godly line of Seth was contaminated by the godless line of Cain. However, the first possibility—that angels are in view—is by far the strongest contender. It is the dominant view throughout Jewish as well as Christian history. It also connects directly with the ancient Near Eastern belief that semidivine beings (like angels) procreated with mortal women. This supports the natural reading of Jude 6–7 and 1 Cor 11:10.[208] Last, it is directly supported by the Greek OT, the Septuagint, which was *the* Bible of the Jews.[209]

Outward Appearance

They "saw" (6:2)—this was also the first step in the sin of Adam and Eve (3:6), as well as of Achan (Josh 7:21) and David (2 Sam 11:2). When we are led by our eyes, bad things happen.

Since the women mentioned are fair, it could be that angels lusted after human flesh—particularly that of beautiful women. If this speculation is on the right track, it would align nicely with the choice of Lamech to marry physically (though perhaps not spiritually) attractive women (4:19).

Although this interpretation may be more difficult for some of us to accept because it is so enigmatic and may not square with our mental or theological categories, as Gen 6 goes on, we will see that God is saying, in effect, "So what if there was once a superior race of giants? So what if fallen angels once mated with humans? The real heroes are the godly—like Noah."

120 Years?

Yahweh has reached the end of his patience. In 120 years, he will flood the earth—if we may assume Noah became a father *after* Yahweh's pronouncement (6:3).[210] As we saw earlier, Noah was 500 when he became a father, and 600 when the flood came (5:32; 7:6). There is another way to read the passage, and that is that Yahweh is reducing human longevity to 120 years.

There are two problems with this interpretation. First, virtually no one reaches such an age.[211] Second, a number of OT figures are credited with lives longer than 120 years (if these ages are literal and not figurative), as we saw in the previous chapter. Of course, the exceptions might prove the rule. Perhaps the explanation lies in sexagesimal mathematics, since 120 = (60 x 2) = (12 x 10). Not all Bible passages are equally clear—some of our interpretations we need to hold provisionally.

Blurring Boundaries

Yahweh's strong reaction is all the more intelligible when we appreciate that, in OT theology, violating or blurring boundaries is reprehensible. One example is mixed crops (Lev 19:19), since plants are ordained to reproduce according to their kind (Gen 1:11–12, 21, 24–25). This also ruled out clothing of more than one fabric (Deut 22:9–11); mediums, who broke the barrier between the living and the dead (Deut 18:11); cross dressing, which blurred the genders (Deut 22:5); copulating with animals (Lev 20:16); and marrying non-Israelites (Deut 7:3). If Israelites were to marry within the people of God (within the tribe, actually, as in Num 36:3), then *a fortiori* they wouldn't have been permitted to marry angels.

Such mythology was prevalent in Egyptian, Greek, Hurrian, Ugaritic, and Canaanite theology. Neither the *Atrahasis Epic* nor the Sumerian flood story have gods marrying humans. However, King Gilgamesh was born of such a marriage. So, when we find angels liaising with women, we expect God's word to comment on this (condemnation, not commendation). Yahweh is highly displeased.

The Nephilim

The offspring of these angel-human unions are the Nephilim (v. 4), a word that in Hebrew means "fallen ones." The writer tells us, "These were the heroes that were of old, warriors of renown" (6:4c). While they may have been well known, and even honored among men, they were fallen from grace.

The Septuagint translates *Nephilim* not as fallen ones, but as giants (*gigantes*). In many ancient religions, various divinities mate with humans, producing demigods—like Heracles (Hercules), son of Zeus by Alcmene, and Perseus, Zeus's son by Danae. The Genesis writer is tapping into familiar tradition not only in Mesopotamia, but throughout the ancient world.[212]

We see throughout Genesis various "foreshadows" of strikingly similar events that come later.[213] The creation, for example, foreshadows a "re-creation" in Gen 9 with Noah. Here we see another event that has been foreshadowed earlier on. Like Eve in the Garden, who "saw" that the fruit was "good" for food and "took" it (Gen 3:6), so the sons of God "saw" that the daughters of men were "fair" (lit. "good") and "took" them as their wives (6:1–2).

Before comparing these towering figures with the type of hero that Yahweh commends, let's focus on an often-missed detail. "The Nephilim were on the earth in those days—and also afterward" (6:4a). After what, it must be asked. In the flow of this part of Genesis, which is the preamble to the flood account, it seems the writer is saying that the Nephilim were on the earth both before *and* after the deluge. If that is hard to imagine, given the global destruction we assume resulted in the cataclysm, maybe we are reading the flood narrative too strictly.

In Jewish tradition, the giants were extremely tall—approximately 5000 feet or 1515 meters.[214] Wherever we land on the nature of the flood (global, regional, or something more enigmatic), we have to contend with Num 13:33. Here the spies scoping out the promised land saw the Nephilim—whom they described as giants. Maybe the spies are saying that the well-fed Canaanites were tall in stature, reminding them of the Nephilim. Or perhaps they were claiming that the Nephilim still lived—although this seems farfetched, given the enormous height of these giants. They felt inferior (like "grasshoppers")—outclassed physically and militarily.

Nimrod

The ancient world glorified those who "lived large" as warriors, hunters, or rulers. Later in Genesis we are introduced to Nimrod. "He was a mighty hunter before Yahweh; therefore it is said, 'Like Nimrod, a mighty hunter before Yahweh'" (10:9). The story of Nimrod has been lost (to us), though apparently the ancients were familiar with it. (The quotation signals a larger work that includes this missing narrative.) Nimrod may mean "we shall rebel."[215] He was no pushover; no one told *him* what to do.

Two Kinds of Hero

There are two kinds of hero, the worldly kind and the godly kind. Modern culture celebrates and even idolizes sports stars, military commanders, Hollywood starlets, and billionaires. The ancient world had the same broad categories—think gladiator, military general, actors in the theater, and aristocrats. Homer wrote of Odysseus, Ajax, and Achilles. Virgil sang of Aeneas, mythic founder of Rome after the Trojan War. The Vikings celebrated Sigmund, Guðmundr, and Ragnar Lodbrok. The Philistines stood in awe of Goliath (1 Sam 17). Whom do *we* praise?

The fallen ones, "warriors of renown" (6:4) (literally, "men of the name")[216] sought *their own* honor and glory—like Cain, who *named* a city after himself, and the architects of Babel, who sought to make a *name* for themselves (11:4). In contrast, followers of Yahweh seek *his* honor and glory. If we want to become truly great, it will be the Lord who brings this about—as he did in the life of Abraham: "I will… make your name great" (12:2).

> In the great epics of the ancient world the hero often stands as a lonely figure. He must overcome obstacles, fight monsters, acquire helpers (whether women, "sidekicks," or magic objects); and his triumph in the end signals man's triumph over his archenemy, Death.... The Bible sees things rather differently. Death is also overcome, but not only by the individual's struggle. It is rather through the covenant community, bound together by God's laws and his promises, that the heroic vision is lived out.[217]

Thus, there are two types of hero, godly and worldly—and godless, to the extent that they follow false gods.

> [5]*Yahweh saw that the wickedness of humankind was great in the earth, and that every inclination of the thoughts of their hearts was only evil continually.* [6]*And Yahweh was sorry that he had made humankind on the earth, and it grieved him to his heart.* [7]*So Yahweh said, "I will blot out from the earth the human beings I have created–people together with animals and creeping things and birds of the air, for I am sorry that I have made them."* [8]*But Noah found favor in the sight of Yahweh.*

With worldly examples of behavior, the succeeding generations drift farther and farther away from God and his ways. The epidemic of sin (line of Cain) has now affected the entire earth, reaching pandemic proportions. Humankind is past the tipping point (v. 5). Yahweh is "grieved" (v. 6)—the same word used when Dinah's brothers found out that she had been raped (Gen 34:7)—a bitter indignation. He plans to start over. And he will do it with the one man who has not corrupted himself: Noah (v. 8). Noah is a true hero, by virtue of walking with God, obeying him, and fearing him more than the judgment of his fellows.

Consider the heroes of the region of Mesopotamia. In the *Gilgamesh Epic*, Gilgamesh meets Utnapishtim (Tablet IX), who, with his wife, had survived the flood (Tablet XI). Utnapishtim resembles another pre-Noahic figure, Atrahasis, hero of the Akkadian *Myth of Atrahasis.* Utnapishtim means "he found life," while Atrahasis means "super-wise." The name of the Sumerian Noah, Ziusudra (king of Shuruppak), means "long life."

Noah is not a hero like them, lucky or super-intelligent. He is the hero of the flood account—yet not all that "heroic." (He doesn't rally the troops, slay the foe, or battle Humbaba.) The narrative skillfully builds up the holiness and greatness of God, not that of the hero.

> [9]*These are the descendants of Noah. Noah was a righteous man, blameless in his generation; Noah walked with God.* [10]*And Noah had three sons, Shem, Ham, and Japheth.*

In contrast to the ungodly marriages of 6:1–4, Noah and his sons are all monogamous. "Blameless" does not mean perfect. (We are given a glimpse of Noah's shortcomings in Gen 9.) See Ps 101:2; Ti 1:6–7; Rev 14:5. Note also that his sons are not listed in birth order (more on that in chapter 14).

Heroes and Zeroes

As we have seen, a worldly hero may be a "zero" in God's eyes. God is the one who will exalt us—or humble us. Paul warns us, "For he will repay according to each one's deeds: to those who by patiently doing good seek for glory and honor and immortality, he will give eternal life; while for those who are self-seeking and who obey not the truth but wickedness, there will be wrath and fury" (Rom 2:6–8). We have a choice: to seek the glory of God, or to seek personal glory. When we depart from God's ways, we are in danger of getting it all wrong. As Jesus proclaimed, "What is prized by human beings is an abomination in the sight of God" (Lk 16:15b).

By the same token, a godly hero may be a "zero" in the world's eyes.[218] Fortunately, God does not require us to be tall, strong, photogenic, or powerful (see 1 Cor 1:26–27). Aligning ourselves with God's will may elicit bewilderment and even scorn among the worldly (1 Pet 4:4, 12–16). Yet standing up for the truth, regardless of how outnumbered or outclassed we may be, makes us heroes in the sight of the only one whose opinion counts.

With this in mind, we are ready to appreciate the character of Noah (next chapter).

RECAP

Biblical Truths

- God defines greatness differently than we humans do. A humble heart and an obedient spirit are of true worth in the sight of the Lord (1 Pet 3:4). Nor is greatness physical; David was the great one, not Goliath (1 Sam 17).
- Since God desires connection (relationship) with humans, it grieves him when worldly behavior and values pull us away.

- Sin is serious. The infection had been gaining momentum ever since the first act of rebellion, mounting to a complete, planetary pandemic. But for the grace of God, no one would have a shred of hope.

Points of Contact with Pagan Culture

- The ancient myths told of angels or gods mating with human females, giving rise to a race of giants of exceptional skill and strength. Gen 6 says, in effect, "So what?" The true hero is Noah, known for little more than his willingness to obey God and follow his instructions.
- The pagan narratives exalt worldly persons–men and women of power, cunning, or wealth. The Bible inverts this valuation completely, in effect mocking the hero cults of the ancient world.

NT Connections

- Though mystifying and theologically odd to our minds, fornication between angels and women is alluded to in Jude 6–7 and 1 Cor 11:10.
- Jesus repeatedly encourages us not to seek human approval or glory, for example in Jn 5:41,44; 7:18; 8:50, 54; 12:43.
- Several times the NT warns us to be ready for the return of the Lord by speaking of the careless and godless ways of the world before the flood (Mt 24:38–39; Lk 17:26–27; 2 Pet 2:5).

Application

- This chapter is meant to challenge us about our own "hero worship." Do we idolize *people*–for their strengths in academics, athletics, acting, or any other area–when they are not living for God? Has anybody in all of history been more impressive or worthy of adoration than Jesus Christ? It is Christ whom we should worship.
- Noah found favor with Yahweh. He was "blameless," exhibiting a quality vital not only for overseers (church leaders), but for all who love God. Let us strive for the same.

I will sing of your love and justice
to you, YAHWEH, I will sing praise
I will be careful to lead a blameless life–
when will you come to me? (Ps 101:1-2 NIV)

---

204. For example, see Josephus, *Antiquities* 1.3.72–74; Philo, *On the Giants* 1.4; 1 Enoch 6:1–6; *Jubilees* 5:1.

> There is further support for the "Angels" theory: In Gen 18–19 three men visit Abraham, but they are the Lord plus two angels, all in human form. They are presumably wearing local dress, they eat a meal and they speak Abraham's language. So angels are capable of being transformed into fully functioning humans. Thus it is entirely reasonable to suppose that some angels of Gen 6 decided to stay on earth in human form and have children by the daughters of men. There is no sex in heaven, but here on earth things are different. Incidentally, this reminds us of Jesus' appearances in Lk 24:36–43 and Jn 20:19–29, where He displays the same capabilities as the angels.

Trevor Cook, Cape Coast, Ghana, personal correspondence with Douglas Jacoby, 3 October 2015. See also Tremper Longman III, *Genesis*, in Story of God Bible Commentary (Grand Rapids, MI: Zondervan, 2016), 114–115. On the other hand, one could argue that these three "men" together represent the presence of the Lord (see 18:3: "my Lord"). See John H. Sailhamer's comments in *Genesis*, rev. ed., in The Expositor's Bible Commentary (Grand Rapids, MI: Zondervan, 2017).

205. Longman and Walton state:

> In Mesopotamian lore there are individuals in the antediluvian period called the *apkallu* [citing Anne Draffkorn Kilmer, "The Mesopotamian Counterparts of the Biblical Nephilim," in *Perspectives on Language and Text*, ed. Edgar W. Conrad and Edward G. Newing (Winona Lake, IN: Eisenbrauns, 1987), 39–44]. These are generally considered semidivine creatures who are the great sages most known for bringing the arts of civilization to humanity from the gods… Though the *apkallu* are never corporately referred to as "sons of God," in the book of Enoch (second century BC) the "Watchers" are the sons of God, parents of the Nephilim, and the ones who brought the arts of civilization to humanity. The book of Enoch therefore has the Watchers in the same role as both the Mesopotamian *apkallu* and the sons of God in Genesis 6… Psalm 82 may add one more piece to this puzzle. Here God addresses the "great assembly" (the divine council who are elsewhere the "sons of God") and reprimands them for their failure to maintain justice. In verse 6 these "gods" are referred to as "sons of the Most High," who will nevertheless die as mortals (bringing to mind Gen 6:3). This could feasibly be understood as related to the primordial, antediluvian era introduced in Genesis 6:1–4.

Lost World of the Flood, 126–127.

206. Walton, Matthews, Chavalas, *IVP Bible Background Commentary: Old Testament*, 36.
207. Sextus Julius Africanus (c. AD 160–240) seems to be the first to propose the idea (*Chronography*, Section II), although it does not become a common view until the early 5th century, with Augustine (354–430), in *City of God*, 15. Though less influential than Augustine, Ephrem the Syrian (306–73) also suggested the Sethian view in his *Commentary on Genesis*, 56.
208. See also 2 Pet 2:4.
209. The LXX was translated in the 3rd cent. BC. LXX (Roman numerals for 70) is *septuaginta* in Latin, the language of Rome.

210. The number 120 may well be symbolic. As Longman and Walton note, "120 is a decimal representation that perhaps could be compared to the 1,200, which is in the sexagesimal notation used in Mesopotamia. Twelve hundred is represented in the Akkadian text of Atrahasis as 600.600." *Lost World of the Flood,* 125.

211. Conceivably one person in 10,000 today lives to the age of 100. In all of recorded history, only one has reached 120, Jeanne Louise Calment (1875–1997), http://anson.ucdavis.edu/~wang/calment.html.

212. In Greek mythology, these giants, the most wicked of spirits, were imprisoned in *Tartaros.* This is the Tartarus referred to in 2 Pet 2:4, sometimes (incorrectly) translated "hell."

213. See John Sailhamer's discussion of foreshadowing in *The Meaning of the Pentateuch* (Downers Grove, IL: IVP Academic, 2009).

214. 1 Enoch 7:1–6:

> And all the others together with them took unto themselves wives, and each chose for himself one, and they began to go in unto them and to defile themselves with them, and they taught them charms and enchantments, and the cutting of roots, and made them acquainted with plants. And they became pregnant, and they bare great giants, whose height was *three thousand ells* [> 2 mi, or 3.5 km]: Who consumed all the acquisitions of men. And when men could no longer sustain them, the giants turned against them and devoured mankind. And they began to sin against birds, and beasts, and reptiles, and fish, and to devour one another's flesh, and drink the blood. Then the earth laid accusation against the lawless ones.

For the conversion of ells into modern measurement units, see https://en.wikipedia.org/wiki/Biblical_and_Talmudic_units_of_measurement.

215. As suggested by some rabbinic commentators, though this etymology is not certain. Nimrod is also a word for a hunter. In American slang, it means "idiot, jerk" (*Merriam-Webster's Collegiate Dictionary*).

216. The same phrase appears in Num 16:2 and Ezek 23:23.

217. Fox, *The Five Books of Moses*, 5.

218. This is not to imply that there aren't some towering figures who combine worldly greatness with godly character. Biblical examples include Joshua, Moses, Rahab, Deborah, Esther, and David and his "Mighty Men" (Hebrew *gibbōrim*, warriors).

IV

Cleansing: Deluge to Babel

In accordance with his holiness, Yahweh cleanses the earth and provides grace for a fresh start. Once again the earth is populated, and yet among the swarms of humanity arises a self-centered competition: who will gain renown? The defiance of God's will is decisively rebuffed at Babel.

The forecast is bleak, and yet God has not given up. Through Abraham, hope is renewed and God's ultimate, unstoppable purposes prevail. (Yet this is outside the domain of *Origins,* which takes us only up to the Tower of Babel.)

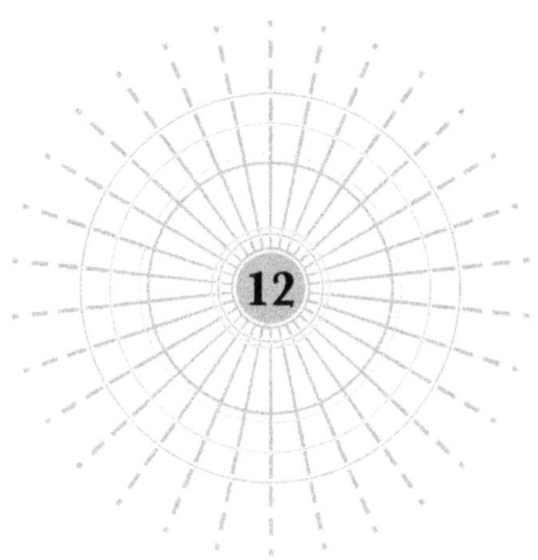

Rescue
Noah's Ark

Before we discuss the flood narrative, let it be said that whatever one's conclusion about the nature of the deluge (literal or not, global or regional), this is not a matter of salvation. Informed men and women hold differing views on this matter—and that doesn't mean they are hardhearted or theologically careless. Since a lot has been written on the topic, and from many different angles, we should strive to maintain a respectful attitude toward those with whom we disagree.

> *6:11 Now the earth was corrupt in God's sight, and the earth was filled with violence. 12 And God saw that the earth was corrupt, for all flesh had corrupted its ways upon the earth. 13 And God said to Noah, "I have determined to make an end of all flesh, for the earth is filled with violence because of them; now I am going to destroy them along with the earth."*

In the Mesopotamian account, the gods attempt to wipe out humans first by drought, then by disease, and finally by deluge. Yet the reason for the extermination is not moral. The noise of human activity has been disturbing the gods' sleep! One of the gods (Ea, or Enki) tips off Utnapishtim, the Babylonian Noah—to the consternation of some of the other gods. The two explanations aren't necessarily incompatible, as violence may well have been noisy. At any rate, Genesis makes explicit what the Mesopotamian accounts leave unstated.[219]

In contrast, Genesis informs us that corruption and violence had escalated—all flesh was affected. While the pagan gods long for quiet and order, Yahweh is concerned with holiness—with righteous living. Humankind was like a lump of clay that has been hopelessly marred (Jer 18:1–4). All the potter could do was start over again. Yahweh himself informs Noah, leaving him specific instructions.

> [14]*Make yourself an ark of cypress wood; make reeds* in the ark, and cover it inside and out with pitch.* [15]*This is how you are to make it: the length of the ark 300 cubits, its width 50 cubits, and its height 30 cubits.* [16]*Make a roof for the ark, and finish it to a cubit above; and put the door of the ark in its side; make it with lower, second, and third decks.*
>
> * According to Longman and Walton, the word often rendered "rooms" probably should be "reeds."[220]

This is not the first ark. The first was the one in the (far more ancient) flood story of Mesopotamia. That ark was described as a cube, whereas Noah's ark was shaped like a barge.[221] There is some evidence, however, that the Mesopotamian ark was envisioned as a giant coracle (a round wicker boat covered with a waterproofing material), in which case traditional depictions are far off the mark.[222]

Interestingly, whereas the heroes of the pagan flood accounts protest the divine action of causing the flood, Noah seems not to demur in the least.

Cubits

In our high-tech world, the term *qubit* (a unit of information in quantum computing) may be more familiar than the old word "cubit." The cubit was a common OT measure. Although scholars are still discussing its exact length, it seems the common cubit was the distance from elbow to fingertip—about eighteen inches (46 cm).[223] Thus, at 300 cubits in length, the ark was approximately 450 feet or 137 meters long. This is larger than any boat in the ancient world, and in fact larger than any wooden craft today—raising the possibility that the description contains hyperbole or symbolism.[224]

> *[17]"For my part, I am going to bring a flood of waters on the earth, to destroy from under heaven all flesh in which is the breath of life; everything that is on the earth shall die. [18]But I will establish my covenant with you; and you shall come into the ark, you, your sons, your wife, and your sons' wives with you. [19]And of every living thing, of all flesh, you shall bring two of every kind into the ark, to keep them alive with you; they shall be male and female. [20]Of the birds according to their kinds, and of the animals according to their kinds, of every creeping thing of the ground according to its kind, two of every kind shall come in to you, to keep them alive. [21]Also take with you every kind of food that is eaten, and store it up; and it shall serve as food for you and for them."[22]Noah did this; he did all that God commanded him.*

All are to die, apart from the occupants of the ark (and presumably marine life). God makes a covenant—a huge theme in Genesis and in both the OT and NT. The covenant is originated at divine, not human, initiative. The animals are to be loaded in pairs, that their species may have a future. Noah is also to load food for all.

Noah obeys, a lone figure, although presumably with the assistance of his family. In the ancient Sumerian version, Utnapishtim's neighbors lend a hand, as he has told them he is attempting to escape destruction at the hands of Enlil. Utnapishtim is told to preserve the seed of all living things. Yet, unlike

Noah, he packs a hoard of silver and gold—objects lacking true intrinsic value. Utnapishtim also invites artisans to board, preserving not only human life, but human culture.

Ancient Near Eastern Flood Stories

Culture	*Hero*	*Rain*
Sumerian	Ziusudra	7 days
Babylonian	Utnapishtim	6 days
Assyrian	Atrahasis	7 days
Israelite	Noah	40 (150) days

Two Arks

The ambiguity of the word "ark" in English—referring to the ark of the covenant (the box containing the Ten Commandments) and Noah's ark (the ship)—has a corresponding ambiguity in Hebrew. The word *tēvāh*, meaning "ark" (the ship, not the chest) is also the word used for the basket in which the baby Moses floated (Ex 2:3). Linguistically and theologically considered, this was no coincidence; the future hope of humanity and of God's people was afloat in this second "ark."

> *7:1Then YAHWEH said to Noah, "Go into the ark, you and all your*
> *household, for I have seen that you alone are righteous before me in*
> *this generation. 2Take with you seven pairs of all clean animals, the*
> *male and its mate; and a pair of the animals that are not clean, the*
> *male and its mate; 3and seven pairs of the birds of the air also, male*
> *and female, to keep their kind alive on the face of all the earth. 4For in*
> *seven days will send rain on the earth for forty days and forty nights;*

and every living thing that I have made I will blot out from the face of the ground." [5]*And Noah did all that* Yahweh *had commanded him.*

Although all animals board the ark in pairs, the "clean" arrive in groups of seven pairs. This is a pointer to the intended recipients of Genesis: the Israelites. According to Lev 11, some animals are clean, others are not. The unclean animals have a right to reproduce, but they may not be eaten by humans. The clean animals are also for sacrifice. Whereas Israel's neighbors sacrificed (and ate) donkeys and dogs, and worshiped rams and bulls, Israel sacrificed rams and bulls, and did not eat ceremonially unclean foods. This explains passages like Gen 43:32 and Ex 8:26. Another pointer that Genesis is written for the Israelites is the recurrence of the number seven—as in the seven pairs of clean animals (vv. 2–3) and the rain to begin in seven days (v. 4). The number 40 is also extremely common in the Hebrew Bible (the OT), showing up 122 times.

[6]*Noah was six hundred years old when the flood of waters*
came on the earth. [7]*And Noah with his sons and his wife and his*
sons' wives went into the ark to escape the waters of the flood. [8]*Of*
clean animals, and of animals that are not clean, and of birds, and
of everything that creeps on the ground, [9]*two and two, male and*
female, went into the ark with Noah, as God had commanded Noah.
[10]*And after seven days the waters of the flood came on the earth.*

Noah's family boards well in advance of the cataclysm.

[11]*In the six hundredth year of Noah's life, in the second month,*
on the seventeenth day of the month, on that day all the fountains
of the great deep burst forth, and the windows of the heavens were
opened. [12]*The rain fell on the earth forty days and forty nights.* [13]*On*
the very same day Noah with his sons, Shem and Ham and Japheth,
and Noah's wife and the three wives of his sons entered the ark,
[14]*they and every wild animal of every kind, and all domestic animals*
of every kind, and every creeping thing that creeps on the earth, and

> *every bird of every kind–every bird, every winged creature. [15]They went into the ark with Noah, two and two of all flesh in which there was the breath of life. [16]And those that entered, male and female of all flesh, went in as God had commanded him; and Yahweh shut him in.*

This is creation in reverse. The waters that were separated in Gen 1:6–7 now flow back together—from above the earth and from below. In later biblical passages we find allusions to Gen 1 and the frightful prospect of "de-creation."[225] For more on the ancient aspects of cosmology (firmament, floodgates of heaven, etc.), see Appendix A.

Yahweh closes the door of the ark (v. 16). In the Babylonian account, Ea tells Utnapishtim to close the door behind him (*Gilgamesh Epic* 11:93). "Noah and his family are entombed in a place of darkness in order to be saved."[226]

> *[17]The flood continued forty days on the earth; and the waters increased, and bore up the ark, and it rose high above the earth. [18]The waters swelled and increased greatly on the earth; and the ark floated on the face of the waters. [19]The waters swelled so mightily on the earth that all the high mountains under the whole heaven were covered; [20]the waters swelled above the mountains, covering them fifteen cubits deep. [21]And all flesh died that moved on the earth, birds, domestic animals, wild animals, all swarming creatures that swarm on the earth, and all human beings; [22]everything on dry land in whose nostrils was the breath of life died. [23]He blotted out every living thing that was on the face of the ground, human beings and animals and creeping things and birds of the air; they were blotted out from the earth. Only Noah was left, and those that were with him in the ark. [24]And the waters swelled on the earth for one hundred fifty days.*

The ark rises higher and higher above the earth (vv. 17–18). Utnapishtim uses a navigator, whereas Noah's rudderless ark requires him to have faith in God. The experience of rescue (from drowning) must not degenerate into anxiety about the direction in which things are going. Though he did not know the future, he knew Yahweh—and that he and his family had been rescued. See 2 Pet 2:9.

Baptism

The waters serve a dual function. They destroy the life on earth, cleansing the earth to facilitate a new beginning. Yet they also *save* the ark, since they raise it above the destruction. Peter notes the parallel with baptism. The ancient world was "buried" under water. After its "death" there is a "resurrection" to new life.[227]

> *God waited patiently in the days of Noah, during the building of the ark, in which a few, that is, eight persons, were saved through water. And baptism, which this prefigured, now saves you–not as a removal of dirt from the body, but as an appeal to God for a good conscience, through the resurrection of Jesus Christ (1 Pet 3:20–21).*

As the apostle reminds us, we are saved through the water of baptism—separating us from the world, lifting us to a new heavenly position (Eph 1:20; 2:6; Col 3:1–11). Despite its symbolic elements, it is not baptism that symbolizes the flood, but the flood that symbolizes baptism.

The rains come down in torrents for 40 days (7:4)—though for only a week in the original Mesopotamian story. The flood level continues to increase for 150 days (7:24). Another difference in the accounts is the place of the gods. Of course, they do not appear at all in the Genesis version, since there is but one true god. A striking line from the *Gilgamesh Epic* speaks of the cowardice of the gods: "frightened… shrinking back…" and cowering "like dogs."

In the pagan flood, the waters rise nearly to the firmament. Pressed against its hard edge, the gods are terrified. Because they are *part of* creation, their existence is threatened. They seem to realize that flooding the world was a huge mistake. Divine vengeance without consideration of the consequences—quite a contrast to the considered and moral mandate of the holy God.

Gilgamesh Epic: The Flood

Overtaking the [people] like a battle,
None can see his fellow,
Nor can the people be recognized from heaven.
The gods were frightened by the deluge
And, shrinking back, they ascended to the heaven of Anu.
The gods cowered like dogs,
Crouched against the outer wall.

Tablet 11:110

> [8:1]*But God remembered Noah and all the wild animals and all*
> *the domestic animals that were with him in the ark. And God made*
> *a wind blow over the earth, and the waters subsided;* [2]*the fountains*
> *of the deep and the windows of the heavens were closed, the rain*
> *from the heavens was restrained,* [3]*and the waters gradually receded*
> *from the earth. At the end of one hundred fifty days the waters had*
> *abated;* [4]*and in the seventh month, on the seventeenth day of the*
> *month, the ark came to rest on the mountains of Ararat.* [5]*The waters*
> *continued to abate until the tenth month; in the tenth month, on*
> *the first day of the month, the tops of the mountains appeared.*

We now come to 8:1, "But God remembered Noah…," at the exact center of the flood narrative, running from 6:9 to 9:17. It is the thirty-ninth verse; there are thirty-eight verses before it and thirty-eight verses after it. Thus, the narrative has perfect symmetry, the analysis of which goes beyond the scope of this book, but which demonstrates the careful composition of the account.[228]

God "remembered Noah." "Remembering" is covenant language. Yahweh is relational. The verse should not be taken to mean that God had literally forgotten Noah—that the builder of the ark had slipped his mind until this point. Remembering/forgiving/forgetting in biblical religion is relational, not mental. That is, when God forgives, he "forgets"—not holding sins against us (Jer 31:34; Heb 8:12). He does not "remember" and "forget" as we might remember and forget, since he is omniscient. For him, remembering (or forgetting) pertains to his acting (or not acting) based on certain facts. This insight also points us to the true nature of forgiveness. We are not necessarily to forget a wrong we have suffered (or to justify it), but we are called to be like God—to remember a wrong only in the nonrelational sense (keeping it in mind, but without bearing a grudge).[229]

The Structure of the Biblical Flood Story

a. Transitional introduction–Noah and his three sons (6:9–11)
  b. First divine speech: Promise to flood and establish covenant (6:12–18)
    c. Second divine speech: Multiplication of life and food (6:19–22)
      d. Command to enter the ark (7:1–3)
        e. 7 days–Waiting for flood (7:4–10)
          f. 40 days–Beginning of flood (7:11–17)
            g. 150 days–Rising flood (7:18–24)
              h. God remembers Noah (8:1)
            g¹. 150 days–Receding flood (8:2–5)
          f¹. 40 days–End of waters' decrease; ark alighting (8:4–6)
        e¹. 7 days–Waiting for earth to dry (8:7–14)
      d¹. Command to leave ark (8:15–22)
    c¹. Third divine speech: Multiplication of life and food (9:1–7)
  b¹. Fourth divine speech: Promise not to flood again and to remember covenant (9:8–17)
a¹. Transitional conclusion–Noah and his three sons (9:18–19)[230]

The wind pushes back the water (8:1), just as the wind will push back the Red Sea (Ex 14:21) and similar to how God pushed back the Jordan when Joshua led the Israelites across (Josh 3:16; 4:18). The upper and lower water sources are sealed off (v. 2). In time, the ark alights on one of the mountains of Ararat (not necessarily Mt. Ararat, as commonly held, since the Bible refers to a range, not a single peak). Ararat (Urartu) is in Armenia. In the *Gilgamesh Epic*, the ark comes to rest on Mt. Nisiri (southern Kurdistan).[231] Soon the occupants of the ark will be released.

> *[6]At the end of forty days Noah opened the window of the ark that he had made [7]and sent out the raven; and it went to and fro until the waters were dried up from the earth. [8]Then he sent out the dove from him, to see if the waters had subsided from the face of the ground; [9]but the dove found no place to set its foot, and it returned to him to the ark, for the waters were still on the face of the whole earth. So he put out his hand and took it and brought it into the ark with him. [10]He waited another seven days, and again he sent out the dove from the ark; [11]and the dove came back to him in the evening, and there in its beak was a freshly plucked olive leaf; so Noah knew that the waters had subsided from the earth. [12]Then he waited another seven days, and sent out the dove; and it did not return to him any more.*

In both biblical and pagan accounts, birds are released to assess whether the land is sufficiently dry for disembarkation. Whereas Noah opens the hatch (door), his pagan counterpart opens up the boat to the four winds—all its doors and windows are opened so that everything can exit.

Creation and Re-creation

The de-creation (destruction) by the flood is followed by re-creation, with Noah presented as a second Adam. Notice the common elements: wind (1:2 = 8:1), waters (1:2 = 8:2), separation of waters (1:6–7 = 8:13–14), and the cycle of night and day (1:4 = 8:22).

[13]In the six hundred first year, in the first month, on the first day of the month, the waters were dried up from the earth; and Noah removed the covering of the ark, and looked, and saw that the face of the ground was drying. [14]In the second month, on the twenty-seventh day of the month, the earth was dry. [15]Then God said to Noah, [16]"Go out of the ark, you and your wife, and your sons and your sons' wives with you. [17]Bring out with you every living thing that is with you of all flesh–birds and animals and every creeping thing that creeps on the earth–so that they may abound on the earth, and be fruitful and multiply on the earth." [18]So Noah went out with his sons and his wife and his sons' wives. [19]And every animal, every creeping thing, and every bird, everything that moves on the earth, went out of the ark by families.

Biblical and Mesopotamian Flood Accounts: Seventeen parallels

1. Divine decision to destroy humankind	Gen 6:6–7; G 14–19; A 2:38–52; 2:8:34; RS 1, 3; S 3:15–4:1 (140–151)
2. Warning to flood hero	Gen 6:13; G 20–23; A 3:1:13–21; RS 12, 14; S 4:2–12 (152–162)
3. Command to build ark	Gen 6:14–21; G 24–31; A 3:1:22–33
4. Hero's obedience	Gen 6:22; 7:5; G 33–85; A 3:2:10–18
5. Command to enter	Gen 7:1-3; G 86–88
6. Entry	Gen 7:7–16; G 89–93; A 3:2:30–51
7. Closing door	Gen 7:16; G 93; A 3:2:52
8. Description of flood	Gen 7:17–24; G 96–128; A 3:2:53–4:27; S 5:1–3 (201–3)
9. Destruction of life	Gen 7:21–23; G 133; A 3:3:44, 54
10. End of rain, etc.	Gen 8:2-3; G 129–31; S 5:4–6 (204–6)
11. Ark grounding on mountain	Gen 8:4; G 140–144
12. Hero opens window	Gen 8:6; G 135; S 5:7 (207)[232]
13. Birds' reconnaissance	Gen 8:6–12; G 145–154

14. Exit	Gen 8:15–19; G 155; A 3:5:30
15. Sacrifice	Gen 8:20; G 155–158; A 3:5:31–33; S 5:11 (211)
16. Divine smelling of sacrifice	Gen 8:21–22; G 159–161; A 3:5:34–35
17. Blessing on flood hero	Gen 9:1–17; G 189–96; S 6:4-11 (254-61); RS r. 1–4

Key: A = *Epic of Atrahasis* / RS = Ras Shamra version of A / G = *Gilgamesh Tablet* 11[233] / S = Sumerian version "*Eridu Genesis*"[234]

In gratitude, Noah prepares to sacrifice to Yahweh, who responds with a promise not to destroy the world ever again (by water). This is not because God expects better behavior, for he is completely realistic when it comes to human nature.

> *[20]Then Noah built an altar to YAHWEH, and took of every clean animal and of every clean bird, and offered burnt offerings on the altar. [21]And when YAHWEH smelled the pleasing odor, YAHWEH said in his heart, "I will never again curse the ground because of humankind, for the inclination of the human heart is evil from youth; nor will I ever again destroy every living creature as I have done."*

Noah presents sacrifices (8:20). In the *Gilgamesh Epic*, a sacrifice is also made—three birds. Yet there is a huge difference. Enlil, god of the earth, wind, and air, who ordered the flood, is infuriated when he discovers that humans have survived it. He comes late to the sacrifice, described in truly memorable terms. The gods buzz like flies around the sacrifices, since they are starving—after all, they have been deprived of food for some two weeks (the duration of the flooding and subsiding of the waters). No humans had been servicing them. The gods then swear not to cause such destruction ever again. (But can anyone really trust them?)

The Genesis account was written in deliberate interaction with the ancient Near Eastern background narrative, highlighting the seriousness of sin, the awesomeness of God, and the grace and renewal offered by the true God. In contrast, in the pagan accounts righteousness is not such a big deal, nor are there any compelling reasons to worship the gods—apart from the benefits they will impart, provided we take care of them.

> [22]*"As long as the earth endures,*
> *seedtime and harvest, cold and heat,*
> *summer and winter, day and night,*
> *shall not cease."*

Things will be normal again. We need not fear a relapse into primeval chaos—and Yahweh guarantees this. One scholar insightfully describes the dynamics of the flood chapters of Genesis:

> With the Flood, order reverts to chaos and creation is undone. Outside the Ark, beneath the silent primordial ocean, the earth again is formless and empty of breathing life. Soon will come a new creation–as was the first, wakened by breath or wind of God. Like the first creation, it emerges step-by-orderly-step out of the primordial Deep, following the general pattern of the Six Days of Gen 1:3–31, to become the home of a new creation and a rescued humankind.
>
> Just as the spirit (or Spirit) of God originally hovered over the chaotic and oceanic Deep (Gen 1:2), now a "wind" from God passes over the flooded earth (8:1). "Wind," "breath" and "spirit" translate the same word in the Hebrew language, and also in the Greek. Day Two had brought into being a firmament, separating the waters above and below the sky. Similarly, the Creator now closes the fountains of the Deep and shuts the floodgates of the sky (8:2–3).
>
> On Day Three, God had separated dry land from seas. As the waters evaporate from the earth, now also dry land appears (8:5). On Day Four, the Creator had ordained cycles of days and seasons. So after the Flood he reestablishes summer and winter, seedtime and harvest, day and night. God blesses birds and animals and

> orders them to multiply. He reminds the human family that they are made in his image, and he assigns them a place of dominion in the food chain (8:17–9:7). All this is reminiscent of his activities on Days Five and Six.
>
> Again God has replaced chaos with cosmos, order in place of disorder, and creation is restored. The Creator promises never again to destroy the earth by water, and, to remind himself of his promise, he places a rainbow in the sky (9:8–17). The Hebrew word for rainbow can also mean a war bow, leading some scholars to suggest another interpretation of the story: the Creator has hung up his war bow, signaling that he is now at peace with all that he has made on the earth.[235]

In the pagan account, there is no certainty that a cataclysm of chaos won't come crashing in again. There is no assurance, no trust corresponding to the faith in Yahweh encouraged in v. 22.

Further

Although we could spend more time on the flood and the controversies surrounding Noah,[236] that is not the purpose of this chapter—or this book. We will stick as much as possible with the ancient agenda. If you want more, there is no shortage of material to study.[237]

In our next chapter, we will read of the renewal of covenant following the deluge, and in the chapter after that of the replenishment of the earth through human migration.

RECAP

Biblical Truths

- Sin is serious–a matter of life and death. God is especially concerned with human violence and corruption.

- The flood is a reversal of creation (Gen 1), as though God were pushing a rewind button.
- "The evil within humankind can, if not restrained, overstep God-given limits, and when it does, it produces giants that human beings can no longer handle. It set free powers which should have no place in this world."[238]

Points of Contact with Pagan Culture

- Whereas the regional flood myth had the gods peeved at mortals for disturbing their sleep, the Bible assures us that it is sin that angers God. Yahweh is not petty, nor is he easily irritated. He is slow to anger–Ex 34:6.
- There are nearly two dozen connections between the biblical flood story and the accounts circulating in the ancient world. The Genesis narrative reads like a rewriting of the familiar and older pagan stories.
- Various flood narratives may be found around the Mediterranean world, not just in Mesopotamia. The Greeks had the story of Deucalion and Pyrrha, the Egyptians the stories of Atum, Ra, and Hathor. Of course, there are flood stories from even farther afield–like the stories of Manu (India), Yu and Yao (China), and the Wawalik sisters (Australian Aborigines).
- The Babylonian Noah loads silver and gold onto the boat. In contrast, Noah brings only his family and the animals; he does not go beyond the divine command.
- Whereas the pagan accounts do nothing to assure post-flood humanity that life will be normal again, *and safe*, Yahweh promises "nor will I ever again destroy every living creature as I have done" (8:21).
- Given the sheer number of flood accounts in the ancient Near East, it is likely that there is a historical core to the flood story (i.e., something big happened).

NT Connections

- The flood provides an apt image for the judgment day, which is taken up by Jesus (Mt 24:37–39; Lk 17:26–27) and Peter (2 Pet 2:5).
- 1 Pet 4:4 alludes to the pouring out, or "flood,"[239] of dissipation (NIV 1984).

- Gen 7:17 connects nicely with 1 Pet 3:21, paralleling the waters of the flood with the water of baptism.

Application

- It is appropriate to worship the Lord when he has delivered us–when we become Christians as well as any subsequent time we experience his grace.
- The return of the Lord will come as a thief in the night. Predicting the event is a waste of time; preparing for it is not.
- On the topic of preparation, the Bible gives no support to "survivalism," which is un-Christian on multiple fronts, even though the example of Noah may be cited.[240]
- Sometimes the cycle of corruption can be undone only by a clean and radical break. In our attitude toward sin, are we sufficiently serious about combatting it, or do we coddle ourselves?
- The Mesopotamian gods were petty. They could be roused to anger by a mere inconvenience, whereas Yahweh becomes indignant over injustice, violence, and corruption. What makes *me* angry–being inconvenienced, or witnessing injustice?

---

219. In the *Atrahasis Epic*, every 600 years the gods send an illness or plague or famine to reduce human population, until a deluge is decreed. Atrahasis asks the god Enki to ensure the salvation of humanity.

220. Longman and Walton write:

> The… term probably does not refer to 'rooms' but to 'reeds.' It would be odd to mention rooms here since the text does not get to the interior of the ark until later. Here the text is addressing building materials. The use of reeds as caulk between the wood (then covered with bitumen) is not only known in the ancient world but is perhaps how the building of the ark in the Babylonian accounts is described. [Compare Akkadian *qa-ne-e to* Hebrew cognate *qānim*. John Day, "Rooms or Reeds in Noah's Ark? *qnym* in Genesis 6:14," in *Visions of Life in Biblical Times*, ed. Claire Gottlieb, Chaim Cohen, and Mayer Gruber (Sheffield, UK: Sheffield Phoenix, 2016), 47–57. Reeds and reed workers are mentioned both in Atrahasis and Gilgamesh.] Whether reeds were used to fill the seams in the wood or for some other purpose, the use of reeds as building material is another similarity between Genesis and the Babylonian accounts. This suggests some use of reeds in the construction. This would stand as the common denominator between this vessel and that of Moses. [There it is a different word for reeds because papyrus, one type of reed, is specified.]
>
> If the second and third terms are both loanwords from Akkadian, the first term, *gōpher*, also unique in Hebrew text, should also be examined as a potential loanword.

> In Genesis we have *gōpher* covered with *kōpher*. The latter, *kōpher*, is a loanword from Akkadian *kupru*. We might expect, then, that *gopher* may be an Akkadian loanword from *gupru*. Intriguingly, in Akkadian, *gupru* is a reed hut. [*CAD* G 118, s.v. *gubru*. is used in the Gilgamesh Epic (1.37), but it is not used in the flood account in the epic, where the word for reed hut is *kikkish* (11.21).] Even though Noah is not told to dismantle anything, it is possible that he is constructing his boat from reed stalks, whether from his house or not. If that is the case, the verse would read: "Make for yourself a vessel of stalks from a reed hut; (with) reeds you will make the vessel and tar it inside and out with bitumen." [The Hebrew word for "stalks," *ʿēts*, can refer to trees, to planks from trees, to wooden implements made from trees, or to stalks of woody plants. Note, for example, "stalks of ax" in Josh 2:6. In the Gilgamesh Epic, one of the materials is "palm fibre" (11.54). If such is the case, the text does not refer to lumber from a *gopher* tree.] If we are correct that the biblical account uses three Akkadian loanwords in the description of the materials used to build the ark, that could add reasons to think that the biblical author is aware of Mesopotamian traditions. Against that claim, however, is that the narrative flow concerning the building materials does not specifically follow any of the Mesopotamian traditions.

Lost World of the Flood, 77–78.

221. The Mesopotamian ark is seven stories in height. There is an intriguing possibility that the ark may have been conceived as a ziggurat (see discussion on Gen 11). A cuneiform tablet from Uruk, or Erech (Gen 10:10) dated to the 3rd cent. BC describes a seven-story ziggurat, each story smaller than the one below it.

222. According to Longman and Walton,

> In 2014 a cuneiform tablet about the size of a cell phone came into the possession of the British Museum. It is part of an account of the flood that features Atrahasis as the hero. The reverse side preserves only some partial lines, but the front side contains a detailed description of the construction of the ark.
>
> In this account the ark is described as coracle-like, specified in the text as a round vessel with a diameter of about 230 feet and 20-foot-high walls. As in the other accounts from Mesopotamia, this vessel is inherently not seaworthy. This boat is like a giant rope basket, using thirty wooden ribs around the circumference.

Lost World of the Flood, 59–60.

223. The royal cubit was 20 inches (51 cm), while the long cubit measured 22 inches (56 cm). To convert from (common) cubits to feet, just multiply by 1.5. To convert roughly to meters, divide by 2. Of course, it is probable that these lengths ought to be reduced somewhat, since modern arms are a bit longer than ancient ones. To illustrate, my "cubit" (Douglas) is 22" (56 cm), while Paul's is 21" (53 cm).

224. Other ancient ark vessels display similar hyperbole. Irving Finkel observes that the round vessel of Atrahasis has 14,400 sq. cubits of floor space, as does the cubical ark of Gilgamesh, while Noah's ark is slightly larger, at 15,000 sq. cubits. Irving Finkel, *The Ark Before Noah: Decoding the Story of the Flood* (New York: Nan A. Talese, 2014), 213; cf. Longman and Walton, *Lost World of the Flood*, 61.

225. When God threatens to use Babylon to punish Israel, the prophet Jeremiah thunders forth using the imagery of creation in reverse. The earth is to become waste and void, the heavens dark. All life is gone, and chaos (disorder) reigns (Jer 4:23–26).

226. Atkinson, *Message of Genesis* 1–11, 140.

227. Paul also speaks of the death, burial, and resurrection in baptism (Rom 6:3–4; see also 1 Cor 15:3–4).

228. Though the verse delineations are manmade, and so we should not overinterpret them, it seems those who added the numbers were aware of the symmetry and numbered the text in a way that reflected and highlighted it.
229. See also Gen 9:15–16. The theme of God's remembering is strong in the book of Nehemiah (1:8; 5:19; 6:14; 13:14, 22, 29, 31).
230. Many readers of Genesis have noticed the *palistophe*, or *chiasm*, in the account (6:9–9:19). This analysis is adapted from Wenham, *Genesis 1–15*, 156–157 and Lamoureux, *Evolutionary Creation*, 219.
231. This is *Nimush* in the *Gilgamesh Epic*.
232. Longman and Walton cite a difference between the Babylonian and biblical accounts:

    > When Uta-napishti opens the window he sees shores/the edge of the sea and fourteen places where landmasses were visible (11.140–41)—so not all was totally submerged. Regarding people, Atrahasis indicates that "total destruction" was called for by the gods, and in Gilgamesh, observing the aftermath of the flood, "all the people had turned to clay" (11.135).

    Lost World of the Flood, 69.
233. Pritchard, *Ancient Near Eastern Texts*, 93–95.
234. Thorkild Jacobsen, "The Eridu Genesis," *Journal of Biblical Literature* 100, no. 4 (December 1981): 522–25. Cited in Wenham, *Genesis 1–15*, 219.
235. Adapted with permission from Edward Fudge (independent scholar), "Out of Chaos New World Emerges," http://edwardfudge.com/2014/04/out-of-chaos-new-world-emerges/. (Note: Fudge passed away during the writing of this book.)
236. Three observations:

    > Westerners (primarily Western Europeans and North Americans) have been fascinated by the geological column any possible connection with a global flood, especially since the 19th-century scramble for fossils—before and after Darwin's *On the Origin of Species* (1859). The entire column had been worked out well before Darwin, so it is an unfair criticism to claim that scholars with an anticreationist bias invented it. Most scientists were creationists in the 19th century anyway.
    >
    > The search for evidence of a global flood was strongly prosecuted during the 19th century. Davis Young has written a superb study on this effort—well worth reading. See Davis A. Young, *The Biblical Flood: A Case Study of the Church's Response to Extrabiblical Evidence* (Grand Rapids, MI: Eerdmans, 1995); see also Davis A. Young and Ralph F. Stearley, *The Bible, Rocks, and Time: Geological Evidence for the Age of the Earth* (Downers Grove, IL: IVP Academic, 2007).
    >
    > A global flood did not create the mountains, valleys, fossils, etc., as these are formed by long and slow processes, not cataclysmic events like floods. Nor could it account for the positions of the fossils—all finely sorted by stratum, whereas floods mix everything without any fine sorting at all. See Carol Hill, Gregg Davidson, Wayne Ranney, and Tim Helble (eds.), *The Grand Canyon, Monument to an Ancient Earth: Can Noah's Flood Explain the Grand Canyon?* (Grand Rapids, MI: Kregel, 2016).
237. Please refer to the bibliography. Also of interest may be the short article at https://www.douglasjacoby.com/?p=16875. Further, the website has a podcast on Noah (login required), as well as a review of Darren Aronofsky's 2014 movie *Noah*, a film that takes many liberties with the story, possibly trying too hard to combine biblical and extrabiblical traditions and to entertain (or shock) the audience (https://www.douglasjacoby.com/noah-the-movie/).
238. Atkinson, *Message of Genesis*, 131.
239. *Anachusis*, rendered "excesses," means pouring out, and hence a flood or wide stream.
240. "Is Survivalism Christian?" at https://www.douglasjacoby.com/qa-1478-survivalism-christian/.

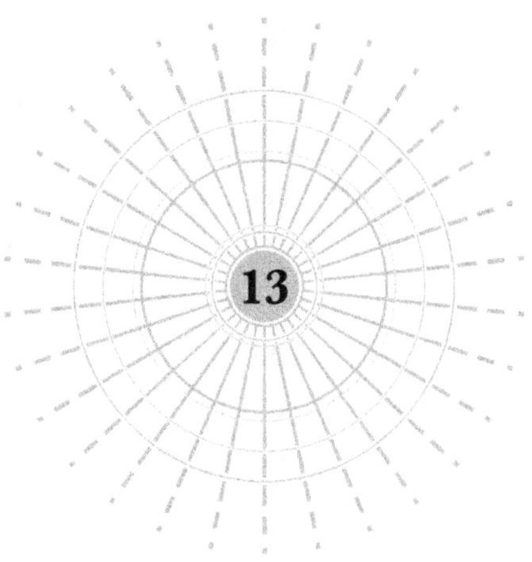

Renewal

After the Deluge

The rains have ended, the earth is dry, and the ark is needed no longer. Noah and family had stepped out on faith, and then stepped out of the ark. Now it is time to keep moving—in the direction of all the points of the compass.

> *9:1 God blessed Noah and his sons, and said to them, "Be fruitful and multiply, and fill the earth. 2 The fear and dread of you shall rest on every animal of the earth, and on every bird of the air, on everything that creeps on the ground, and on all the fish of the sea; into your hand they are delivered. 3 Every moving thing that lives shall be food for you; and just as I gave you the green plants, I give you everything. 4 Only, you shall not eat flesh with its life, that is, its blood. 5 For your own lifeblood I will surely require a reckoning: from every animal I will require it and from human beings, each one for the blood of another, I will require a reckoning for human life."*

Humankind's relationship with the animal kingdom has changed. God created the food chain from the outset, which is called "good" (Ps 104:20–28; cf. Job 38:39–41; 39:28–29; 41:1, 10, 14). Now, not everything is "good" or "very good." Rather, we find "fear and dread." Moreover, eating flesh is explicitly permitted, provided it has been drained of its blood. This is a Levitical prohibition—one of the food laws of Leviticus.[241] When we view the ark as a container of kosher and nonkosher animals, we appreciate Genesis as a Jewish work.

Permission to eat meat after the flood doesn't necessarily mean there was no meat for humans before. After all, God had made skins of animals to cover Adam and Eve, presumably requiring their deaths; and ruling over the fish of the sea (Gen 1:28) suggests the possibility of meat eating. While Gen 1 seems to preserve the beauty and harmony theme and avoids any hint of the existing food chain, we have explicit mention of meat eating here.

> *6"Whoever sheds the blood of a human,*
> *by a human shall that person's blood be shed;*
> *for in his own image*
> *God made humankind.*
> *7And you, be fruitful and multiply, abound on the earth and multiply in it."*

Notice that the image of God remains after the flood. All human life is special—which raises a pertinent question.

Death Penalty?

Interpreters often read 9:6 as a divine mandate for capital punishment in cases of premeditated murder. It is true that the OT law has capital punishment for a number of crimes—but is this the point being made in Genesis? Was the death penalty universally required from the beginning? It isn't necessarily a mandate for the death penalty; it may be an observation. The murderer ultimately must face God.

Gen 9:6 could be read as describing (or predicting) the imminent death of the murderer—as opposed to requiring it. To illustrate, Rom 13 warns criminals that they may face the sword (beheading, the normal means of execution for Roman citizens). While it is morally permissible, God is not commanding the Romans to kill anyone. They could have opted for a different penalty.[242]

> *[8]Then God said to Noah and to his sons with him, [9]"As for me, I am establishing my covenant with you and your descendants [seed] after you, [10]and with every living creature that is with you, the birds, the domestic animals, and every animal of the earth with you, as many as came out of the ark. [11]I establish my covenant with you, that never again shall all flesh be cut off by the waters of a flood, and never again shall there be a flood to destroy the earth."*

As the passage repeatedly emphasizes, Yahweh is a God of covenant. The covenant with Noah is sometimes called the Noahic. Covenants were also made with Adam, Abraham, David, and Moses (the Adamic, Abrahamic, Davidic, and Mosaic covenants), not to mention the new covenant (Jer 31:31–34; Heb 8:8–13).

> *[12]God said, "This is the sign of the covenant that I make between me and you and every living creature that is with you, for all future generations: [13]I have set my bow in the clouds, and it shall be a sign of the covenant between me and the earth. [14]When I bring clouds over the earth and the bow is seen in the clouds, [15]I will remember my covenant that is between me and you and every living creature of all flesh; and the waters shall never again become a flood to destroy all flesh. [16]When the bow is in the clouds, I will see it and remember the everlasting covenant between God and every living creature of all flesh that is on the earth." [17]God said to Noah, "This is the sign of the covenant that I have established between me and all flesh that is on the earth."*

The rainbow is the sign of the covenant. Sometimes it is claimed that before the flood it had never rained, and that therefore the rainbow was the first ever. Yet the rainbow doesn't have to be something new. Consider, for example, the sign of circumcision (Gen 17:11). Circumcision had been practiced for centuries. The Philistines never adopted this custom, but the Phoenicians and Ethiopians did—and the Egyptians had been circumcising since at least 2400 BC.

Walton comments on the rainbow:

> In the Gilgamesh Epic the goddess Ishtar identified the lapis lazuli (deep blue semiprecious stones with traces of gold-colored pyrite) of her necklace as the basis of an oath that she will never forget the days of the flood. An eleventh-century Assyrian relief shows two hands reaching out of the clouds, one hand offering blessing, the other holding a bow. Since the word for rainbow is the same word as that used for the weapon, this is an interesting image.[243]

With these divine assurances, a covenant, and the memory of the old world fresh in their minds, Noah's family repopulates the earth.

> *18The sons of Noah who went out of the ark were Shem, Ham, and Japheth. Ham was the father of Canaan. 19These three were the sons of Noah; and from these the whole earth was peopled.*
>
> *20Noah, a man of the soil, was the first to plant a vineyard. 21He drank some of the wine and became drunk, and he lay uncovered in his tent. 22And Ham, the father of Canaan, saw the nakedness of his father, and told his two brothers outside. 23Then Shem and Japheth took a garment, laid it on both their shoulders, and walked backward and covered the nakedness of their father; their faces were turned away, and they did not see their father's nakedness. 24When Noah awoke from his wine and knew what his youngest son had done to him, 25he said,*
>
> *"Cursed be Canaan;*
> *lowest of slaves shall he be to his brothers."*

Noah was an earthy character (literally)—a man of the soil. (Of course, so was Adam—formed from *'adāmāh.*) He plants a vineyard, drinks, and eventually passes out (or is in a drunken stupor), lying unclothed in his tent. On seeing his father in his inebriated state, Noah's youngest son, Ham, responds perversely (Lev 18:6; Hab 2:15). When his father compromises himself, Ham does not honor his father. He does not have the welfare of the family in mind (Ex 20:12). Rather, he exposes him to shame—which drives Noah to curse his grandson, Ham's son Canaan. Ham behaves worse than outsiders to God's covenant; even they know better, according to writings of the time.[244] Drunkenness, perversity, and cursed progeny—these are not promising developments.

There are other parallels between Noah and Adam. Both were tillers of the soil (2:15), and both get in trouble over fruit (3:6). Yet whereas Adam is naked but without shame (2:25), Noah's nakedness ends with shame on him, his son, and his grandson. In both cases, a curse is part of the aftermath of the sin committed.

The point of the passage is not so much to recount the first act of perversion. There will be plenty more in Genesis, and thereafter throughout the Scriptures, since they accurately reflect human behavior. The point is that Canaan, Ham's son, was the ancestor of the morally degenerate Canaanite tribes. The Phoenicians, with such city-states as Carthage (North Africa) and Tyre and Sidon (north of Israel, in modern Lebanon), were the last vestige of the Canaanite race. Even the Romans, hardly innocent in the area of sexual perversions, were shocked by the immorality of the Phoenicians who lived at Carthage.

The "Curse of Ham"?

It was through Christian influence that slavery eventually disappeared in the Roman Empire, and through Christian influence yet again it was outlawed in Britain, through the work of Wilberforce and others in the early 1800s. Yet churches espousing the "curse of Ham"—possibly the most repeated "biblical" racist argument in the history of (lapsed) Christianity—used it to justify apartheid, white supremacy,[245] slavery, and other forms of institutionalized prejudice. Slaveholders, and even the occasional missionary, taught that Shem, Ham, and Japheth represent the races of Asians, blacks, and whites. Jesus was presumed white, though this is fallacious, since the people of the Near East are dark-complected Asiatics. Ham was black, so it is claimed, and Gen 9:18 states that he was the ancestor of the Canaanites, whom God commanded Israel to annihilate, so we are under no obligation to treat these inferior specimens of humanity with compassion or even justice. Historically, this interpretation has encouraged genocide, slavery, and exploitation.

26 He also said,
"Blessed by YAHWEH my God be Shem;
and let Canaan be his slave.
27 May God make space for Japheth,
and let him live in the tents of Shem;
and let Canaan be his slave."

The Curse on Canaan

Canaan, Ham's son, is mentioned five times in ten verses (9:18–27). At the time of Abraham (12:6), the Canaanites were in the (future) land of Israel, yet their behavior was not yet as egregiously wicked as we witness later, in Deut 7:1–6. This is yet another indicator that the account was written from the perspective of, and for the benefit of, God's people of the old covenant.

In v. 27 there is another wordplay (*yapht*, a play on *Yapheth* or *Japheth*). Noah has spoken his only words in the entire narrative—a curse. In sum, the "curse of Ham," which landed on Canaan (the *man*), must be seen in historical context. It is meant to prove that the inhabitants of Canaan (the *land*), into which the Israelites in Moses' day are to enter, do not deserve to live there. There was abundant evidence that this was the case—although not in the time of Abraham, when the sin of these people had not reached its full measure (Gen 15:16).[246]

28 After the flood Noah lived 350 years. 29 All the days of Noah were 950 years; and he died.

The "first family" of Adam, Eve, Cain, and Seth has its counterpart in a second "first family," consisting of Noah, his three sons, and the four wives. The areas into which they spread, and the peoples descended from them, are presented in Gen10, in the Table of Nations.

RECAP

Biblical Truths

- Yahweh, who initiates, loves, covenants, and forgives, takes no pleasure in destroying the wicked (Ezek 18:1–32). Yet at some point, even though he is slow to anger (Ex 34:6), divine judgment must fall.
- Sin affects multiple generations. Consider the impact of Noah's sin: Noah-Ham-Canaan-Canaanites-Israelites.
- Yahweh graciously relates to his people through covenants.

Points of Contact with Pagan Culture

- Population growth in accordance with the command to multiply (1:28) is something to be celebrated. This goes against the tenor of pagan mythology–with gods annoyed because there are too many humans. We may also recall Exodus 1, where population growth is suppressed by the Egyptians. The Hebrews had multiplied to the point of becoming a political threat, and Pharaoh wanted their growth to decelerate.
- In terms of sexual perversion in the ancient world, Ham does not rate favorably. Unfortunately, God's people are often negatively (fairly) compared to outsiders–who serve as a sort of mirror–to keep them humble. See Deut 9:4-6.

NT Connections

- Noah is described as "a herald of righteousness" (2 Pet 2:5). Whether by word or by example, he represented God in the midst of a corrupt society.

- While the NT does not reiterate the charge to "be fruitful and multiply" (Gen 1:28; 9:1, 7), Jesus does charge Christians to take the message to all creation–a different sort of multiplication (Mt 28:19; cf. Acts 5:14; 12:24).
- Christians are in a covenant relationship with God, the new testament in Christ's blood. See Heb 8.

Application

- If even a righteous man like Noah could become intoxicated, we need to be especially careful when it comes to the use of alcohol and pain medication.
- Sexual immorality should not even be rumored among followers of Christ (Eph 5:3). It is destructive, addictive, and easy to slip into. Whatever the nature of the perverse behavior of Ham, Gen 9 shows a negative impact affecting numerous generations.
- Love does not delight in evil, and it always protects (1 Cor 13:6-7 NIV)–the opposite of Ham's behavior (9:22).

---

241. Lev 7:26; 17:12; 19:26; also Deut 12:16, 23, 24; 15:23.
242. For several pieces on crime and punishment, see https://www.douglasjacoby.com/category/podcasts/various/crimepun1mp3/.
243. Walton, *Lost World of Adam and Eve*, 39. See also Laurence A. Turner, "The Rainbow as the Sign of the Covenant in Genesis XI.11–13," *Vetus Testamentum* XLIII (January 1993: No. 1): 119–122.
244. The *Aqhat Epic*, a Ugaritic work that would have been familiar to those first reading or hearing Genesis, says that the good son takes his father "by the hand when he is drunk, carries him when he is sated with wine" (Pritchard, A 1.32–33, *Ancient Near Eastern Texts*, 150). Various scholars see Ham's sin as homosexual incest (e.g., Wenham, Rethinking *Genesis 1–11*, 36n).
245. How may we counter white supremacy? It is assumed that Adam was a white man. Here is the thinking: Since "Adam" in Hebrew is the same word for both "mankind" and "red," and since blacks and other races don't have pinkish skin, nonwhites don't classify as human beings. They may belong to the animal kingdom, but they have no *soul.* Thus, it is unreasonable to claim that nonwhites have equal rights with whites. "Edom," another name for Esau and the nation of which he is ancestor, means "red, ruddy," and this is the same word as that for "man."

    Refutation: We're dealing with two different words in Hebrew. They have the same consonants (*'*, *d*, *m*) but different vowels (*ā*, *ā* vs. *ā*, *o*) and may be related etymologically, but they are listed separately in the Hebrew lexicon: (*'* is the consonant *aleph*, like the glottal stop.) The confusion arises because Hebrew words are normally written without vowels.

    'ādām = man, mankind; *'adāmāh* = ground, from which man was made

    'ādom = red, as the skin color of Esau. From an obsolete word for "tawny"

    As an illustration of our unfamiliarity with Hebrew, take the English words fever and favor. The consonants are the same (f, v, r), but the vowels are different (e, e vs. a, o). Are the two words related? No, but if you took out the vowels (as Hebrew was written without vowels) they could be confused. So it is with *'ādām/'adom*.

246. In its "full measure," the Canaanites were guilty not only of "squatting" on land deeded to the people of Israel, but also of human sacrifice, gang rape, bestiality, incest, and a wide range of injustices. For more, see Paul Copan, *Is God a Moral Monster? Making Sense of the Old Testament God* (Grand Rapids, MI: Baker, 2011); also, Paul Copan and Matthew Flannagan, *Did God Really Command Genocide?* (Grand Rapids, MI: Baker, 2014).

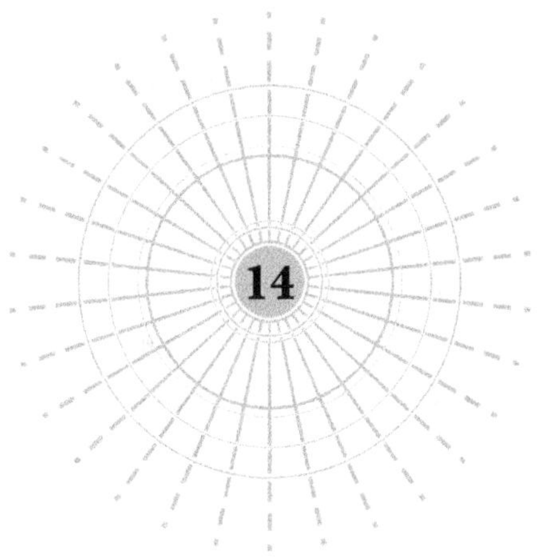

Repopulation

Table of Nations

Genesis 10 features a genealogical and geographical table commonly called the Table of Nations, focusing especially on the land of Canaan (10:15–19). This is because (1) the Canaanites are the people Israel had to deal with early in her history (the other nations would become more significant later in the OT), and (2) Noah's curse on Canaan must be located in a broader perspective. The Israelites, hearing Gen 9–10 read aloud, would have been strengthened in their conviction to fulfill their mission to claim the promised land and to live in obedience to Yahweh.

The list of seventy nations isn't intended to be comprehensive. Furthermore, it doesn't actually reflect Noah's generation but rather Moses' generation while Israel was a fledgling nation. Also, its primary focus is on the ancient Near East during the middle of the second millennium BC rather than nations beyond it.

[10:1]These are the descendants of Noah's sons, Shem, Ham, and Japheth; children were born to them after the flood.

[2]The descendants of Japheth: Gomer, Magog, Madai, Javan, Tubal, Meshech, and Tiras. [3]The descendants of Gomer: Ashkenaz, Riphath, and Togarmah. [4]The descendants of Javan: Elishah, Tarshish, Kittim, and Rodanim. [5]From these the coastland peoples spread. These are the descendants of Japheth in their lands, with their own language, by their families, in their nations.

Japheth

Japheth's line is detailed first. He is the eldest of the sons. It seems that in several instances, "sons of" pertains to a political or geographical connection, not direct blood relationship. In ancient times, sonship could refer to several kinds of relationships: by blood, adoption, or treaty.

Sometimes names do not refer to people at all, so much as to *peoples* or tribes (e.g., Kittim and Rodanim; Gen 10:4 and 1 Chr 1:7), and even to nations (e.g., Canaan, the grandson of Noah is said to have begotten the Jebusites, Amorites, etc.; Gen 10:16–18).[247] Other names are simply geographical references (e.g., Elishah, Tarshish; Gen 10:4 and 1 Chr 1:7) or cities (e.g., Sidon; Gen 10:15)—and yet the Jebusites are considered a distinct people group. Inclusion in genealogical records may be an implicit honor or a condemnation, as opposed to a fact requiring immediate biological connection.[248]

This first group consists of recognizable peoples. For example, Javan (v. 4) are the ancient Greeks. Notice they all have their own languages—more on this in our next chapter in the discussion of the tongues at Babel.

"These are the descendants of Japheth in their lands, with their own language, by their families, in their nations—*and their gods*" (v. 5). Those three words do not appear in the text, yet they are true insofar as each city, region, and country had their own distinctive divinities (as we discussed in Chapter 4).

Next, we come to the descendants of Ham, the youngest son.

> *[6]The descendants of Ham: Cush, Egypt, Put, and Canaan. [7]The descendants of Cush: Seba, Havilah, Sabtah, Raamah, and Sabteca. The descendants of Raamah: Sheba and Dedan. [8]Cush became the father of Nimrod; he was the first on earth to become a mighty warrior. [9]He was a mighty hunter before YAHWEH; therefore it is said, "Like Nimrod a mighty hunter before YAHWEH." [10]The beginning of his kingdom was Babel, Erech, and Accad, all of them in the land of Shinar. [11]From that land he went into Assyria, and built Nineveh, Rehoboth-ir, Calah, and [12]Resen between Nineveh and Calah; that is the great city.*
>
> *[13]Egypt became the father of Ludim, Anamim, Lehabim, Naphtuhim, [14]Pathrusim, Casluhim, and Caphtorim, from which the Philistines come. [15]Canaan became the father of Sidon his firstborn, and Heth, [16]and the Jebusites, the Amorites, the Girgashites, [17]the Hivites, the Arkites, the Sinites, [18]the Arvadites, the Zemarites, and the Hamathites. Afterward the families of the Canaanites spread abroad. [19]And the territory of the Canaanites extended from Sidon, in the direction of Gerar, as far as Gaza, and in the direction of Sodom, Gomorrah, Admah, and Zeboiim, as far as Lasha. [20]These are the descendants of Ham, by their families, their languages, their lands, and their nations.*

The Hamites—Egyptians, Assyrians, Philistines, and Canaanites—troubled the Israelites throughout OT history. They were the ones whom God used to chasten Israel. These names may mean little to us, but they were full of meaning for the Jews who read this part of Genesis. Later, the Babylonians, Assyrians, Greeks, and others played a larger role in Israelite history (10:10–11 [cities in Assyria and Babylon] and 10:14 [Philistines]). A complete commentary on Genesis would take each nation in turn and relate it to the flow of history in the OT.

Once again, the "sons of Ham" are not necessarily biologically related. Political bonds, linguistic commonalities, and other social connections often constituted sonship in the biblical sense. Many of the men mentioned are also actual nations (Cush, Egypt,[249] Put, and Canaan, for example, in 10:6). This is one more reason to be cautious in interpreting genealogies; a name doesn't necessarily mean just one person.

Nimrod (vv. 8–9) is a mighty hunter, with the possible implication that he was one of the Nephilim (6:4). (Refer to our discussion on hero figures in Chapter 11.)

It is unshocking that Sodom and Gomorrah are connected with Ham, given the sexual perversion and lack of love for their fellow humans about which we read in Gen 19. (See also Ezek 16:49.)

> *[21]To Shem also, the father of all the children of Eber, the elder brother of Japheth, children were born. [22]The descendants of Shem: Elam, Asshur, Arpachshad, Lud, and Aram. [23]The descendants of Aram: Uz, Hul, Gether, and Mash. [24]Arpachshad became the father of Shelah; and Shelah became the father of Eber. [25]To Eber were born two sons: the name of the one was Peleg, for in his days the earth was divided, and his brother's name was Joktan. [26]Joktan became the father of Almodad, Sheleph, Hazarmaveth, Jerah, [27]Hadoram, Uzal, Diklah, [28]Obal, Abimael, Sheba, [29]Ophir, Havilah, and Jobab; all these were the descendants of Joktan. [30]The territory in which they lived extended from Mesha in the direction of Sephar, the hill country of the east. [31]These are the descendants of Shem, by their families, their languages, their lands, and their nations.*

Last, the sons of Shem, the middle child, are listed. Cities (like Asshur) and countries (like Aram and Sheba) will be familiar to veteran Bible readers. The children of Eber (v. 21) are the Hebrews.

The lineage of Shem, although he is the youngest son of Noah, is given prominence. Again, this is a common biblical inversion: the elder or eldest child is not the most blessed, the honor going instead to the younger or youngest. (Isaac was younger than Ishmael, Jacob younger than Esau, Joseph younger than all his brothers except Benjamin, David also the youngest—of eight sons!) In this case, it is the middle child that is blessed. The blessings don't go only to the children born at the "ends" (eldest and youngest)—which itself would be a form of prejudice.

> [32]*These are the families of Noah's sons, according to their genealogies, in their nations; and from these the nations spread abroad on the earth after the flood.*

The "earth" over which the offspring of Noah spread out was the land within 1000 miles of the mountains of Ararat.[250] These mountains are about 800 miles (500 km) north of Babylon. Note that in 41:57 the area of the eastern Mediterranean (the ancient Near East, including part of North Africa) is called "all the world."

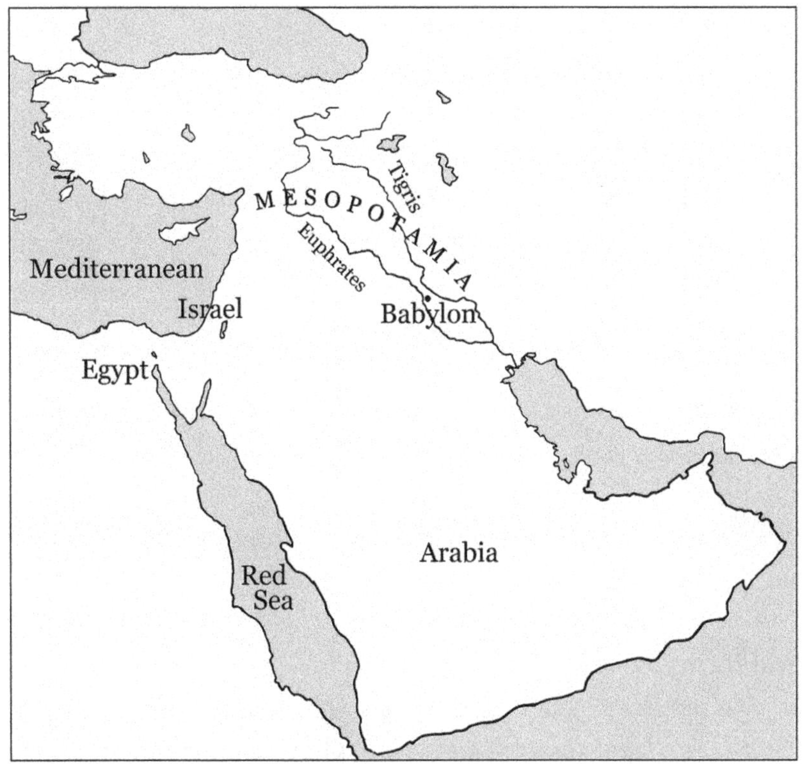

The World of Genesis 1-11

Here (v. 32) ends the fourth of the generations *(toledoth)* passages. (The fifth is at 11:10, just outside the range of our study in this book.) Remember, the book of Genesis is constructed around ten "generations."

Further Perspectives

- Chronologically, chapter 10 of Genesis *may follow* chapter 11, since the nations in chapter 10 have already acquired their own languages (10:5, 20, 31). Yet could this have happened in 11:9? The stories do not appear to be connected. It is probably best to let each account stand on its own, rather than risking a forced harmonization of the texts.
- There are 70 nations mentioned, just as there are 70 descendants of Noah's sons and 70 descendants of Jacob who go to Egypt (46:27).[251] This is probably no coincidence.
- The Table of Nations, inserted in the chapter before the birth of Abraham, spiritual father of the Jewish people, served as a reminder that God loves the Gentiles too—that he had purposes for them as well. Israel did not drop down out of heaven, but was taken right out of the heart of these heathen nations. Deut 9:4–6 was a later reminder of this fact, though it generally failed to elicit the intended effect: to keep Israel humble. A valuable lesson for us all.

In our next (and final) chapter, we will probe another narrative about the nations. On to Babylon.

RECAP

Biblical Truths

- We all belong to the same world and share common origins. We may not *act* like a "brotherhood of man," but it is God's will that we acknowledge our common origins and live like neighbors (not enemies).

- True kinship is not national or tribal, but association with kindred spirits. Some of these "spirits" are allies or trading partners of God's people (like Sidon and Sheba); most are not (like Magog, Assyria, and Canaan).
- God does not show favoritism. The firstborn may receive special treatment in traditional culture, but the Bible is full of countercultural inversions: the younger eclipsing the elder, women overshadowing men, smaller armies conquering larger ones, and so forth.
- Despite the destruction of the flood, God preserved the human race. The world is repopulated. God ensures the preservation of humankind.

Points of Contact with Pagan Culture

- Multiple names in the Table of Nations are cities in the eastern Mediterranean world: Nimrod (Nimrud), Nineveh, and Babylon.
- Multiple names in the Table are countries or lands, like Egypt, Aram (Syria), Cush, Havilah, Ophir, Magog, and Sheba.

NT Connections

- Just as "every nation under heaven" (Acts 2:5) doesn't refer to all the earth literally (rather, to the eastern half of the Roman Empire), so it is with the "earth" of Gen 10:32.
- Some of the peoples in the Table of Nations are known by different names or have been subsumed into other people groups by the time of the NT (the first century AD). For example, Uz[252] becomes part of Edom, and Javan (Ionians) are the Greeks.

Application

- Not everything is as it appears. A cursory reading of the Table of Nations would lead one to suppose the names refer to individual persons. Healthy respect for ancient culture, patience in studying the past, and openness to reconsidering cherished opinions all go a long way in learning how to read the Bible. And that is an activity and area in which none of us has "arrived."
- Let's make an effort to appreciate the different people groups of our own time. Becoming familiar with maps and atlases enables us to care for people

outside our immediate circle and to be more confident sharing our faith with persons from other nations.

---

247. Hill, "Making Sense of the Numbers of Genesis," 248.
248. If this strikes you as odd, consider this: Jesus called some of the Jewish leaders the sons (descendants) of Satan (Jn 8:44), just as John the Baptist called many of his generation a "brood of vipers" (Mt 3:7; Lk 3:7).
249. If we were demanding genetic accuracy, the Egyptians are Semites like the Hebrews. They are not Hamitic.
250. All these peoples lived in the Eastern Mediterranean region, at the intersection of Europe, Africa, and Asia. Why is there no mention of the people of India, who were known to people in the OT, and whose land is mentioned in Esth 1:1; 8:9? What about the aboriginal Australians, who have lived for 70,000 years on that island-continent? Or the New World, which never appears on any of the ancient maps? The "world" of Gen 10 is the *biblical* world—not necessarily coextensive with the entire landmass of the earth.
251. As we have often noticed, numerical motifs are common in Genesis—in this case, seven and its multiples.
252. Hebrew '*Ûts*.

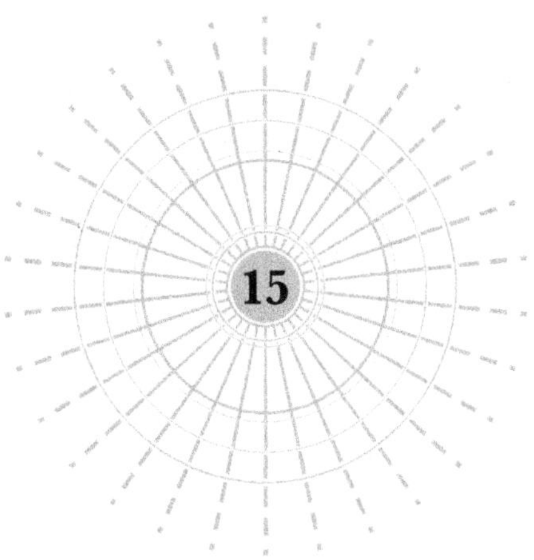

Recognition
Babel

We have arrived at the final segment in our study of Gen 1:1–11:9, to Babel.[253] The phrase "Tower of Babel" is familiar the world over, yet the account is far richer than most realize. This story, as with every biblical story, must be appreciated in its context. God had rescued the family of Noah, his descendants spreading out and repopulating the world. They grew strong in numbers, but weak in spirituality. They failed to appreciate Yahweh's grace, and in time, a self-assured, humanistic outlook on life took root. Somewhat predictably, people soon quested after the same object sought by Eve and Adam: the right to be master of one's own destiny.

> *11:1 Now the whole earth had one language and the same words.*
> *2 And as they migrated from the east they came upon a plain in the*
> *land of Shinar and settled there. 3 And they said to one another,*
> *"Come, let us make bricks, and burn them thoroughly." And they had*
> *brick for stone, and bitumen for mortar. 4 Then they said, "Come, let*

> *us build ourselves a city, and a tower with its top in the heavens, and let us make a name for ourselves; otherwise we shall be scattered abroad upon the face of the whole earth."*

The whole world (as sketched in Gen 10) had one common language (which is not the picture in Gen 10). They understood one another. They came to the plain of Shinar (Sumer, land of the Sumerians)—which is to say, they congregated in Babylon.

Were they restless? Recall that Adam had to leave Eden, an "exile." Cain became a fugitive too. Noah was carried far away by the surging flood. And now *his* descendants are wandering, seeking security. If only they would seek a city with *true* foundations (Heb 11:10). Instead, weary of travel, they aim to put down roots—urban roots (see 4:17)—and make a name for themselves.

Their project will be rendered in brick.[254] Their common cause: to build a city, and particularly a tower. In this cause, they were united. Unity is desirable, provided those unified are inclined toward God. But this was hardly the situation at Babel. Humankind was still on the run from Yahweh. The Tower of Babel was to be a monument to human ego and reputation ("make a name"), not a memorial to Yahweh. No tower—or system, state, or political power—has the right to lay claim to the soul, for this undermines faith, creativity, authenticity, and other elements of human thriving. Yahweh will not tolerate the tyranny of totalitarianism.

The tower was almost certainly one of the dozens of ziggurats (stepped pyramids) discovered in the region of Babylonia, for example, the great stepped pyramid of Etemenanki. These were massive, sacred mountains (not natural, but manmade). Unlike pyramids, ziggurats were filled with rubble—there are no tunnels and chambers within. An inscription relating to a later ziggurat in Babylon describes it as "the building whose top is in heaven." Archaeologists have also identified stepped pyramids outside Mesopotamia and in Egypt, Guatemala, Indonesia, Italy, Mexico, Nigeria, Peru, and even the United States (Illinois). The steps make the pyramids easier to construct and easier to ascend—no need to posit the activity of aliens.

Ziggurats

Ziggurats were temple-topped towers. To help us visualize, the *Zondervan Cultural Backgrounds Study Bible* has an excellent online graphic.[255]

Facts about Ziggurats

- Ziggurat is from the Akkadian *ziqqurat*, meaning "temple tower" or "mountain peak."
- These were stepped pyramids.
- They were stairways from the heavens so that the gods could come down to earth, visit the temple and its town, and bring blessing.[256]
- They included a place (at the top) for the divine visitors to eat and rest. Note: followers of the god were not allowed inside the complex (except for priests).
- Babylonian religion was heavily focused on astrology, which was facilitated atop the ziggurats.[257]
- They dominated the skyline of the region from roughly 2100 BC till sometime in the Persian period (6th–4th centuries BC).
- The Ziggurat of Ur (c. 2100 BC), birthplace of Abraham (c. 2000 BC), was a site of moon worship.[258]
- The cuneiform text *Summa Alu* (literally, "If a city...") speaks of impending doom hanging over cities or towers built too high.[259]
- Such stepped pyramids appeared in numerous regions of the ancient world, not just in the ancient Near East.

As we have seen, Gen 1–11 is in dialogue with ancient Near Eastern culture, although it has radically reworked the story. What about Babel? *Enuma Elish* begins with the creation account of the Babylonians, proceeds with the building of Babylon, and ends with the construction of the temple of

Marduk, king of gods in the Babylonian pantheon.[260] There is a loose literary connection. The temple of Marduk, built by the Annunaki gods, was made using special bricks. This raises the possibility that Gen 11:1–9 is a spoof on *Enuma Elish.*[261]

There is no tower among the polytheistic background narratives, but there is still a direct connection between the Tower of Babel and ancient Babylonia, and it is archaeological. It is written in bricks—not stone.

> *5YAHWEH came down to see the city and the tower, which mortals had built. 6And YAHWEH said, "Look, they are one people, and they have all one language; and this is only the beginning of what they will do; nothing that they propose to do will now be impossible for them. 7Come, let us go down, and confuse their language there, so that they will not understand one another's speech." 8So YAHWEH scattered them abroad from there over the face of all the earth, and they left off building the city. 9Therefore it was called Babel, because there YAHWEH confused the language of all the earth; and from there YAHWEH scattered them abroad over the face of all the earth.*

Even though the Tower was meant to reach the heavens, its penetration into the celestial sphere was minuscule. Strictly speaking, ziggurats were more for the gods to visit the world of humans than for humans to ascend to the heavens. The Lord has to "come down" to see the tower—so small is it, so far short of the lofty purpose for which it was built. The tower in Babel must not be completed; the God of love refuses to let man self-destruct again. After the fall, God set cherubim in place, flaming swords brandished. At Babel, he confounds the common tongue of the human race and creates division—which functions as a form of protection against ourselves. After God's intervention, work on the city grinds to a halt. People spoke past one another. Without clear communication, no major undertaking can be accomplished.

God is not scattering them because he condemns unity or unified action, so much as because together his unruly children were engaging in mischief.

(At times parents must separate children who are misbehaving.)[262] They had removed their faith from Yahweh and placed it in self.

Confounding of Tongues

Throughout Gen 1–11 the pagan myths have been parodied. The Babylonian god Enki is making mischief,[263] preventing humans from speaking the same language—for no *moral* reason. He is not protecting humans from the consequences of foolish decisions, as Yahweh does in Gen 11:1–9. So it is with the Babylonian flood, sent to drown the noisy humans, heedlessly disturbing the gods' sleep.

In the Bible there is a moral reason for the flood: the sin of violence (6:5, 11). And at Babel, human pride is the reason the tongues of humankind are confounded. Indeed, we get a hint of something negative early on as the people of the land migrated "eastward" (11:2 NIV)—the direction you *don't* want to go in Genesis, as we've noted earlier.

The Sumerian epic entitled *Enmerkar and the Lord of Aratta* tells of a time when all spoke the same tongue, as do the Epic Tales of Lugalbanda and Gilgamesh (the original forms of which were circulating during the twenty-first century BC). The confounding of tongues, then, was well known in the Mesopotamian religion.[264]

There's a play on the Hebrew word *bābel*. In the Akkadian original, it may be intended to mean "gate of God." In the wordplay, it is connected with *bālal*, the verb "to confuse."[265] They are really "babbling" now, their message "blah, blah, blah." In the consistent style of Genesis, heathen notions and names are parodied and exposed as powerless and empty. God's word effectively strips the mythology from the pagan beliefs and accounts. Having removed the clutter of manmade religion and superstition, he brings his word to us.

As we've seen, another wordplay is on Shem (*shēm* means "name"). One line of Shem brings us to Babel, where they say, "Come, let us… make a name [*shēm*] for ourselves" (11:4). The other line leads to Abraham, who by faith leaves the Babylonian region; he obeys the God who promises to "make [Abraham's] name [*shēm*] great" (12:2).

Dangerous Parallels

What was so dangerous about the brewing situation in Babel that God had to "go down" and act so dramatically? Babel was where "the wicked prowl, as vileness is exalted among humankind" (Ps 12:8). It doesn't take any special genius to notice the parallels with modern society. If we could voyage back through time, the city would seem eerily familiar:

- Haughty, humanistic thinkers who flatter themselves "too much to detect or hate" their own sin (Ezek 16:50; Ps 36:2 NIV). As with the king of Babylon, overweening pride precedes a fall (Isa 14:13–15).
- "Guilty people, whose own strength is their god" (Hab 1:11 NIV). Instead of humbly trusting Yahweh, people place confidence in money (economic power), might (military power), muscle (physical power), and mind (brain power).
- A place where family is sacrificed for career, lust is confused with love, free time is lived for self, and faith seasons—but does not guide—everyday life.
- A time when the system of technology is honored more than people. "The fusion of science and technology means that increasingly the moral decision as to the uses of truth will be made preemptively before the truth is even sought; we seek only truth which fits our purposes."[266]

None of us is immune to the attractions of Babel. It's easy to be wowed by technology, whether the latest iPhone or the space program to Mars. And how easy it is to live life in modern society without a sense of dependence on God. With automation, convenience, and control in an increasingly depersonalized, fragmented, and alienated society, we can fall into the trap of becoming practical atheists, despite the Christian creeds we verbally confess. Yet technology is not our savior! We live longer, but are humans today happier emotionally than 200 years ago? 2000? We must be realistic about science, with all its limitations and the narrow strip of reality it engages; it must not be worshiped as some sort of redeemer. Indeed, living by science alone will result in a stripping away of our own humanness—purpose, meaning, human dignity and rights, personhood, awe, wonder, beauty, goodness, moral duties, loving. Our world has been disenchanted and needs reenchanting.

It's also easy to compare one Christian to another and one church to another, and to commend or criticize them depending on the criteria we have assumed God values most. Yet when we slip into humanistic thinking, when we Christians measure ourselves by ourselves, we are not wise (Col 2:4, 8; 2 Cor 10:12).

We are not to be overawed by human institutions, nor are we to preach a system, but Christ alone. As Paul declared, "For we do not proclaim ourselves; we proclaim Jesus Christ as Lord and ourselves as your slaves for Jesus' sake" (2 Cor 4:5).

Of course, pride resides not only in "church people," but to some extent in all of us. It is arrogant to claim all the credit for who we are and what we possess (1 Cor 4:7). God exposes the Babylonians' arrogance—even as ancient Rome later came under the judgment of God and fell. And like Rome, so Western culture today is reeling under a spreading moral rot threatening to undermine its very foundations. Today it seems our "advanced" society is "united"—in hedonism, narcissism, ingratitude, and moral compromise (Rom 1:21). Naturally, unity can be a terrific blessing—or a terrible curse. Unity is a blessing if the cause is noble and just. Otherwise, it is a menace.

Babylon in the Bible

According to the Greek historian Herodotus, "In magnificence there is no other city that approaches [Babylon]." The city was famed for its Hanging Gardens–one of the Seven Wonders of the Ancient World–in addition to its numerous canals, massive walls, beautiful temples, and proud citizens. Yet Babylon is more than just an ancient kingdom whose capital city bears the same name. In both testaments, Babylon is associated with the folly of human pride and the vanity of achievement apart from God:

- The story of the Tower of Babel (Gen 11) is a satirical, biting tract against the hubris of Babylon.
- The overthrow of Babylon is compared to the demise of Sodom, which itself is like the original fall from grace (Isa 13:19; 14:12).
- The prophets Jeremiah and Habakkuk continue the theme of God's opposition to human pride. Daniel, too, exposes the vanity of power and sovereignty apart from God (Dan 4–5).
- Peter refers to Rome as "Babylon" (1 Pet 5:13). The book of Revelation also compares the Roman Empire to Babylon, which by extension serves as a symbol of the world. We are warned, "Come out of her" (Rev 18:4).[267]

Pentecost: Babel in Reverse

Things look gloomy. Fortunately, thanks (again) to God's initiative, the future isn't necessarily completely bleak. The next section of Genesis brings us to the life of Abraham, the towering figure of the second part of the book, a man of faith and father of the faithful (Rom 4:16).

Yet from the perspective of Genesis, the full, grand reversal of Babel is yet to take place long after the era of Abraham—at Pentecost (Acts 2). The scattered nations (with their manifold tongues) will once again be united, with communication clear and purpose pure. Pentecost is Babel in reverse.[268] The vision of the prophet would be fulfilled:

> *At that time I will change the speech of the peoples*
> *to a pure speech,*
> *that all of them may call on the name of YAHWEH*
> *and serve him with one accord (Zeph 3:9).*

As long as we trust the Lord, instead of putting our faith in structures, plans, and systems—there is hope.

Recognition and Renown

With the warnings of Babel resounding in our minds, let us keep our eyes fixed on Christ as we run with determination the race before us (Heb 12:1–2). He calls us to preserve the unity of the Spirit in the bond of peace (Eph 4:3), and he himself models self-sacrificial humility to inspire us toward spiritual like-mindedness.

RECAP

Biblical Truths

- God is ultimate, not the state.
- Technology is to be used first of all in the service of God, not for self or even for society.
- As with the flood, the intervention at Babel takes place not because of pettiness or caprice, but because humans inhabit a moral universe and threaten to destroy themselves.
- The Lord may intervene when our schemes and poor decisions spell ruin. This should be seen as a gracious act more than a punitive one.

Points of Contact with Pagan Culture

- Several ancient sources refer to a confounding of tongues.
- Ziggurats, towers to the heavens, were common in the ancient Near East. The Babel story parodies this aspect of Babylonian religion.
- Shinar (Sumer), brickwork, and the word *bālal* all connect the reader (or listener) with Babylon.

NT Connections

- Pentecost (Acts 2) is Babel (Gen 11) in reverse.
- Babylon in the OT is Rome in the NT. (Is there a "Babylon" today?)

Application

- We should check ourselves from time to time to ensure we are not in greater awe of any person, organization, economic system, or social or political cause than we are of God. Christ is the Savior, not science, technology, intellect, education, or society.
- Religion and superstition that aim to divine the future (astrology and horoscopes, bogus "prophecy," etc.) are failures to have faith in God. We may not know what the future holds, but we know him who holds the future.
- The Genesis story was well informed by the thought systems of its day, with which it intelligently interacted. We should do the same.
- It is God's name that is supreme. Therefore, seeking a name for oneself will generally conflict with the pursuit of holiness. As the Lord warned Baruch, "And you, do you seek great things for yourself? Do not seek them" (Jer 45:5a). Godly greatness is not the same as worldly greatness.

The Rest of Genesis

As for the rest of Genesis, a supplement to these fifteen chapters is accessible (and free) online.[269]

A Final Word

We have seen that Genesis 1–11 runs close to the pagan background narrative: the creation of the cosmos, the creation of humans, the mortality of the human condition, the long ages of the antediluvians, notions of heroism, the flood, and the tower (ziggurat). These points of contact serve to strengthen our faith, once we realize that many facets of the primeval narrative were recognized by ancient peoples.

As discussed near the beginning of the book, biblical theology is most visible at the points where the story has been recast. We also noted that we can spot the differences from the original *only* if we are familiar with the original. By now the background narrative should be abundantly familiar, and the conclusion is obvious: the pagan idolatries have nothing to offer. Compared to the true religion of Yahweh, the false gods are exposed as worthless.

The true God towers far above the false gods in every way. Where they show caprice, he offers compassion; where they are unpredictable, he is logical; where they are inconsistent, he is trustworthy; where they are immoral, he is righteous; where they are dependent upon human support, our God is the One upon whom humans can forever depend; where they are weak, he is powerful beyond reckoning.

The opening book of Scripture is hardly our only resource for knowing and engaging the world, for we have in our possession far more than just Genesis. We have the entire OT and NT, the record of twenty centuries of church history (the successes and blunders of which should make us more effective—and humble), and a more profound knowledge of the natural world—a world that strongly suggests a Creator. He is willing to adapt his terminology and presentation of complex concepts to help his creations better embrace his truth.

Genesis shined a spotlight on the empty human religion, philosophy, and tradition of its day (see Col 2:8; 1 Pet 1:18). And now that you better grasp the broader cultural context in which Genesis was written, we hope you will never read—or share—Genesis the same way again.

---

253. Much of the discussion of Babel has been adapted from https://www.douglasjacoby.com/the-tower-of-babel/.
254. There is a wordplay in v. 3: *'eben* (stone) and *chomer* (mortar) are the building materials in Israel. But in Mesopotamia, where stone is rarer, builders use *lebhenah* (brick) and *chemar* (bitumen). Josephus informs us that some of the walls of Babylon were built of brick and bitumen, others of brick only (Josephus, *Against Apion* 1.19.139).
255. http://d3iqwsql9z4qvn.cloudfront.net/wp-content/uploads/2017/08/11134517/NIV-CBSB-Babel-Infographic1.jpg.
256. Longman and Walton clarify:

    > The idea that the stairways of the ziggurat were meant for the god to come down is evidenced in the Mesopotamian myth "Nergal and Ereshkigal," where the messenger of the gods descends from heaven down to the netherworld by means of a stairway... The connection of this mythical stairway to ziggurats is specified by the name of the ziggurat at Sippar: "Sacred Place of the Pure Stairway to Heaven." The Akkadian stairway is *simmiltu*, cognate to Hebrew *sullām*—the word describing the ladder/ stairway that Jacob sees in his dream, Gen 28:10–12.

    Lost World of the Flood, 136.
257. Until the last few centuries, there was no distinction between astronomy (a legitimate science) and astrology (pure superstition).
258. The moon god is *Sin*, or *Nanna*.

259. For one of the websites where you may see ancient cuneiform texts (Akkadian), explore http://ccp.yale.edu/omen-series-summa-alu.
260. The temple of Marduk was named *Ésagil* ("the great house"), and Babylon's ziggurat was called *Étemenanki* ("the house of the foundation of heaven and earth").
261. "The Ésagila was the temple of Marduk, king of the gods and protector of Babylon. The Ésagila complex was supposed to be 'the Mecca of Mesopotamia.'" Wenham, *Genesis 1–15*, 244.
262. As suggested in Walton, Matthews, and Chavalas, *The IVP Bible Background Commentary: Old Testament*, 42.
263. Enki is not unlike Loki, the trickster god in the Norse pantheon.
264. Sparks notes, "Folded into the tale [of Emmerkar] are two linguistic etiologies, one that made Emmerkar the inventor of written language and letters, and another that credited the wise god Enki for the origins of human languages, which he apparently created by confusing languages in a manner akin to that described in Gen 11." Sparks, *Ancient Texts*, 273. Sparks is referring to the Mesopotamian account of *Enmerkar and the Lord of Aratta*, as found in Walter Beyerlin, *Near Eastern Religious Texts Relating to the Old Testament* (Philadelphia, PA: Westminster Press, 1978), 86–87.
265. *Bālal* also sounds like the words for folly and flood!
266. W. Thorson, "The Spiritual Dimensions of Science," in C. F. Henry, ed., *Horizons of Science* (New York: Harper and Row, 1978), 217–218. Cited in Atkinson, *Message of Genesis 1–11*, 180.
267. Frank Viola expresses it well:

    > All said, Babylon is not your native habitat. It's a counterfeit of the house of God. If we learn nothing else from the Babylonian captivity, let us learn this: Many of God's people are living in Babylon today.... The Lord will never build His house in a foreign land. His ultimate passion can only be fulfilled when His people leave that fallen system.... In essence, the principle of Babylon is to declare independence from God and to build community without Him. This is the principle that drove Cain, the first city builder. Cain left the presence of God and built a city on his own (Gen 4:16–17). It's what drove Nimrod, Cain's descendant, to build Babel (Gen 10:9–10).

    Frank Viola, *From Eternity to Here: Rediscovering the Ageless Purpose of God* (Colorado Springs, CO: David C. Cook, 2009), 187.
268. Further evidence that in Acts 2 Luke is thinking of Babel are his use of three terms from the LXX of Gen 11:7: *glōssan*, language; *phōnēn*, sound; *syncheōmen*, confound.
269. Access from http://www.paulcopan.com/articles/ or directly at https://www.douglasjacoby.com/rest-of-genesis.

Postscript

A Caution to Teachers

Those of us who teach must take special care when we aim to shape the ideas of our students—whether they are children in a Sunday school class, young believers, or even older Christians who are uncomfortable breaking out of paradigms that have been shown to be inaccurate. We are responsible for how we affect others—which is why James tells us teachers will be judged more strictly (Jas 3:1). Paul urged us not to let our knowledge become the means of destroying someone else's faith. Jesus said our carelessness may cost us dearly (Mt 12:36–37).

Even if God's word is a like a hammer (Jer 23:29), we are not to club people with the truth—but gently bring them into the kingdom (Mt 11:28–30). With this in mind, the following is a word of admonition.

Knowledge Can Be Dangerous

Why the caution? Because if you're a Bible lover, you desire to share what you have learned with anyone who will listen, and as soon as possible. Granted, most of what we learn in the Bible may not be inherently dangerous; still, we are to handle it with care.

While many of you are familiar with most of the stories of Genesis, we suspect there are those of you who have encountered much new content here. We have learned about polytheistic pagan narratives, the interpretation of creation accounts, the meaning of numbers like 930 and 120, ancient cosmology, and symbolism in Gen 1–11. (Let's be realistic: how many members of your church have you heard talking about ziggurats or Gilgamesh or Marduk?) Hence the caution—really, an appeal for pastoral sensitivity—is in order. Let's be careful not to teach anything that may be perceived as an attack on the faith.

> *Jesus said to his disciples, "Occasions for stumbling are bound to come, but woe to anyone by whom they come! It would be better for you if a millstone were hung around your neck and you were thrown into the sea than for you to cause one of these little ones to stumble" (Lk 17:1–2).*

The Lord expects us to be considerate not just to children or new believers, but to anyone who could end up stumbling (falling). While we can cause others to stumble by our example—what we *do*—it is often what we *say* that brings them to spiritual harm.

> *So, whether you eat or drink, or whatever you do, do everything for the glory of God. Give no offense to Jews or to Greeks or to the church of God, just as I try to please everyone in everything I do, not seeking my own advantage, but that of many, so that they may be saved. Be imitators of me, as I am of Christ (1 Cor 10:31–11:1).*

"Be imitators of me" does not refer to Paul's knowledge of philosophy or his travel schedule. Consider the context. In the three chapters spanning 1 Cor 8:1–11:1, Paul calls on us to waive our rights. The subject here is eating meat sacrificed to idols, a practice that promotes idolatry and damages many believers spiritually. (Paul says don't!) In Rom 14–15 the focus is broader. We have taken the liberty of tweaking several parts of the following passage. (This is not a new translation, or even a paraphrase; it's an application.)

> [14:1]Welcome those who are weak in faith, but not for the
> purpose of quarreling over opinions...
>
> [13]Let us therefore no longer pass judgment on one another,
> but resolve instead never to put a stumbling block or hindrance in
> the way of another. [14]I know and am persuaded in the Lord Jesus
> that God accommodated Genesis for an ancient audience. It makes
> perfect sense to me that appreciating symbolism brings us closer to
> understanding God's revelation—that "symbolic" in no way means
> "untrue." Yet my teaching is both false and dangerous for the one
> who cannot imagine it could be biblical. [15]If your brother or sister
> is being injured by your theology, you are no longer walking in
> love. Do not let your viewpoint cause the ruin of one for whom
> Christ died.... [17]For the kingdom of God is not about history and
> geography and theology, but righteousness and peace and joy in
> the Holy Spirit. [18]The one who thus serves Christ in this spirit is
> acceptable to God—and to others. [19]Let us then pursue what makes
> for peace and mutual upbuilding. [20]Do not, for the sake of correct
> formulations or scientific accuracy, destroy the work of God.... [22]The
> faith that you have, have as your own conviction before God. Blessed
> are those who have no reason to condemn themselves because of
> what they approve....
>
> [15:1] We who are strong ought to put up with the failings of
> the uninformed, the vulnerable, or those with a simple faith—and
> not to please ourselves. [2]Each of us must please our neighbor for
> the good purpose of building up the neighbor. [3]For Christ did not
> please himself....
>
> [5]May the God of steadfastness and encouragement grant you
> to live in harmony with one another (Rom 14:1, 13–15, 17–20a, 22;
> 15:1–3a, 5a).

Stumbling or Grumbling?

Of course, there is a difference between stumbling and grumbling. Some people are simply disagreeable, and they expect everyone to concur with their opinions. They may claim that you have offended their religion, when all you have done is to point out weaknesses in their thinking. You cannot please the grumblers—with their ranting, fuming, and labeling—so don't worry about it (Rom 12:18). On the other hand, the Lord forbid that we should cause someone to stumble.

Teaching on Two Levels

Jesus taught what people could absorb—which means he frequently instructed on two levels. He spoke to outsiders, but seldom the same way he spoke to insiders. Nor did he share everything he knew on a subject, in accordance with the audience and their capacity to take in what he was saying.

> *With many such parables he spoke the word to them, as they were able to hear it; he did not speak to them except in parables, but he explained everything in private to his disciples (Mk 4:33-34).*

To teach in such a manner requires self-control. It is easy to say too much, whether overloading a class or sermon, going off on tangents, or bringing up subjects that deserve a full class or two—not a minute or two! We know all about teaching something we now wish we could take back—many times over.

Teaching on two levels is in no way deceptive, but *selective*. We seldom present every aspect of a passage or a doctrine or a biblical theme. Every teacher makes choices—what to include and what to exclude. Besides, as we see in the ministry of Jesus, there are often further opportunities for those with more-than-average interest in the subject to learn more.

The teacher or preacher has no choice: for a class or sermon to have maximum impact, it must be simplified, although often to us who teach it may feel oversimplified. We will serve our hearers best if we keep this in mind: "Wise men always know more than they tell, but fools tell more than they know."

Other Useful Materials

In the final section of the book, you will find two diagrams to help us envision the world as conceived by most people living in biblical times and before, followed by a closer look at the genealogies found in Genesis 5–11.

Next comes an appendix on the nature of God's revelation. The belief under review is that God only communicates in one way—through Scripture. The notion that God's truth is restricted to only one location (the Old and New Testaments) is itself not a biblical idea, as will be demonstrated. This is not to undermine the authority of Scripture, but to enhance it.

At the very end of the book you will find a short bibliography of useful books, websites, videos, and courses.

Appendix A

Ancient Cosmology

An Appeal for Honesty

It is highly tempting for us Bible believers to read our own interpretation into Scripture. We have all done it. And it's especially easy to read modern scientific concepts into ancient texts, particularly the Bible. Instead, let's take a (perhaps corrective) look at the common cosmology of ancient times.[270]

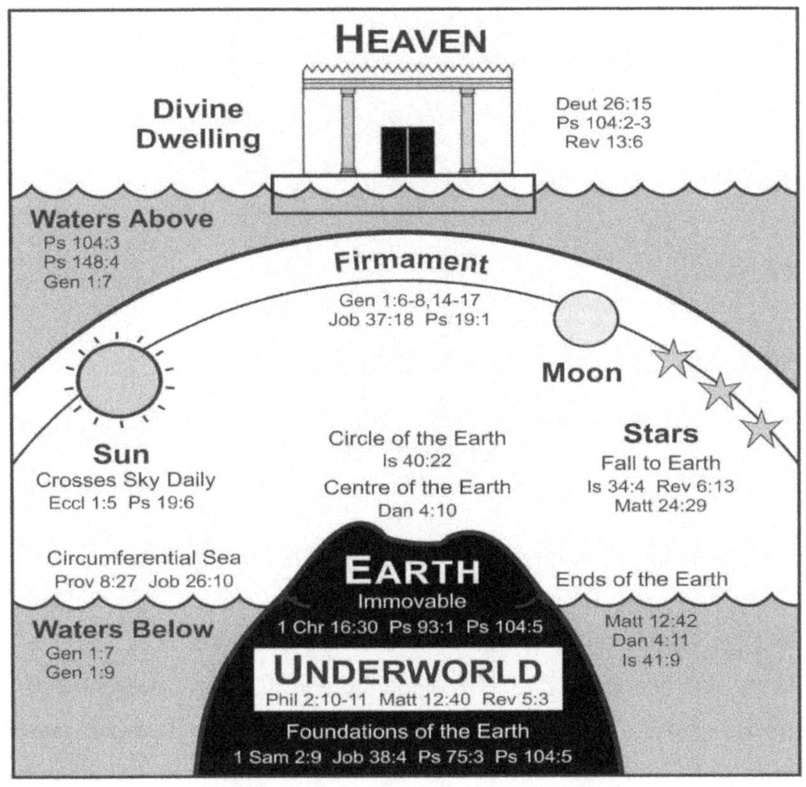

Gen 1 speaks of a firmament ("dome" in the NRSV). Some of us were taught that this was an old-fashioned word for the sky. Later, once we had studied Hebrew, we learned that these are different words—and they are not synonyms.[271] The firmament is *firm.* But there's more. Genesis speaks of a celestial freshwater ocean above the firmament (for which reason the sky is blue). Floodgates in the firmament allow the passage of water as rain. There are also floods beneath the earth, fountains of the deep. In Noah's flood, both sources are opened up, the waters converging on and overwhelming the earth—which was flat.[272] The Babylonian *Imago Mundi* map (written in cuneiform and dating to the sixth century BC) is one of several ancient sources demonstrating this view of the cosmos.[273]

Imago Mundi (image of the world) map, Babylonia, 6th cent. BC

Does This Clash with What You've Been Taught?

There is abundant scriptural evidence for the view presented in this appendix, besides the evidence of ancient maps and drawings (not presented in this book).[274] Not that this is the only area where what was accepted as plain fact in ancient times cannot be harmonized with modern ideas. Views on the functions of human organs give us one such example.[275] Honesty requires us to weigh all the scriptural material, not to support a twenty-first-century view, but to see the world as the ancients saw it and to grasp how God accommodated his revelation to speak first to an ancient people who had this world picture. Perhaps we could compare it to meteorologists using the phenomenological (appearance) language of "sunrise" and "sunset," though these terms are not technically accurate.

---

270. This diagram also appears in Stanley N. Gundry, ed. *Four Views on The Historical Adam* (Grand Rapids, MI: Zondervan, 2013), 44. Used with permission.
271. Sky is *shāmayim*—which also means heaven and heavens. Firmament is *rāqiya'*, and refers to beaten metal. Its literal meaning is "extended solid surface," as in Gen 1:6 (see entry in *The Enhanced Brown-Driver-Briggs Hebrew and English Lexicon*). In English Bibles it is rendered "sky" (inaccurate—although closely connected [Gen 1:8]), "expanse" (misleading), "vault" or "dome" (correct though interpretive as to its shape), and "firmament" (Lat. for an extended solid surface). Sometimes translators devise highly clever explanations. In commenting on Gen 1:6, the NET Bible claims, "The Hebrew word refers to an expanse of air pressure between the surface of the sea and the clouds, separating water below from water above" (NET [New English Translation]: Second Beta Edition [www.netbible.com, 2003], p.3, n11). Yet there is nothing about "air pressure" in Gen 1, or for that matter anywhere in the Bible; this is obviously a move to prevent Gen 1 from clashing with modern science. The ancient versions are generally more faithful. The Greek OT (LXX) translated *rāqiya'* as *stereōma*, from *stereos*, the adjective for solid, hard, firm. Thus, Jews and Christians reading Greek, Latin, and Hebrew originally shared a common understanding.
272. For more on the Flat Earth, you might enjoy Q&A 1487, at https://www.douglasjacoby.com/qa-1487-flat-earth/.
273. Cuneiform inscription and map, BM 92687, British Museum, London, used with permission. Accessible at https://traveltoeat.com/wp-content/uploads/2012/08/wpid-Photo-Aug-31-2012-435-PM.jpg. See also Wayne Horowitz, *Mesopotamian Cosmic Geography* (Winona Lake, IN: Eisenbrauns, 1998), 321.
274. (1) Waters above the firmament (Gen 1:7; Ps 104:3; 148:4). (2) The sun moving across sky daily (Eccl 1:5; Ps 19:6; Josh 10:13). (3) The circle (not sphere) of the earth (Isa 40:22)—from above the earth appears circular. (4) The center of the earth (Dan 4:10). (5) The waters beneath the earth (Gen 1:7, 9). (6) The firmament—a solid, hemispherical dome (Gen 1:6–8, 14–19; Ps 19:1; Job 37:18). (7) Stars falling to the earth—therefore much smaller than the earth (Isa 34:4; Rev 6:13; Mt 24:29). (8) The earth has "ends" (50x, e.g., Isa 41:9; Dan 4:11; Mt 12:42). (9) The earth is immovable (1 Chr 16:30; Ps 93:1; 104:5). (10) There is a literal underworld (Phil 2:10–11; Rev 5:3, 13). (11) The earth is set atop foundations (25x, e.g., 1 Sam 2:8; Job 38:4; Ps 75:3; 104:5). (12) Heaven is above the firmament and the celestial ocean (Ps 104:2–3; Deut 26:15).
275. The Egyptians preserved most of the mummy's organs—but threw away the brain. The heart is rarely referred to in the OT, but the kidneys ("reins" in the KJV) were considered the site of emotion and intellect. Paul assures Philemon that Onesimus is Paul's very bowels (not heart, in the NT Greek). Many more examples could be given. For more on the kidneys, see the article at https://www.douglasjacoby.com/kidneys-in-the-bible/.

Appendix B

The Geocentric Universe

An Appeal for Honesty (Again)

Just as it may be difficult to unlearn what we have been taught about the (ancient) biblical view of the earth, so again it may be challenging (embarrassing?) to admit that the Bible never bothers to correct the geocentric view, which was common in most cultures until the seventeenth century. Yet God is the God of truth. This may be put another way: all truth is God's truth—as Augustine and Aquinas pointed out.

Scriptures Supporting the Geocentric View

A multitude of Bible passages justify the geocentric view (Greek *gē*, earth + *kentron*, sharp point [center]), as opposed to the heliocentric view (Greek *hēlios*, sun). The sun moves across the sky daily (Eccl 1:5; Ps 19:6; Josh 10:13), while the earth is immovable (1 Chr 16:30; Ps 93:1; 104:5). It was on the basis of passages like these that Galileo was challenged by some senior churchmen, convinced that their interpretation was the most logical, literal, scientific, and biblical. (How might *we* have reasoned had we lived in the early seventeenth century?) Eventually the weight of new discoveries and the simplicity of the new paradigm led to wholesale abandonment of the clunky system of cycles and epicycles relied upon to bolster the "biblical" view of the cosmos, depicted below.[276]

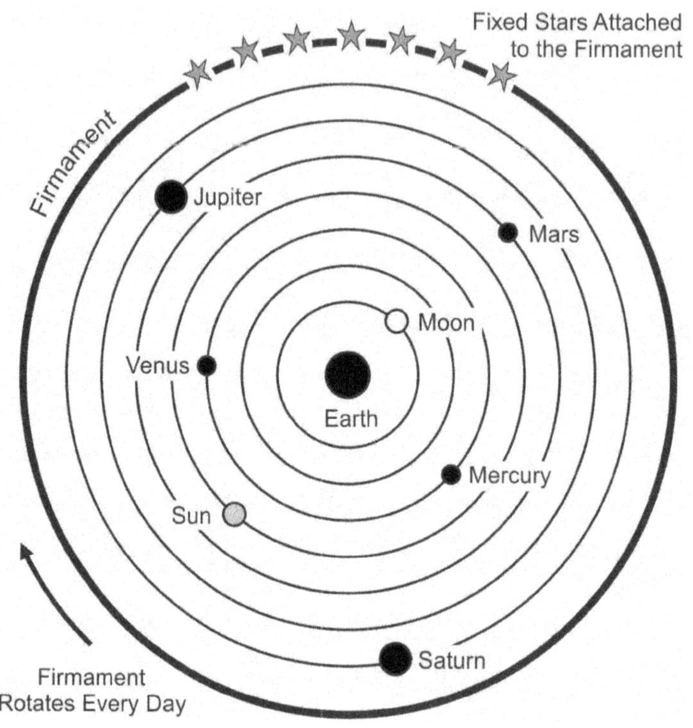

Clarity

Galileo, building on the work of Copernicus,[277] gave us not only the telescope, but also a more comprehensive appreciation of our part of the universe.[278] The truth is, Galileo's observations did not discredit the Bible; rather, they discredited the wrong way in which it was being interpreted at the time. Both sides of the uproar believed in God and the Bible; the debate wasn't over whether God created the world.[279] In fact, Galileo, in a 1615 letter to the Duchess Christina of Tuscany, claimed that when properly interpreted, the Scriptures will not conflict with genuine discoveries of science. God reveals his wisdom and power in both his "books": his word and his works.

Let the following words be Galileo's contribution to clarity when Scripture and science seem to be in conflict: "The Holy Spirit intended to teach us in the Bible how to go to heaven, not how the heavens go."[280]

276. Diagram used with permission from Denis O. Lamoureux. This diagram appears in his *Evolution: Scripture and Nature Say Yes!* (Grand Rapids, MI: Zondervan, 2016), 136.
277. It was the name of Nicolaus Copernicus (1473–1543) that was given to the new astronomy, the Copernican Revolution overthrowing the Ptolemaic model.
278. Among Galileo's many inventions were also the pendulum clock and the astronomical telescope. Technically speaking, the German scientist Hans Lippershey invented the telescope in 1608, but this was useless for looking at the heavens. Galileo's vastly improved model (1610) allowed him to see the major moons of Jupiter—strong evidence for the heliocentric model of the solar system. Up until this time, the geocentric model prevailed, with the support of biblical passages literally understood. Thus, Galileo led scientists and churchmen (nearly always the same persons) to reread the Bible.
279. Kidner again: "It was Galileo's telescope, not his church, that conclusively refuted the interpretation of Ps 96:10 as a proof-text against the earth's rotation. Galileo incidentally realized that the new astronomy discredited only the expositors, not the Bible." *Genesis: An Introduction & Commentary*, 31.
280. Galileo Galilei (1564–1642), citing Caesar Baronius (1538–1607).

Appendix C

Genesis Genealogies

Genesis 5, 10–11: The Spreading of the "Seed"

In Gen 3:15, God promises that there will be a *crushing seed* from a woman who will defeat Satan. We see the unfolding of this promise in the early chapters of Genesis—particularly in the genealogies.

A. Genesis 5: If you compare the genealogy here with Shem's genealogy in 11:10–26, it is written the same way except that this section includes "and he died" at the end of each of the names. Why mention this? In light of the rebellion and the fall (Gen 3), and the aftereffects of the fall (Gen 4), the outcome is death ("in the day that you eat of it you shall die"). The author, however, notes a significant omission: the seventh from Adam, Enoch, *did not die*. He "was no more, because God took him" (v. 24). The author draws to our attention why this was so: Enoch walked with God (vv. 22, 24). Despite the curse of death, Enoch avoided death because he walked with God (just as Adam and Eve were to walk with God in the garden [Gen 3]). One finds life by walking with God. To walk with God implies *a way of life* (Deut 30:15–16: "See, I have set before you today life and prosperity... by… walking in his ways, and observing his commandments").

Later, the author mentions that Abraham and Isaac *walked before God* (Gen 17:1; 24:40; 48:15). In 17:1–2, to walk with God is to fulfill one's covenant obligation with God. Walking with God was not following a code. Rather, it was living a life of faith. We see that faith enabled Abraham to please God (15:6). Heb 11:5 tells us Enoch pleased God because he lived by faith. Although the Hebrew says Enoch *walked with* God, the Greek translation (Septuagint) says that Enoch *pleased* God.

What number in the genealogy is Enoch? He is seventh (the biblical number for fullness—not perfection). The number ten is also biblically noteworthy. Who is tenth? Noah. In Gen 5:29 we read that his father named him Noah (which means "comfort") because "he will comfort us in the labor and painful toil of our hands caused by the ground the Lord has cursed" (NIV). Then in v. 32, we are told that after Noah was 500 years old, he became the father of Shem, Ham, and Japheth. What should come next? *And then he died.* But it's missing. Why? We are told that Noah walked with God too (6:8–9). Thus, the genealogy is interrupted by the account of Noah to show that if you want to escape the consequences of the fall, walk with God.

We are told in Hebrews 11 that Noah was a man of faith who trusted the promises of God regarding the future even though his experience could not testify to the likelihood of a massive flood. Remember that the flood came 120 years after God spoke to him about it. This means that Noah, whose sons were born after he was 500 (the flood came when Noah was 600) worked by himself building the ark well before he had any children to help him. This is quite a picture of faith.

Didn't Noah die? Yes. But only after the account in chapter 9 of his sin of drunkenness, bringing shame upon himself, does the genealogy continue: "After the flood Noah lived 350 years.... and then he died" (vv. 28–29). It is the author's way of saying that rebelling against God's ways brings death.

B. Genesis 10–11:[281] There are exactly 70 nations in the list given here (10:1–32).[282] Note the parallel with the 70 Israelites (Jacob's family) who end up in Egypt (Ex. 1:5.

The sons of Japheth are named in 10:2–5, then the sons of Ham in 10:6–20,[283] and then the sons of Shem in 10:21–31. It is interesting that in chapter 11, the sons of Shem (which is where we get the word "Semite") are listed again (11:10–26). Why is this? Shem's line goes in two directions after Eber. Look first at the list in chapter 10. Eber is the fourteenth from Adam (7 x 2 = 14). Incidentally, Abraham is twenty-first from Adam (7 x 3 = 21). These numbers highlight the theological significance of these men.

Eber is the father of the Hebrews; this is where we get the name. He has two sons—Peleg and Joktan (v. 25). The name *Peleg* means "division," and the author makes a point of showing a division of humanity here: “One was Peleg, for in his day the earth was divided.” The author goes on to give the genealogy of Joktan rather than that of Peleg. Then in chapter 11, Peleg’s genealogy is picked up:

EBER (10:25)
↓ ↓
Joktan (ch. 10) Peleg (ch. 11)

The critical question here is, “Where do these genealogies lead us?” Joktan’s line migrates and moves eastward (11:2 NIV). East in Genesis, as we’ve noted, generally has negative connotations: Adam and Eve are driven east of Eden (3:24); so is Cain after he kills Abel (4:16; cf. 10:30, where some of Shem’s line go east toward Babylon); 13:11, when Lot goes east; 16:12, where God says that Ishmael will live to the east (NIV); 25:6, when Abraham sends his sons (by Keturah, his second wife) eastward and “away from his son Isaac.” East in Genesis suggests judgment and separation from God. Going west is associated with connotations of God’s blessing and presence.[284] Peleg’s line in chapter 11 leads to Abraham, who moves westward—to the land God has promised him.

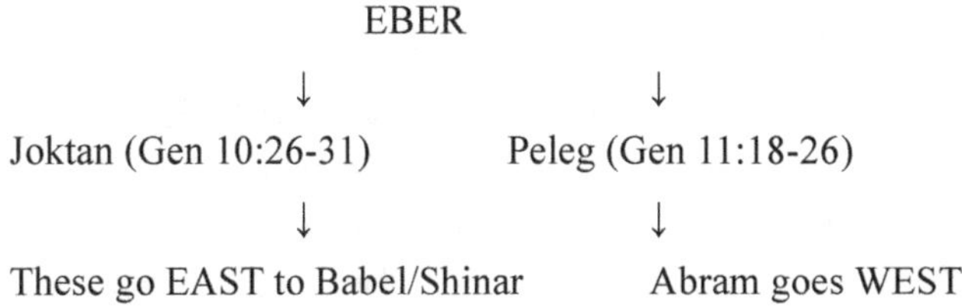

Now, it is noteworthy here that both of these—Peleg and Joktan—are from the line of Shem, which in Hebrew means “name.” The author is going to use this word *shēm* (“name”) in a significant way. Those coming from Joktan’s line are in Shinar or Babylon, where they say, “Come, let us build ourselves a city, and a tower [*migdāl*—related to *gādal*, meaning ‘to be great’], and let us make a name [*shēm*] for ourselves” (11:4). “Name” has to do with fame and progeny.[285] God says in response, "Come, let us go down, and confuse their language" (v. 7).[286] These people, who were probably building a ziggurat (which looked like the Aztec temples in Mexico), didn't build it to get close to God, but to make a name for themselves. And although they had their own individual dialects, there was still a common language that brought them together and enabled them to communicate[287] (like the many dialects in Austria—although German is the common means of communication). God would "come down" to disrupt their communication.

But Peleg's line is different. Rather than human initiative to make one's name great, God tells Abram—who moves westward—in 12:2: "I will make your name [*shēm*] great." Hebrews 11:10 tells of Abraham, who looked for a city with foundations, "whose architect and builder is God." What we see here is a man-centered ambition contrasted with an exaltation that comes from God. The one who humbles himself will be exalted, but the one who exalts himself will be humbled. This genealogy points us to the importance of a God-centered existence instead of human pride and ambition. Two responses to human guilt and disobedience are represented.[288]

The City of God and the City of Man

	A wordplay on "name" (*shēm*)	
Gen 11:4: "Let us make a *name* for ourselves."	Motivation: Self-centered	Result: Confusion and scattering
Gen 12:2: "I will… make your *name* great."	Motivation: God-centered	Result: Blessing for all the families of the earth

So, in this section of Genesis (with the unfolding of the "seed" of the woman), we have the foreshadowing of what will take place in Christ: the *seed of Abraham* will bring blessing to the ends of the earth and oppose the self/human-centered Babylons of history.

281. Note: There are gaps in these genealogies. The author wasn't aiming at linear precision ("son" or "beget" can refer to descendants [e.g., "sons of Israel"]). Compare the longer genealogies in Scripture to shorter ones (e.g., Ezra 7:1–5 omits six names that are given in 1 Chr 6:3–14).
282. There are four terms that go along with the genealogies of Japheth, Ham, and Shem: "lands," "families," "nations," and "language" (10:5 [Japheth]; 10:20 [Ham]; 10:31 [Shem]). This language is later used when the curse is reversed, when there are worshipers of the Lamb from every "tribe," "language," "people," and "nation" (Rev 5:9). Isa 66:19 (in the LXX) appears to refer back to the table of nations of Gen 10: Lud (Libya) from Shem; Put from Ham; and Tarshish, Tubal, Meshech, and Javan from Japheth.
283. Note that the descendants of Ham include many of Israel's traditional foes. They include the Canaanites but also the Egyptians (10:13), Babylonians (10:10), and Assyrians (10:11). In 9:26, Noah curses Canaan, Ham's son, declaring, "Let Canaan be [Shem's = Israel's] slave." Wenham writes:

    > It has often been thought odd that Noah does not curse Ham, who was the guilty son, but instead singles out Ham's son, Canaan, who did not do anything. However, once the curse is read in the light of chapter 10, it is apparent that nations like Egypt and Assyria were never Israel's slaves as the Canaanites and their sub-groups [Hittites, Jebusites, Amorites, Girgashites, Hivites, etc.] were. In this respect, it would certainly have been inappropriate for Noah to have said, "let Ham be Shem's slave," but "let Canaan be his slave" does describe the fate of the Canaanites.

    Gordon Wenham, *Story as Torah* (Grand Rapids, MI: Baker, 2000), 36.
284. John Sailhamer, *The Pentateuch as Narrative* (Grand Rapids, MI: Zondervan 1993), 98.
285. Bruce Waltke, *Genesis: A Commentary* (Grand Rapids, MI: Zondervan, 2001), 179.
286. The use of words tells the story of Babel: "Let us make bricks [*nilbena*]" (11:4) is made into "confusion" when God says, "Let us confuse [*nabela*]" (11:7).
287. John Goldingay, *Old Testament Theology: Israel's Gospel*, vol. 1 (Downers Grove, IL: IVP Academic, 2003), 189.
288. Sailhamer, *Pentateuch as Narrative*, 130.

Appendix D

God's Two Books

"To conclude, therefore, let no man... think or maintain that a man can search too far or be well studied in the book of God's word, or in the book of God's works..."

–Francis Bacon

Most Bible-believing Christians think of the Bible as the primary way—even the *only* way—God speaks to us. Or at least it's the only surefire way to know his will. And yet the Bible itself declares that the Lord has spoken in *various* ways in the past (Heb 1:1). He continues to do so in the present, as we shall see.

Of course, it's easy to counter with, "The truth of the Bible is obvious—even self-interpreting—while the other means of discerning God's will are more subjective." There is truth in this perspective, and yet Scripture *does* require interpretation. That is, it must be pondered, evaluated in context, and carefully applied. We strive to grasp what the Scriptures meant to those who heard them first and then carefully make the connections to our own lives. Similarly, it's all fine and well to say, "What would Jesus do? That's all we need to do." But even when we are examining the life and words of Christ, there is no skipping over interpretation. (Are we to imitate him in his dress? miracles? preaching style? itinerant lifestyle? celibacy?)

This is not to say we can make the Bible mean whatever we want it to mean. Truth is not flexible, despite postmodernist opinion that all should find and embrace "their own truth." What it does mean is that studying Scripture requires effort. But then, so does listening to a conversation partner—and some of us are better than others at being listeners (Jas 1:19). Peter admitted that Paul's thoughts were sometimes difficult to follow—yet he still regarded them as true, and as Scripture (2 Pet 3:15–16).

General and Special Revelation

Theologians distinguish between general revelation and special revelation. General revelation is accessible to all human beings. This includes the natural world, as well as things like conscience, reason, human experience, and collective wisdom. Special revelation, on the other hand, is that part of God's saving communication available only in Scripture (including the history of biblical Israel and the life and teachings of Jesus Christ).

God Speaks

Scripture (Bible)
The person of Jesus Christ (NT)
The history of Israel (OT)
Nature
Conscience
Wisdom of the elders
Spiritual counsel[289]

In this appendix we compare two means of divine revelation, one special and the other general: Scripture and nature, sometimes called the "two books."

Book of Works

The Book of Works (nature) is a message expressed in the grandeur of the universe, in mathematics (the universal scientific language for expressing the laws of God), and in DNA (the biological "language of God.")[290] The Bible itself speaks of this "book," as Christian thinkers through the ages have observed. Pss 19; 104; 111:2, and Rom 1 are four passages affirming the Book of Works. There are limitations, of course: the natural world teaches us about God's power (as the apostle Paul noted in Rom 1:20), but not his mercy (which is not a cardinal virtue in the animal kingdom). But then, Scripture has limitations too: it does not tell us when the world began, or how many galaxies there are, or how to cure cancer.

Some of the best in the field of science in recent centuries have been top-notch scientists who were *also* well-educated biblically. Through the course of history, hundreds have approached nature with this thought in mind: doing science is akin to thinking God's thoughts after him. There are atheist and agnostic scientists in our day, possibly more than at any time in the past, but the trend used to be just the opposite. Modern science is grounded on a faith in the rationality of God. It is only since the Enlightenment that a significant minority of scientists no longer believes in the Bible. Most intellectuals believed in a rational God. Because he is a rational God, he created a rational universe; the laws of the universe are knowable and testable. Since he is not capricious, we can have confidence that experimentation will yield results consistent with reality. Most prominent men of science were theists, or believers in an intelligent God.[291] Of course, great minds of faith are not only a thing of the past.[292]

Book of Words

The Book of Words (Scripture) is, of course, the testimony of the Bible. The Bible contains a message (consisting of words), and it is the message that is inspired, not the individual words, which must be translated—unless we read Hebrew, Aramaic, and Greek, the three languages of the original texts.[293]

Psalm 19 is helpful in that it affirms knowledge of God through both nature (Ps 19:1) and Scripture (vv. 7–11).

Studying God's Two Books

Book	*Consisting of*	*Language*	*Understood through*
Scripture	Words & sentences, documents (a library)	Hebrew, Aramaic & Greek	Bible study & theology
Nature	Matter & energy, space & time	Mathematics, DNA & chemical symbols	Scientific investigation & experimentation

An apt quotation on science and faith comes from Francis Bacon (1561–1626): "To conclude, therefore, let no man… think or maintain that a man can search too far or be well studied in the book of God's word, or in the book of God's works; divinity or philosophy; but rather let men endeavor an endless progress or proficience in both."[294] We have made it our practice to cultivate relationships not only with biblical scholars but also with scientists, and have learned a lot from them. Yet it is not often that scientists are Bible experts, or that theologians have advanced degrees in the sciences.

Accommodation

Although science education is an important part of academic training for children and adults alike, and teachers may simplify complex concepts when they are first introducing them to the class, for the fully trained scientist, there is no ignoring formulas or equations just because they are difficult. Nature is what it is, so science does not accommodate itself to the intellect of the observer. Physical, chemical, and biological processes may be only partially known, yet because we have confidence in the consistency and universality of scientific laws, we keep probing. Our theories and approximations are getting closer and closer to describing the nature of reality.

Scripture is another thing altogether. It is not a science book written for academics. Even when topics related to science are touched on in Scripture, everything *has to be* simplified. The Lord accommodates his message to the people of ancient times. Of course, any time an omniscient being communicates with finite creatures like you and me, he is coming down to our level. Even if the Bible were written to include modern science, this would be out of date in a few centuries—perhaps even in a few decades.

- An effective lecturer accommodates the lesson to the audience, aiming for clarity, even if this means occasional generalization or oversimplification. No principle is likely to be remembered (or followed) once it has died the death of a thousand qualifications.
- Schoolteachers take care to impart knowledge that is age appropriate. They may "push" the students, but they do not talk over their heads.
- Jesus told parables, generously provided examples and illustrations, and he took care not to speak past the capacity (and receptivity) of his audience (unless it was for his purpose, e.g., Mt 13:10–23; Mk 8:14–21; Lk 18:31–34; Jn 11:7–16).

Accommodation and the Incarnation

The incarnation itself is a splendid example of accommodation. So that we could relate to God, the Son of God took on human flesh (Phil 2:5–8). Coming down to our level, he emptied himself. God not only came down to our level in Christ; he also came down to our level in his revelation.

The gospel was delivered not in the fine dialect of Attic Greek (the language of Socrates and Plato), but in the street language of the Mediterranean world.[295] (This is not to say the NT contains no Greek of fine literary style—but it is rare, most of it found in parts of Luke–Acts and in [all of] Hebrews.) This is God's way: to relate, connect, illuminate, simplify—whatever it takes to focus us on his message, with minimal secondary information or corrections of common opinions.

Further Thoughts about Science and Theology

Hopefully the thoughts expressed so far will prove useful as you think through the issues. With this concept of the nature of God's revelation in mind, let's consider ten more thoughts about science and faith.

I. Theology Resembles Science

As Solomon (a botanist, zoologist, ornithologist, herpetologist, and ichthyologist in his own right—1 Kings 4:33) rightly remarked, "It is the glory of God to conceal things, but the glory of kings is to search things out" (Prov 25:2). The glory of science is not that different from the glory of theology. Both require patient study and honest processing of the data. [296]

II. The Problem of Specialization

More often than not, scientists are specialists, not "all-rounders." Although specialization has many benefits, it can be problematic. One might even argue that the more minutely focused one is on an area of expertise, the less qualified he or she is to comment on the rest of science. This means that most scientists are not Renaissance men or women—they aren't necessarily qualified to throw their weight around in other disciplines, and should not belittle those who may differ. This is especially true for comments well outside their area of scientific expertise.

Of course, the case is no different for nonscientists. Theologians may be extremely familiar with Genesis—having read it dozens of times—but this does not mean that all others must yield to their opinions. Augustine (AD 354–430) calls us to humility as well as to an awareness that carelessly proclaimed opinions may discredit the faith.[297]

III. Science or Faith: A False Choice![298]

Science and theology are not in some sort of competitive or contrarian relationship with each other. Rather, with the doctrine of the Two Books in mind, they are complementary.[299]

While we should not apply the dictum too rigidly, it might be helpful to think about science as more concerned with the "How" question—namely, physical processes involved in the natural world. The Christian faith helps us with our existential "Why" and theological "Who" questions.[300] That is, purpose and meaning ("why") as well as the nature of God and humanity ("who"). Furthermore, there are "How" questions in theology—for example, "How can humans become right with God?" We could also speak of the "how" when it comes to God's activity in history—how water was turned to wine or how Jesus could walk on water. We can also ask "Why" questions about science ("Why does water freeze at 32°F/0°C?"). However, overall, it's helpful to distinguish the "how" of physical processes from the "why" of purpose and meaning and the "who" of both divine and human persons and natures.

IV. About Evolution

The belief in atheistic or naturalistic evolution (denying that there is a Creator God as the Bible describes) is a serious error. That is because naturalism or atheism is a metaphysical, not a physical, theory. By itself, the truth or falsity of evolution turns on *scientific* facts—just like gravity or quantum physics. These are not inherently atheistic or naturalistic. If it turns out that the facts point us to evolution, then we are left with the question of how to interpret those facts, and there are some Christians who claim the facts support evolution, while others deny this.[301]

So, even though Christians disagree on the question of evolution, it is important to keep the main thing the main thing. There is nothing problematic in principle to believe that God works in the biological world through natural processes. Job claimed that God's hands "fashioned" him (Job 10:8–9), and the psalmist said that God knit him together in his mother's womb (Ps 139:13)—although these things were done according to the natural, biological processes the Creator had put in place. Thus, as Christian philosopher Alvin Plantinga contends, the fundamental problem is *unguided* evolution, not *guided* evolution.[302] Of course, it is possible that God set up the initial parameters, knowing that the universe would evolve (Douglas considers this plausible). Yet even on that assumption, there is no chance the universe would exist or could support life on its own. His intelligence is still clearly visible. Whether God brought the world—or life—into being instantaneously or through a lengthy process is beside the point, since he can do anything he wills. It is the denial of God that is the issue, not where one stands vis-à-vis genuine discoveries of modern science.[303]

V. Bible = Science Textbook?

The Bible is not a science book. To approach it as such disregards its literary and theological nature. A telephone book contains many words, and they are arranged alphabetically—the same arrangement found in a dictionary. Yet the telephone book was never meant to be used as a dictionary. And if you want to order a pizza, don't waste your time searching under "P" in the dictionary. Some think that the Bible is a treasure trove of scientific facts. This is a wrong approach to the Scriptures.

Now imagine for a moment that the Bible *were* a science textbook, and God explained biology, chemistry, and physics exhaustively. It would be very, very long. Millions of pages of articles, books, lectures, and lab reports of a scientific nature have been published. If God had made his word scientifically comprehensive, you would need a crane to lift your Bible. And there would be several other serious problems (outlined in this endnote[304]).

If God had wanted to correct the cosmology of the ancient peoples, he could have. In a time when everyone believed the earth was the center of the world, perhaps he could have set them right—without diminishing or obscuring the essential message. Yet apparently this was not his intent. In the Bible, the earth does not orbit the sun; it does not move (Ps 104:5). Scripture is written for people to read and understand. This explains why it is composed in simple, down-to-earth language.

As we've noted, the words "sunrise" and "sunset" are often used, even though technically speaking they are inaccurate. Yet even the newspaper and the weatherman say "sunrise." The Scriptures describe phenomena as they appear, not necessarily as they actually are. Three biblical examples of phenomenological description are sunrise (Mk 16:2); rabbits chewing the cud (Lev 11:6), whereas actually they practice refection (eating partially digested fecal matter); and bats being included with the birds (Lev 11:19), whereas they are, zoologically speaking, flying mammals. The Bible was never intended to be a science book.[305]

VI. The Antiquity of the Universe

The universe gives every appearance of being immensely ancient. Some stars and galaxies are so far away from us that their starlight would not have reached us—they would be invisible—unless 10 billion years (or more) had already elapsed since the genesis of the cosmos.

Couldn't God have created all this instantly, or fast-forwarded the process to "save time"? Of course he could (Ps 115:3). Yet it seems that God's normal way of working is through prolonged processes. The cosmos required billions of years before it was ready to support a planet like Earth.[306]

VII. Appearance of Age?

Sometimes it is argued that God created the earth with an appearance of age. The "Omphalos Theory," popularized by British zoologist Philip Gosse in 1857, is named after the Greek word for "navel," *omphalos*. Since (it is claimed) Adam was formed as a fully adult male, he had a belly button. He may have appeared to be twenty-five or thirty years old, but in fact he was only seconds old. The trees of Eden, by the same token, would have shown tree rings (annual growth rings). Simply put, God made the earth with a built-in appearance of age.

But there is a problem here. Scientific evidence cannot be claimed for both a young earth *and* an appearance of age, which is precisely what the Young Earth advocates are doing. There should be no shred of evidence for a "young earth" if the Omphalos Theory is correct. Moreover, this approach makes God a party to deceit, since through the physical world he is misleading us. And yet the Scriptures affirm over and over that God *reveals truth* through the creation (Ps 19:1; Rom 1:20). You just cannot have it both ways.[307]

VIII. Complexity

With recent advances in astrophysics (on the macro scale of study) and quantum physics (on the micro scale), as well as strides in microbiology, genetics, and many other complex fields, it is a fair guess that the cosmos appears to be millions of times more complex now, in the new millennium, than it did at the turn of the last century. The deeper we probe, the more stunning the intricate mechanisms and systems we discover. Now more than ever, scientists need the "big picture" assistance that a personal Creator can provide.

IX. Conclusion

So, then, although the Lord communicates in multiple ways, for our purposes in this appendix there are two "books" of God:

- His *Book of Words* (Scripture)—a message expressed in sentences and stories. Careful Bible study, reverent theology, and a sincere intent to obey (to follow the truth wherever it leads) are the soundest strategy for plumbing the Book of Words.
- His *Book of Works* (Nature)—a message expressed in the grandeur of the universe. Careful scientific inquiry opens up the wonders of God's world.

The opinions we hold concerning the relationship of science to Scripture ought to be tempered by a humble awareness of the limits of our knowledge. No single person can know all there is to know. We need each other and must value the contributions of both science and theology. We allow Conrad Hyers the last word:

> If one wishes to argue for deeper meanings and mysteries in Scripture, they are certainly there. But they are not scientific in character. They are theological and spiritual. They are not meanings and mysteries hidden from the ancients, but now revealed to [twenty-first] century scientists, which lie along the horizontal plane. They are rather inexhaustible depths of meaning and mystery which lie along the vertical plane.[308]

289. In addition, in the past God has spoken in dreams and visions, and (even more rarely) in an audible voice or through angels. Though all these means of communication are visible in the OT and NT, many Christians doubt that they still occur today. Usually it is fruitless to argue against someone's experience. (They "saw" or "heard" what they saw or heard.) At the least, we should agree that God is not restricted; he can make his will or presence known in any number of conceivable ways.
290. Well worth reading is Francis S. Collins's apologetic piece, *The Language of God: A Scientist Presents Evidence for Faith* (New York: Free Press, 2006). For a different perspective, see J.P. Moreland, et al., eds., *Theistic Evolution* (Wheaton, IL: Crossway, 2017).
291. This was the case throughout the last four hundred years. Robert Boyle (1627–1691), familiar to any chemistry student, was probably the first to use the scientific method; he was also a theologian who wrote commentaries on the Bible. Polish astronomer Nicolas Copernicus (1473–1543), the first modern scientist to propose the sun as the center of the solar system, was also a deeply committed Christian. He believed that God had set the heavens in motion. Consider where the world would be without the following disciplines. Then consider that their reputed founders were men who believed in God, like Boyle (chemistry), Newton (physics), Babbage (computers), and Kelvin (thermodynamics). To this distinguished company could be added many others, e.g., Simpson (gynecology), Pascal (hydrostatics), Agassiz (ichthyology), Ramsay (isotropic chemistry), and Steno (stratigraphy).

    In brief, the scientific method arose *because of* the theistic (and later also deistic) worldview of the "Enlightenment" culture (beginning in the 17th cent.). It was considered ludicrous to think that the universe, as immense and complex as it seemed to be, could possibly be the product of chance alone, as some modern scientific theories assume. Anyone who rejected God as the Creator was suspected of not having all their marbles.

    See also Mark Noll, "How Did the Reformation Reform the Study of Nature?" http://biologos.org/blogs/guest/how-did-the-reformation-reform-the-study-of-nature? Accessed 31 Oct 2017.
292. Eric C. Barrett and David Fisher have written an intriguing book, *Scientists Who Believe: 21 Tell Their Own Stories* (Chicago: Moody Press, 1984). All the writers featured in this book are scientifically trained and believe in God. Several are well known, like Astronauts James Irwin and Jack Lousma; Dr. Everett Koop (former US Surgeon General); and Dr. Boris Dotsenko (former head of nuclear physics at the Institute of Physics, Kiev). Eight of the 21 are from countries outside the United States. Several carry out their work in nations where belief brings persecution. A fascinating study, and only adding to the wealth of evidence that reason and faith are not mutually exclusive.
293. This is not to deny the inspiration of Scripture, only to caution that no single translation is perfect. Bear in mind that as both the original languages and the translation languages have evolved over time, the nuances of both present a challenge to interpreters. So, even learning the original Greek, Hebrew, and Aramaic today still presents a challenge as to how best to translate the text into modern languages. The key is to remain humble and open to alternative revelations from other scholars! Fortunately, the message of God is robust enough that it is nearly always conserved when translated. Scribal slips have never been a problem, not because the scribes never made mistakes, but because no copying error ever undid the message of Scripture.
294. Francis Bacon, *The Advancement of Learning* (1605). Further, since the "books" deal with separate provinces, Bacon warned, "We must not unwisely mingle or confound these learnings together."
295. Christians used to think that the Greek of the NT—since it is no longer spoken today, and no ancient specimens had been discovered—was a special language inspired for divine use (a "Holy Ghost" Greek). We suspect this assumption was partly responsible for the fondness

in the 18th and 19th centuries of "thee" and "thou" lingo in prayer. Such pronouns were originally common—say, in 1555—but by 1855 few spoke that way except in church—especially in prayer. Since about 500 of the approximately 5000 Greek words in the pages of the NT were unknown from any other source, many thought that the Spirit had supplied a special vocabulary suitable for these documents. Then in 1897 Bernard Grenfell and Arthur Hunt discovered scraps of Greek papyri in a garbage dump in Oxyrhynchus, Egypt. These were *everyday* documents of common people: invoices and receipts, shopping lists, notes from parents to children, etc.

296. "In the beginning was the Word," proclaims the prologue of John's Gospel (Jn 1:1), echoing the opening lines of Genesis. Not "In the beginning was Feeling," or "In the beginning were Electric Sensations." The word comes first; feeling follows. To come to terms with God means coming to terms with his word (1 Sam 3:1; Jn 12:47–48).

297. In his own words,

> Usually even a non-Christian knows something about [astronomy and biology]… Now, it is a disgraceful and dangerous thing for an unbeliever to hear a Christian, presumably giving the meaning of Holy Scripture, talking nonsense on [scientific] topics…. The shame is not so much that an ignorant individual is derided, but that people outside the household of faith think our sacred writers held such opinions, and, to the great loss of those for whose salvation we toil, the writers of our Scripture are criticized and rejected as unlearned men…. For then, to defend their utterly foolish and obviously untrue statements, they will try to call upon Holy Scripture for proof and even recite from memory many passages which they think support their position, although they understand neither what they say nor the things about which they make assertion [alluding to 1 Tim 1:7].

Augustine (354–430) in *On the Literal Meaning of Genesis.* For the entire quotation, see https://www.ancient.eu/article/91/st-augustine-from-the-literal-meaning-of-genesis/.

298. More at https://www.douglasjacoby.com/?p=16792.

299. For more on the faith-science relationship, see Paul Copan, Tremper Longman III, Christopher L. Reese, and Michael G. Strauss, eds., *Dictionary of Christianity and Science* (Grand Rapids, MI: Zondervan, 2017). Denis Lamoureux's MOOC (massive open online course) *Science and Religion* is well done and thought provoking. It is available at https://www.coursera.org/learn/science-and-religion-101#. For something lighter, there is the DVD by Douglas Jacoby, *Science and Faith: Enemies or Allies?* (Spring, TX: Illumination Publishers, 2014).

300. A professor in the biological sciences offers further perspective:

> In the field of animal behavior (my specialty), there is also the distinction between ultimate (why) and proximate (how) questions, but both are the realm of science. For example, *How does a bird sing?* may require an explanation of how the brain sends signals to the syrinx (sound-producing organ) to produce the behavior. But *Why does a bird sing?* may require an explanation of why it is adaptive for males to sing (singing males attract females and so reproduce) and thus why this behavior developed in the first place. So science deals with both proximate and ultimate questions, but Scripture deals with spiritual questions and provides supernatural or divine explanations—even for natural phenomena (e.g., lightning: Jer 51:16; rain: Mt 5:45; earthquakes: Nah 1:5, your lunch: Deut 8:10–18).

Javier Monzón, personal correspondence (adapted), 25 Oct 2017. We can also add that Scripture is making historical statements as well, speaking of actual events (e.g., 1 Cor 15).

301. For example, see both sides discussed in Kenneth Keathley, et al., eds., *Old Earth or Evolutionary Creation?* (Downers Grove, IL: IVP Academic, 2017). Further, some "evolutionary creationists" have dismissed the fall as unhistorical, maintaining that our tendency toward sin and self is nothing more than the instincts and impulses of our animalist natures that have

not been overcome by evolution and civilization. Apart from the problem of denying this important part of biblical history, assuming the fact of evolution—even if merely for the sake of argument—I (Paul) could respond in this way: just as at the fall God withdrew his grace that sustained inherently mortal human bodies so they would eventually experience death, God likewise took away certain capacities that enabled humans to rise above those animalistic instincts and live in obedience to him—an ability that was withdrawn when they rebelled.

302. See Alvin Plantinga, *Where the Conflict Really Lies: Science, Religion, and Naturalism* (New York: Oxford University Press, 2011).

303. Resources on the creation-evolution issue may be found at https://www.douglasjacoby.com/creation-evolution-reading/.

304. If Scripture included up-to-date (21st-cent.) science:
   - No one would have been able to understand it at the time it was written. Those poor Hebrews three or four thousand years ago—what chance would they have had to comprehend Genesis 1 in modern scientific jargon? Few people today would be able to understand it either, since (1) science requires an education inaccessible to many, and (2) the frontiers of science are always being pushed back. Some facts that may be widely known in fifty years may be beyond the present capacity of today's Nobel Prize winners to comprehend!
   - It would have encouraged the confused notion that "scientific truth" is synonymous with "truth"—that truth must be scientific or else it isn't truth. This is manifestly false! Science deals only with quantifiable phenomena. It has nothing to say about such scientifically unverifiable realities as love and justice. Even if scientists one day can explain the neurochemistry connected to falling in love, all they will have done is to describe it from the physical perspective. This no more explains the reality of love than does analyzing a symphony of Beethoven in terms of acoustical physics "explain" the symphony. The whole is much greater than the sum of the parts, and the human intention gives shape to the formation of the arrangement of notes and their acoustical outcomes.
   - The central message about God and humans would be buried under mountains of information. We are designed for relationships: with God, with family members, with one another. Yet technological innovations have no doubt made our lives more comfortable physically. Who would ever want to return to the days before anesthesia?

305. Wenham's caveat is apropos:

   > Though historical and scientific questions may be uppermost in our minds as we approach the text, it is doubtful whether they were in the writer's mind, and we should therefore be cautious about looking for answers to questions he was not concerned with. Genesis is primarily about God's character and his purposes for sinful mankind. Let us beware of allowing our interests to divert us from the central thrust of the book, so that we miss what the Lord, our creator and redeemer, is saying to us.

   Wenham, *Genesis 1–15*, liii.

306. The cosmos required many eons:
   - To expand to a sufficiently large volume that it would not collapse under the force of its own gravity.
   - To expand to a size large enough for heat and radiation not to kill all (future) living creatures.
   - For H (the first element of the cosmos) to be converted by nuclear fusion into He and the other 90 naturally occurring elements.
   - For the formation of stars, which are nuclear fusion ovens for producing heavier and heavier elements.
   - For stars to run their course, and those exploding into supernovae to disseminate the contents of their nuclei throughout the universe.

- For planetary formation to take place.

Further, the ancient earth was not fit for man's arrival on the scene. Billions of years were required:

- For an atmosphere supportive of mammalian life (e.g., avoiding extreme oxidation and reduction, as well as containing N_2, O_2, Ar, H_2, CO_2, etc. in the right proportions).
- To arrive at the right balance between land and ocean for the sustainability of stable meteorology on the planet.
- For volcanism to bring the heavier elements (metals) from the core of the earth toward the surface—for eventual metallurgical purposes. Man is unique in his technological ability. But without metal and fire, there would be no metallurgy, and no electronics. Follow the stimulating discussion of this theme throughout Michael Denton's *Nature's Destiny: How the Laws of Biology Reveal Purpose in the Universe* (New York: The Free Press, 1998).
- For ancient fauna and (especially) flora to be converted into fossil fuels.
- For various evolutionary processes to run their course in providing a physical body suited to man's aptitudes and purpose.

See Q&A 1506, "Is the earth young, only 1000s of years old?" at https://www.douglasjacoby.com/?p=16701.

307. Some claim that radiometric dating techniques are inherently unreliable—revealing a lack of familiarity with the science (and time in the field). The utility and general accuracy of dating techniques like ^{14}C (for relatively young ages, with a half-life of only 5730 years), ^{40}K–^{40}Ar, ^{238}U–^{206}Pb, etc. are impressive. Further, there are dozens of dating techniques that all indicate a world immensely older than a literal reading of Genesis would indicate. Tree rings (dendrochronology) yield an unbroken record going back over 12,000 years. Stalagmites take us back 40,000 years, while glacial core samples reveal over 100,000 years of history. Many methods indicate ages in the millions and even billions of years. Alan Hayward's *Creation and Evolution* (London: Triangle, 1994) provides a comprehensive overview of the various dating methods.
308. Hyers, "Narrative Form," 215b.

Bibliography

Aharoni, Yohanan and Michael Avi-Yonah. *The Macmillan Bible Atlas.* New York: Macmillan, 1993.

Alexander, Pat, ed. *The Lion Encyclopedia of the Bible.* Tring, UK: Lion, 1978.

Alexander, Pat and David, eds. *The* New *Lion Handbook to the Bible*, 3rd ed. Oxford: Lion Hudson, 1999.

American Scientific Affiliation. Website http://www.asa3.org.

Anderson, Bernhard W. *Understanding the Old Testament.* Englewood Cliffs, NJ: Prentice Hall, 1975.

Atkinson, Davis. *The Message of Genesis 1–11: The Dawn of Creation.* The Bible Speaks Today series. Downers Grove, IL: InterVarsity, 1990.

The Bible Project. https://thebibleproject.com/explore/genesis-1-11/. Accessed 1 Oct 2017.

Biologos website: http://www.asa3.org.

Blocher, Henri. *In the Beginning.* Downers Grove, IL: InterVarsity, 1984.

Bonhoeffer, Dietrich. *Creation and Fall, Temptation: Two Biblical Studies*. New York: Macmillan, 1959.

Brenton, Sir Lancelot C. L. *The Septuagint with Apocrypha: Greek and English.* Grand Rapids, MI: Zondervan, 1982.

Brown, Francis, S. R. Driver, and Charles A. Briggs. *A Hebrew and English Lexicon of the Old Testament.* Oxford: Clarendon Press, 1979.

Brueggemann, Walter. *Genesis.* Interpretation: A Bible Commentary for Teaching and Preaching. Louisville, KY: Westminster John Knox Press, 2010.

_____. *Theology of the Old Testament: Testimony, Dispute, Advocacy.* Minneapolis, MN: Fortress Press, 1997.

Childs, Brevard. *Introduction to the Old Testament as Scripture.* Minneapolis, MN: Fortress Press, 1979.

Clifford, Richard J. *Creation Accounts in the Ancient Near East and in the Bible.* Washington, DC: Catholic Biblical Association of America, 1994.

Colling, Richard G. *Random Designer: Created from Chaos to Connect with the Creator.* Bourbonnais, IL: Browning Press, 2004.

Collins, C. John. *Reading Genesis Well: Navigating History, Science, Poetry, and Truth in Genesis 1–11.* Grand Rapids, MI: Zondervan, coming autumn 2018.

Collins, Francis S. *The Language of God: A Scientist Presents Evidence for Faith.* New York: Free Press, 2006.

Copan, Paul and William Lane Craig. *Creation ex Nihilo: A Biblical, Philosophical, and Scientific Exploration.* Grand Rapids, MI: Baker, 2004.

Copan, Paul, and Christopher L. Reese, eds. *Christianity and Science: Three Views*. Grand Rapids, MI: Zondervan, forthcoming.

_____. Tremper Longman III, Christopher L. Reese, and Michael G. Strauss, eds. *Dictionary of Christianity and Science*. Grand Rapids, MI: Zondervan, 2017.

Denton, Michael J. *Nature's Destiny: How the Laws of Biology Reveal Purpose in the Universe.* New York: The Free Press, 1998.

Drane, John. *Introducing the Old Testament*, rev. ed. Minneapolis, MN: Fortress Press, 2001.

Elliger, Karl. *Biblia Hebraica Stuttgartensia.* Stuttgart: Deutsche Bibelgesellschaft, 1997.

Falk, Darrel R. *Coming to Peace with Science: Bridging the Worlds Between Faith and Biology.* Downers Grove, IL: IVP Academic, 2004.

Fee, Gordon D. and Douglas Stuart. *How to Read the Bible Book by Book: A Guided Tour*. Grand Rapids, MI: Eerdmans, 2002.

Fox, Everett. *The Five Books of Moses: The Schocken Bible, Volume 1.* New York: Random House, 2000.

Gibson, John C. L. *Genesis, Volume 1.* The Daily Study Bible Series. Louisville, KY: Westminster John Knox Press, 1981.

Glover, Gordon J. *Beyond the Firmament: Understanding Science and the Theology of Creation.* Chesapeake, VA: Watertree Press, 2007.

Gonzalez, Guillermo and Jay Richards. *The Privileged Planet: How Our Place in the Cosmos Is Designed for Discovery.* Washington, DC: Regnery, 2004.

Graves, Robert and Raphael Patai. *Hebrew Myths: The Book of Genesis.* New York: McGraw Hill, 1964.

Gundry, Stanley N., ed. *Four Views on The Historical Adam.* Grand Rapids, MI: Zondervan, 2013.

Harrison, R.K. *Introduction to the Old Testament.* Grand Rapids, MI: Eerdmans, 1971.

Heidel, A. *The Babylonian Genesis.* Chicago, IL: University of Chicago Press, 1972.

_____. *The Gilgamesh Epic and Old Testament Parallels.* Chicago, IL: University of Chicago Press, 1973.

Hyers, Conrad. "The Narrative Form of Genesis 1: Cosmogonic, Yes; Scientific, No." *Journal of the American Scientific Affiliation* 36.4 (1984): 213a. Accessible at http://faculty.gordon.edu/hu/bi/ted_hildebrandt/otesources/01-genesis/text/articles-books/hyers_gen1_jasa.htm.

Holland, Glenn S. *Religion in the Ancient World.* The Great Courses. Chantilly, VA: The Teaching Company, 2005. Audio series with accompanying book.

Jacoby, Douglas. *Compelling Evidence for God and the Bible: Finding Truth in an Age of Doubt.* Eugene, OR: Harvest House, 2010.

_____. *A Quick Overview of the Bible.* Eugene, OR: Harvest House, 2013.

_____. *Exodus: Night of Redemption.* Spring, TX: Illumination Publishers, 2017.

Johnson, Dru. *The Universal Story: Genesis 1–11* (Transformative Word). Bellingham, WA: Lexham Press, 2018. (Unfortunately this title came to our attention only after our manuscript was completed.)

Jordan, Michael. *Encyclopedia of Gods: Over 2500 Deities of the World.* New York: Facts on File, 1993.

Kaiser, Walter C. Jr. *A History of Israel, from the Bronze Age Through the Jewish Wars.* Nashville, TN: Broadman & Holman, 1998.

_____. *The Old Testament Documents: Are They Reliable and Relevant?* Downers Grove, IL: InterVarsity, 2001.

Keener, Craig S. and John H. Walton. *Zondervan Cultural Backgrounds Study Bible: Bringing to Life the Ancient World of Scripture.* Grand Rapids, MI: Zondervan, 2017.

Keil, C. F. and F. Delitzsch. *Commentary on the Old Testament* (originally published by T. & T. Clark of Edinburgh, 1866–91). Peabody, MA: Hendrickson, 1996.

Kidner, Derek. *Genesis: An Introduction & Commentary.* Tyndale Old Testament Commentaries. Downers Grove, IL: InterVarsity, 1967.

Köstenberger, Andreas J. and Patterson, Richard. *Invitation to Biblical Interpretation: Exploring the Hermeneutical Triad of History, Literature, and Theology.* Grand Rapids, MI: Kregel, 2011.

Lamoureux, Denis O. *Evolutionary Creation: A Christian Approach to Evolution*. Eugene, OR: Wipf & Stock, 2008.

LaSor, William Sanford, David Allan Hubbard, Frederic William Bush. *Old Testament Survey: The Message, Form, and Background of the Old Testament*. Grand Rapids, MI: Eerdmans, 1996.

Levine, Amy-Jill. *The Old Testament.* The Great Courses. Chantilly, VA: The Teaching Company, 2001.

Longman, Tremper III. *Genesis.* The Story of God Bible Commentary. Grand Rapids, MI: Zondervan, 2016.

_____ and John H. Walton. *The Lost World of the Flood: Mythology, Theology, and the Deluge Debate*. Downers Grove, IL: IVP Academic, 2017.

Mallory, J. P. *In Search of the Indo-Europeans: Language, Archaeology and Myth.* New York: Thames and Hudson, 1991.

McCall, Henrietta. *Mesopotamian Myths.* London: British Museum Press, 1990.

McGrath, Alister. *The Big Question: Why We Can't Stop Talking about Science, Faith and God.* New York: St. Martin's Press, 2015.

McGuiggan, Jim. *Genesis and Us.* Fort Worth, TX: Star Bible Publishers, 1988.

Middleton, J. Richard. *The Liberating Image: The* Imago Dei *in Genesis 1.* Grand Rapids, MI: Brazos, 2005.

Moberly, R. W. L. *Old Testament Theology: Reading the Hebrew Bible as Christian Scripture.* Grand Rapids, MI: Baker, 2013.

A New English Translation of the Septuagint. Oxford: Oxford University Press, 2007.

Numbers, Ronald L. *The Creationists: The Evolution of Scientific Creationism.* Berkeley, CA: University California Press, 1992.

Polkinghorne, John. *Faith, Science and Understanding.* New Haven, CT: Yale University Press, 2011.

Price, Randall. *The Stones Cry Out: What Archaeology Reveals about the Truth of the Bible.* Eugene, OR: Harvest House, 1997.

Pritchard, James B. *The Times Atlas of the Bible.* London: Times Books, 1987.

Provan, Iain. *Seriously Dangerous Religion: What the Old Testament Really Says and Why It Matters.* Waco, TX: Baylor University Press, 2014.

Reyken, Leland. *A Complete Handbook of Literary Forms in the Bible.* Wheaton, IL: Crossway, 2014.

Rosenberg, David, ed. *Genesis As It Is Written: Contemporary Writers on Our First Stories.* San Francisco, CA: HarperCollins, 1996.

Sailhamer, John. *Genesis Unbound.* Sisters, OR: Multnomah Books, 1996.

_____. *The Meaning of the Pentateuch.* Downers Grove, IL: IVP Academic, 2009.

Sparks, Kenton L. *Ancient Texts for the Study of the Hebrew Bible: A Guide to the Background Literature.* Peabody, MA: Hendrickson, 2005.

Stouffer, Lauren and Ted Hildebrandt. *Getting Started with Genesis.* Video class series (2012). https://faculty.gordon.edu/hu/bi/ted_hildebrandt/digitalcourses/00_digitalbiblicalstudiescourses.html#Hildebrandt_OTLit, also found at http://biblicalelearning.org/old-testament/ot-literature-dr-ted-hildebrandt/.

Venema, Dennis R. and Scot McKnight. *Adam and the Genome: Reading Scripture after Genetic Science.* Grand Rapids, MI: Brazos, 2017.

Waltke, Bruce. *Genesis: A Commentary*. Grand Rapids, MI: Zondervan, 2001.

Walton, John H. *The Lost World of Adam and Eve: Genesis 2–3 and the Human Origins Debate.* Downers Grove, IL: IVP Academic, 2015.

_____. *The Lost World of Genesis One: Ancient Cosmology and the Origins Debate*. Downers Grove, IL: IVP Academic, 2009.

_____. Victor H. Matthews, and Mark W. Chavalas. *The IVP Bible Background Commentary: Old Testament.* Downers Grove, IL: InterVarsity, 2000.

Wenham, Gordon J. *Genesis 1–15.* World Bible Commentary, Volume 1. Waco, TX: Word, 1987.

_____. *Rethinking Genesis 1–11: Gateway to the Bible*. Eugene, OR: Cascade, 2015.

Whiston, William, tr. *The Works of Josephus: Complete and Unabridged.* Peabody, MA: Hendrickson, 1987.

Willis, John T. *Genesis.* The Living Word Commentary on the Old Testament. Abilene, TX: Abilene Christian University, 1984.

_____. *The Message of Old Testament History, Volume One: Adam to Moses.* Abilene, TX: Biblical Research Press, 1977.

Young, Davis A. *The Biblical Flood: A Case Study of the Church's Response to Extrabiblical Evidence.* Grand Rapids, MI: Eerdmans, 1995.

Special thanks are due to:

Our editors and proofreaders, Joe Sciortino (you're amazing), Steve Jacoby, Gilbert Kimeng, Becky Nelson, Lisa Sawhill, Elizabeth Thompson, Katie Wenta, and especially the eagle-eyed Amy Morgan.

To fellow explorers of Genesis: Richard Averbeck, Henri Blocher, John Collins, Richard Hess, the late Derek Kidner, Tremper Longman III, Iain Provan, John Walton, Gordon Wenham, and John Willis—as well as to other prominent thinkers, including Francis Collins, Michael Denton, Denis Lamoureux, Amy-Jill Levine, Ronald Numbers, and Davis Young.

To Camille Anjilivelil and Kedamawit Atsbeha—you too have patiently and effectively contributed in important ways.

Last, we are deeply grateful to the staff at Morgan James, particularly Tiffany Gibson, David Hancock, Jim Howard, and Terry Whalin.

ABOUT THE AUTHORS

Paul Copan (PhD Philosophy, Marquette University) is the Pledger Family Chair of Philosophy and Ethics at Palm Beach Atlantic University, West Palm Beach, Florida. For six years, he served as president of the Evangelical Philosophical Society.

Paul is author and editor of over thirty books, including works such as *The Rationality of Theism*, *The Routledge Companion to Philosophy of Religion*, *Creation out of Nothing*, *Philosophy of Religion: Classic and Contemporary Issues*, *The Zondervan Dictionary of Christianity and Science*, *A Little Book for New Philosophers*, and *The Cosmological Argument* (a two-volume anthology). He has also contributed essays to over thirty books, both scholarly and popular, and he has authored a number of articles in professional journals. In 2017, he was a Visiting Scholar at Oxford University.

Paul and his wife, Jacqueline, have six children and reside in West Palm Beach, Florida. His website is www.paulcopan.com.

Douglas Jacoby is an international Bible teacher, having spoken in over 125 nations (and over 100 universities). After serving as a minister on church staff for 20 years in Britain, Sweden, Australia, and the US, he now works as a freelance teacher and consultant, with a special focus on apologetics.

Douglas has debated numerous well-known atheists, agnostics, imams, and rabbis (like Michael Shermer, Rabbi Shmuley Boteach, and Sheikh Shabir Ally). Since the 1990s he has led annual tours to the biblical world. Douglas has written over 30 books, including *Compelling Evidence*, *Jesus & Islam*, *Answering Skeptics*, and *What About Heaven & Hell?* and has recorded 600 podcasts. Douglas also serves as Adjunct Professor of Bible and Theology at Lincoln Christian University. He holds degrees from Drew, Harvard, and Duke.

Douglas and his wife, Vicki, have three children, and reside in the Atlanta area. His website is www.douglasjacoby.com.

Printed in the USA
CPSIA information can be obtained
at www.ICGtesting.com
JSHW022217140824
68134JS00018B/1101

9 781683 509509